T0265197

CATASTROPHIC
IMPACT
AND LOSS

The Capstone of Impact Assessment

CATASTROPHIC
IMPACT
AND LOSS

The Capstone of Impact Assessment

KEVIN D. BURTON

CRC Press
Taylor & Francis Group
Boca Raton   London   New York

CRC Press is an imprint of the
Taylor & Francis Group, an **Informa** business

CRC Press
Taylor & Francis Group
6000 Broken Sound Parkway NW, Suite 300
Boca Raton, FL 33487-2742

Printed and bound in Great Britain by TJ International, Padstow, Cornwall
Version Date: 20120731

International Standard Book Number: 978-1-4665-0464-6 (Hardback)

Library of Congress Cataloging-in-Publication Data

Burton, Kevin D.
  Catastrophic impact and loss / Kevin D. Burton.
    p. cm.
  Includes bibliographical references and index.
  ISBN 978-1-4665-0464-6 (hardcover : alk. paper)
  1. Emergency management. 2. Risk assessment. I. Title.

HV551.2B8698 2013
658.4'77--dc23   2012028551

Visit the Taylor & Francis Web site at
http://www.taylorandfrancis.com

and the CRC Press Web site at
http://www.crcpress.com

CONTENTS

PREFACE

With the publication of *Managing Emerging Risk, The Capstone of Preparedness* in 2011 by CRC Press, my publisher and I set out to deeply consider the notion of risk and what constitutes a risk assessment. In that volume we explored the complexities and wild variance found in what passes for many risk assessments today. We developed scenarios to introduce the reader to areas of critical thinking around probability and possibility, and ultimately proscribed a method that evoked an admixture of data-driven risk modeling and structured narrative around new risk.

Amazingly, in the six months after *Managing Emerging Risk* was published, many of the scenarios came true, and other, more menacing risks emerged. The publisher and I agreed that the volume was a timely and important piece of literature in the ever-changing field of emergency management.

This volume, *Catastrophic Impact and Loss,* is the second stone to be laid in a path toward a more mindful practice of emergency management, with a focus on the impacts caused by risk. Unlike risks, which are hard-to-quantify future events, impacts can be measured, and this book illustrates a complete approach to doing so. While we can only wonder to what standard our industry will ultimately hold impact assessments, it is safe to say that, until now, there has been no such material presented that so completely considers what it means to understand impacts.

The reader should consider this volume with its sister book, *Managing Emerging Risk,* to truly understand the twin capstones of our work as emergency managers; to prepare for risk both probable and possible; and to understand impacts that are utterly knowable.

ACKNOWLEDGMENTS

First, this book is for Athena, my daughter and own Goddess of Wisdom and War, and my wife Adriana, who supports me on a sea of strength and adoration. Next, I thank my father, Dr. George Burton, to whom much is owed in his support and contribution to my thinking around the challenging matters found in this volume. Finally, Jason Philo, my editor and research assistant, is owed a fantastic debt of gratitude for suffering many long days working and reworking this book so that it comes to the reader as clear as a clarion call.

ABOUT THE AUTHOR

Kevin D. Burton has been an active practitioner of the business continuity and disaster recovery disciplines since 1994. As a senior consultant at one of the "big two" disaster recovery consultancies, he had the responsibility of servicing the unique needs of E-businesses and highly mature n-tiered application architecture frameworks in the late 1990s. During this period, his clients included May Company Stores, Cattelus Corporation, Sun America Financial, Homestore.com, Dole Foods, Science Applications International Corporation (SAIC), and PeopleSoft.

In 2001, he was an advisor to the CEO of Toyota Motor Sales as an expert in information technology strategy and governance with respect to business continuity and disaster recovery. After 9/11, his role was enlarged and he became responsible for building a sustainable governance process for business resiliency worldwide and delivering a redundant data center solution for Toyota's U.S. operations.

Building on the concept that 9/11 pushed disaster recovery practitioners into the realm of emergency management within the private sector, Mr. Burton began to develop a broader, more holistic approach to private sector emergency management and created a small firm called Burton Asset Management. As the principal of this firm, he has served as an executive coach, trusted advisor, and program manager for Oakley, The Arizona Department of Transportation, Maricopa County Department of Health, Pulte Homes, Standard Pacific Homes, and Triad Financial Corporation. In addition, he enjoys deep relationships with consultancies in the disaster recovery community including IBM, SunGard, and Gartner Group. He directly advised the Gartner Group and Cisco Systems in and around global systems deployment and risk management for American Express, Caterpillar, and Baxter Pharmaceuticals.

Burton's experience ranges from G100 companies with revenues in the billions to regionalized medium businesses and local small businesses with 5 to 25 employees. His projects consistently include architecting and delivering business and technical requirements for strategic, sustainable, and cost-effective disaster recovery. His broad range of experience has helped clients address many issues to increase their IT process efficiencies or to address business process needs, staff and governance issues, and business-to-IT communication. Direct relationships with agencies in the public sector and other organizations have a built-in tradition of employee safety, risk mitigation, and a clear foresight into the risk of today as well as tomorrow.

Articles by and about Mr. Burton and his company have been published in *GQ Magazine Australia*, *Continuity Insights*, and *Disaster Recovery Journal*. Apple Computers recently profiled Burton Asset Management because of the company's innovative approach to risk management.

Today, Mr. Burton is an avid practitioner, speaker, and student in the field of emergency management who has most recently consulted for Honeywell, Inc. and other financial institutions and large publicly traded companies.

In Mr. Burton's first published textbook, *Managing Emerging Risk* (CRC Press, Boca Raton, FL, 2011), he developed a theme that has emerged from his clinical experience; namely, that a new paradigm for evaluating and "connecting the dots" is necessary if we are to successfully deal with emerging threats. This paradigm relied heavily on lessons that can be learned from what (at least at first) may have seemed to be a strange bedfellow: the marketing industry.

Here in *Catastrophic Impact and Loss* Burton introduces a whole new lexicon of terms that will intrigue and inform the reader, and a solid prescription for conducting impact assessments that is thorough, complete, and unlike any other published materials in the field.

Taken together, the two volumes, *Managing Emerging Risk* and *Catastrophic Impact and Loss*, signal that the emergency management student and practitioner can move beyond the threats and impact du jour and into a mindful state of critical practice in the opposing worlds of managing the probable and possible risks of our futures, and understanding the knowable impacts of our present.

1

The Postmodern Impact Assessment and Problems of the Mind

1.1 KEY TERMS

1.2 OBJECTIVES

After reading this chapter you will be able to:

1. Describe the difference between a *risk assessment* and an *impact assessment*.

2

2. Discuss how the current period in which we practice has given rise to a new set of circumstances in the area of impact assessments and the unique challenges these changes present.
3. Illustrate an understanding of the fundamental flaw in our current approach to impact assessments and provide examples of specific factors that quantify the underlying problem.
4. Provide an example of the evolution of impacts as they have manifested themselves in today's practice of impact assessments.
5. Discuss how looking back at similar times of change in history can yield clues for critical thinking and exploration to the way in which impact assessments could be conducted looking forward.

1.3 OVERVIEW: RISK AND IMPACTS

This is *not* a textbook about **risk**. Risks are both probable and possible threats and hazards that place what is valued in harm's way. This is a textbook about **impacts**. Impacts are best understood as *that which will be lost or damaged* as a result of a risk manifesting itself. The two terms are easily confused and often mistakenly taken to mean the same thing. However, the important difference between the two is that risks can be estimated based on probability or projected as scenarios based on possibility, whereas impacts can be enumerated as value lost, capacity lost, capability lost, or other values that are not probability based at all—we can estimate impacts much more accurately than risks because impacts are not enumerated based on what might be in harm's way; impacts are, when well analyzed, enumerated on what *will* be in harm's way.

Simply put, to consider risk is to consider what *might* bring us harm, whereas considering impacts brings into focus what *will* be in harm's way. Risk is best understood in terms of probability and possibility. Impacts are best understood in terms of actuality and fact.

Given this understanding, it is important to differentiate between a risk assessment and an impact assessment (Figure 1.1).

Risk, according to *Merriam-Webster*, is:

1. The possibility of loss or injury (peril),
2. Someone or something that creates or suggests a hazard,
3. The chance of loss, or the perils to the subject matter of an insurance contract; also, the degree of probability of such a loss.[1]

Figure 1.1 Key concepts in this chapter include understanding the difference between risk and impact studies and a discussion regarding the broader context of impacts in our field.

As understood and managed in the fields of business continuity, emergency management, and counterterrorism, risk is most readily expressed as "someone or something that creates or suggests a hazard." The emphasis on *something* or *someone* posing a hazard is a definitive element across the three professional fields and is most often captured in the work product referred to in our profession as a **risk assessment**. Threats and hazards are estimated in a risk assessment, e.g., computer hardware outages to the catastrophic possibilities of tornados and terror attacks. Risk assessments are often completed by building scenarios[2] and creating risk assessments that inform stakeholders about the *threats and hazards that put their organizations at risk*.

Impact assessments are entirely different in that they inform our stakeholders about what goods, persons, or other important items *are in harm's way*. Neither a risk assessment nor an impact assessment is a disaster recovery plan (DRP), business continuity plan (BCP), or an emergency response plan (ERP).

* * *

A risk assessment tells us what might cause harm, and an impact assessment tells us what would be damaged, destroyed, or otherwise *lost*, as a result.

* * *

To be *at* risk is to be in harm's way. A risk assessment expresses *what will bring our constituents and us harm*. Impact assessments inform us about *what is in harm's way and what is at risk of being damaged or lost*. There are many possible imagined and unimagined risks that threaten our organizations, communities, and nations. There are also many ways to evaluate the people, processes, properties, and perceptions that are in harm's way and how they can be *impacted* by the manifestation of risk.

Impacts are much more realistic manifestations of threats than the notion of risks. While risks may or may not materialize, once they do, the reality of the impacts (however we have calculated them in an impact analysis) become very real. Any professional who has assessed the impact of a pandemic, pathogen-based attack knows that this work is much more specific than any imagined risk. The work of an impact assessment in this area moves from the abstract to a specific reality.

To elaborate on the example just given, working on an impact assessment for a pandemic or pathogen-based attack brings several vague concepts into sharp focus: the closure of schools, the near-immediate surge on medical facilities and hospitals, the gruesome task of separating a healthy parent from the family to care for an infected child, the red tagging of homes and mandatory quarantines, and ultimately the massive loss of life. The impact assessment shifts abstract ideas from the risk assessment into real impacts. As professionals these are the hard truths and inescapable impacts we must consider when discussing them (Figure 1.2).

* * *

In short, to conduct an impact assessment is to consider the profanity of havoc. The job at hand requires professionals who are able to objectively measure what happens when objects degrade from order and fall into chaos—even when required to do so under duress!

* * *

5

Figure 1.2 The differences between risks and impacts are not apparent, as this photo illustrates. A baby playing with an electrical outlet has a risk of being injured. However, to what degree, if any, would those impacts be felt?

Managing Emerging Risk, written by this author in 2011, was about the current world of risk and the necessity to change our methods in order to predict postmodern risks, thereby providing more valuable and true-to-life risk assessments. In that textbook, the term *disaster halo effect* is introduced to clarify the knotty problem of one manifested risk creating another manifested risk. The **disaster halo effect** is "the recognition that modern threats exhibit more than one 'event' and multiple outcomes that can be emergent or evolving."[3] The disaster halo effect establishes that an earthquake (one risk) leading to a tsunami (another risk) is *not an impact—* it is part of a larger disaster halo effect. The tsunami striking another island is *still* not an impact; again, this event *is part of the larger disaster halo effect.*

To understand impacts is to understand what damage was done (not what caused it) as a result of all the events within the disaster halo. Therefore, the economic loss, damage to environment, and loss of life resulting from the tsunami would be *impacts* of the tsunami, with *impacts* from the earthquake being enumerated separately, while all being part of the larger disaster halo event.

1.3.1 Why Risk Assessments and Impact Assessments Are Different

This book is about understanding what is *truly* in harm's way, to what degree, and creating a means of providing a more accurate impact assessment. An impact assessment is a key program deliverable that informs our objectives and shapes our practice, based on understanding the common values and goods at risk belonging to our stakeholders. Risk assessments are only the first part of understanding potential terror attacks and disasters; impact assessments are the other half of that equation, i.e., understanding the impacts that stem from those events. Taken together, the risk assessment and the impact assessment are *the foundations for building a sound response program*. If both of these deliverables are not completed, we have only done half of our job, and we could well be starting off our programs on the wrong footing, leaving us unbalanced and ultimately, unprepared.

People, processes, property, and perceptions are the common values and goods that are in harm's way. These values and goods can be treated as assets and enumerated based on geographical location, value, and density. Inaccurate understanding of impacts can misinform the response effort and unhinge the objectives of any business continuity, emergency management, or counterterrorism planning effort that is undertaken once risks and impacts are understood.

* * *

In the fields of business continuity, emergency management, and counterterrorism the objectives influenced by an impact assessment may be very different from one field of practice to the other.

* * *

However, to be clear:

1. A risk assessment calculates and establishes probable and possible scenarios and rates them based on likelihood.
2. An impact assessment gathers data about the valued people, processes, technologies, and other goods in harm's way and ranks them based on importance or criticality.

7

1.3.2 Approaching the Impact Assessment

While it is often assumed that the current approaches to impact assessments are effective, reflection on recent catastrophic events (both manmade and natural) reveals that our current practice in these fields should be critically examined with an eye toward improvement. Recent events, such as the Amazon cloud computing data center outage of April 21, 2011; the Japanese earthquake on March 11, 2011; and the attempted assassination of Congresswoman Gabrielle Giffords by Jared Lee Loughner on January 8, 2011, have invigorated the national conversation, as well as our professional dialogue, regarding impact assessments due to the scale and scope of impacts felt from these catastrophes.

The nature of impact has evolved across the practices of emergency management— from private sector business continuity planning, to information technology disaster recovery planning, to public sector emergency response planning and counterterrorism. The original goals of scenario planning and the historical roots of our profession were to protect shareholder value. Today, there is no question that we have progressed from simply measuring potential financial, brand, or compliance impacts, or loss of life, injury, and property damage impacts, to giving consideration to a much wider array of impacts.

Not understanding impacts creates a gap in the response planning process that leads to the potential for impacts that *were not even considered as part of the original plan preparation process.*

We are charged with stewarding our profession toward better levels of performance, inclusive of the challenges we face. This requires critical thinking, critique, and an honest measure of our past results. In turn, it also requires that each of us, on our own terms and under the consideration of our current constraints and willingness, choose to move our thinking forward, consider future changes to the current form of standard practice, and implement new ideas. This book proposes evolutionary ideas and concepts for the reader's consideration. Meanwhile, the rapid change surrounding the dynamics of risks and impacts soldiers on.

* * *

Ignoring that impacts have evolved is to put our head in the sand and ignore that the world has changed around us, and that our practice must evolve with it.

* * *

When we accept that a comprehensive impact assessment captures our objectives, we must then confront the notion that our objectives may be very different now than they were 20 years, or even 2 years, ago. In this chapter we will consider some of the evolutionary changes we've seen in impacts and the drivers behind them.

The key lesson of this chapter is that the impact assessment is an essential piece of information that informs our objectives and shapes our practice. Tragically, the real cost of a catastrophe is often underestimated. The value of what is in harm's way has *evolved*, and while business continuity, emergency management, and counterterrorism may have different roles, professional practice in these fields should reflect this evolution.

Impact assessments are one of the most challenging tasks of intellectual analysis in our field. They ask professionals in business continuity, disaster recovery, emergency management, and counterterrorism to confront realities that are often beyond their control and scope of knowledge, including how an organization functions, what value it places on varied outputs it creates, and how those valuable outputs might be impacted by a disaster or terror attack. **Loss of value** is the comparative object at risk, or in harm's way. These impacts can affect finances, brand, and customer relationships. In emergency management and counterterrorism, an impact assessment measures impacts as serious as mortality rates, massive financial losses, and even the complete loss of governmental control.

Few professionals in these fields lose sleep over the risk assessments we conduct. Most practitioners have grown accustomed to considering the potential and possible risks that might manifest themselves should a disaster or terror attack occur. Most practitioners and professionals have come to understand there are risks that we can calculate based on probability and those that can only be understood in terms of their possibility. It is important to note that what might keep us up at night is *not* wondering if we are properly calculating the risks that constantly evolve in a difficult and ever-changing field. What might keep us up at night *is if we are calculating the impacts incorrectly.*

1.4 THE EVOLUTION OF IMPACTS

In order to better understand the modern impact assessment, we must consider the context in which many public and private enterprises now operate. This context is referred to as the **digital age** or the **information**

Figure 1.3 With advances in technology over the last century, our business models have changed as we shift from the industrial age to the digital age.

age, which is the notion that we now operate in a period in which the primary output of the enterprise or organization is information and services. This is a considerable change to the industrial and enterprise outputs of the **industrial age**, in which the primary item of output of the organization was a physical product (Figure 1.3).

The digital age includes the concepts of labor distribution, the globalization of the supply and distribution chains, a growth in emerging markets, outsourcing, and a variety of other permutations of new private and public policies purpose-built for these new realities. In addition, business, and perhaps life itself, seems to have accelerated with the arrival of the digital age, with real-time reportage, global communications networks, a deeper interdependency between trading and cash systems, and the overarching monetary policies and governance that guides them.

The terms **Fordism** and **Taylorism** refer to managerial and operational systems that had a high degree of local focus and brought raw materials through the front of a factory, with workers delivering finished products at the end of a manufacturing line. Fordism, named after Henry Ford, and Taylorism, named after Frederick W. Taylor (a scientist who focused on synthesized workflows), informed much of the thinking of the industrial age. In both models of factory management, worker output was designed and integrated in highly localized forms, managed by "the numbers," and optimized for rapid manufacturing of products and their delivery through a factory.

Today, parts, materials, talent, information, and craftsmanship come to most organizations from all over the world with the "digital superhighway" of the Internet and private networks enabling the management of vast, globalized supply chains and the delivery of highly skilled knowledge work (such as product design, innovation, and management) to low-skilled workers, often to be made in countries other than the ultimate country of consumption. The life cycle of a product today can start as design and prototyping in the United States and be outsourced to any number of companies for refinement and sample creation, delivered in pieces to China or India for manufacture, and finally packaged and delivered to the end consumers back in the United States.

This complex system of management, design, and output is rapidly becoming the norm in U.S. organizations—and not only in business. Much of the public sector now relies on foreign computer chips, internationally networked systems, and even celestial information from satellites to operate and deliver public safety and counterterrorism capabilities. This highlights the primary condition of the economy of the digital age, which is that every piece of the factory is now a globalized point of service rather than a localized process. The digital age is often described as exhibiting a cultural condition known as **postmodernism.** To be postmodern is to be less tethered to location and more attached to time, context, and conditions that are fluid. One way to understand this shift is to consider a recent television commercial featuring a lemonade stand and the evolution of impacts that occurs as this small business grows.

1.4.1 Susie's Lemonade Stand

Do you recall Verizon's television commercials about Susie and her "lemonade empire"? The commercials were created by McCann Erickson for Verizon and went **viral** (spreading rapidly across many different media platforms) in 2011. In fact, they became so popular that the only known bottle of Susie's Lemonade was auctioned on eBay in June 2009 for $162.50[4] in support of Alex's Lemonade Stand Foundation (all proceeds go to find a cure for children with cancer), and you could also find a Facebook page for Susie's Lemonade. McCann Erickson knocked the marketing ball right out of the park with its campaign for Verizon by adding something to a technology advertisement that just couldn't be beat—a kid with a dream.

The commercials in this campaign worked on so many levels that there were over half a million write-ups and blog posts on the topic online, and the print ad earned accolades from Adweek, calling the campaign "exceptional."[5] The commercial unleashed an arsenal of "cuteness" and cut to the core of the American dream, and it all started with the iconic lemonade stand.

Originally airing in March 2011, the first commercial was a study in postmodern business growth. In just under a total of 60 seconds (two 30-second commercials) we watched Susie's business explode into a complex network of machines and human interactions. Going beyond Verizon's marketing, the cute kids, and the "feel good," small-town appeal of the commercial, we found a business case for mobile business encapsulated within a wonderful business model. The first commercial was a 30-second microcosm of any executive's dreams of business expansion in the digital age.

1.4.1.1 The First 30 Seconds

Within 5 seconds Susie went from a bored little girl sitting at a quiet lemonade stand to a girl with a dream. Her dad handed her a cell phone and said, "Hey, Susie, why don't you use this—it has a calculator." The ad was a commercial ploy on how adults and kids see technology completely differently, and Susie delivered on her vision of just what the digital age had in store for her. Within 2 seconds, Susie was holding up the phone with a Global Positioning System (**GPS**) map of the neighborhood and delegating the expansion of her lemonade stands to groups of her friends. Within the first 10 seconds Susie's Lemonade Stand had gone from a stand-alone business to a technology-driven, multilocation retail organization with three locations and five or six employees; all of the workers in her organization depended on GPS to track their growth. By the 11th second, they were are all using a credit card reader attached to their phones to accept electronic payments through electronic funds transfers (**EFT**s).

At one stand, the customer lines grew long. By the 13th second, Susie was using a tablet computer to present her future growth plans to a set of investors. Sales were charting up, "and that's just the first quarter," she said confidently. Apparently Susie got her seed capital, because at 17 seconds she was video chatting on a wireless notebook with an architect who asked, "So you want a slide in your office?" Susie replied confidently, "Or monkey bars— either one." Soon, Susie was buying a building and supporting a notebook-driven, wireless enterprise.

At the 21-second mark, Susie was marching through a warehouse, complete with forklifts and storage racks, conducting supply train tracking of her inventory on a tablet. At 23 seconds, one of Susie's friends from the beginning of the commercial was sporting a shirt and tie, a tablet, and a Bluetooth® earpiece. Susie's dad came home and asked, "Where's Susie?" The boy cocked an eyebrow and asked, "Is she expecting you?" From the 25-second mark to the end, we see Susie, replete in her new business attire, standing in front of her house-turned-offices, with her lemonade delivery truck backing in. Looking at the camera, arms crossed with cell phone in hand, she was confidently staking her ground in the information age.

Within Susie's world a stand-alone business (the lemonade stand) acquired the following objects and systems in a mere 30 seconds: the phone, a GPS, credit card readers and EFT systems, tablet computers, Wi-Fi, and presentation software, an office, a notebook infrastructure, and video chatting, a warehouse, a supply chain management system, and a scheduling or calendaring system with unified communications capabilities. Finally, Susie's empire is in its first stage of growth with an office in place and delivery trucks doing their work. Of course this is only a commercial, but it did something very well—it tracked the postmodern growth of Susie's business in microcosm. Considering this, what happened in the next 30 seconds is not at all surprising.

1.4.1.2 The Second 30 Seconds

In the first 5 seconds of the second commercial, Susie had a crisis; one of her vending machines was nearly out of lemonade! "There's only one bottle left!" observed one of her diligent young employees. "I've gotta tell Susie!" and he's off on his bike to warn her about a failure in the distribution system. Back in her office, Susie was tracking her inventory on her tablet computer (with her slide and monkey bars in full view); she was already aware of the shortage and had a warning on her screen. "The vending machine on Elm is almost empty," she told an adult employee. "I'm on it, boss," he replied, as kids bounced on a trampoline in the background. As an aside, when the adult moved away from Susie's executive desk he noticed something, "New pony?" he asks Susie. Clearly, business was booming.

Meanwhile, Susie's (apparently loyal) young employee rode his bike as fast as he could through town to warn Susie of the shortage. Riding through a freshly laid sidewalk, he shouted, "Sorry!" to the construction workers, single-minded as he was on a mission. Meanwhile, having already addressed the problem, Susie moved on to her next appointment, announcing, "We are open for business!" as she cut the ribbon on her first retail store. Unknowingly, her loyal employee pressed on, dodging through trees in a park to desperately get to Susie before the lemonade vending machine on Elm Street completely failed and was out of lemonade. Susie was still on the move, rerouting one of her trucks by asking a young employee in the warehouse to do a bit of work on the supply chain system on his notebook, "Let's reroute Greg from Fresno," she suggested.

Twenty-one seconds into the commercial, Greg, an adult in a "Susie" uniform, was walking toward his next delivery with a Susie truck in the background when his phone beeped and he got a message. He did a quick, albeit disgruntled, U-turn to handle the inventory problem back at the vending machine. At 23 seconds, Susie's loyal employee arrived at the warehouse on his dirty bike, disheveled and worn. "Susie! The vending machine...." Susie cut him off, "Already filled," she said, verifying it on her tablet.

From this simple act on Susie's part we can deduce that she has added a USA Technologies **telemetry** system (telemetry involves tracking merchandise and locating the nearest pickup and drop-off points for any given truck or delivery mechanism in the supply chain) and ePort cashless payment system (an electronic wireless cash card system) to her ever-growing business.

"Cool bike," she told the exhausted boy in her warehouse as she left for her next conquest. The boy looked after her in stunned amazement, as if to say, "How does she do it?" The final shot in this 30-second spot showed Susie without any gadgets at all—she's simply smiling and standing in front of her "Susie's Lemonade" building complete with loading bays and trucks being filled.

Within the second 30-second commercial, we find a Susie transformed. Her supply chain and payment systems have become fully integrated, she has unified communications, and she is using advanced telemetry and cashless payment systems. She has her office, adult employees, a warehouse, and a fleet of trucks. All within 30 seconds. These two commercials, when viewed back-to-back, show an encapsulated view of a rapidly growing business. Even if the reader extrapolates Susie's business growth over 60 days, 120 days, or even a year—we can see how rapidly a thriving business can evolve in the digital age.

Regardless of the length of time for a business to grow, this wonderful commercial is a case study in postmodern business growth. It shows how a product (even one as simple as lemonade) can expand into a thriving enterprise and, as that happens, what changes occur in the technology landscape and Susie's relationships. Notice how her shareholders change from those few friends who helped her start her business to the investors and the technology partners she now has to satisfy. Notice how her supply chain grows from three lemonade stands to vending machines and retail stores supported by a warehouse and a fleet of trucks. Notice how her cash handling needs evolve from simple cash payments to EFT.

If an impact analysis were conducted in the first 5 seconds of Susie's enterprise, we would focus on the core of her business—lemons, sugar, water, her friends, and the stand. Within the first 30 seconds, that focus would expand to include multiple suppliers, a distribution channel, a fairly complex IT infrastructure, telemetry, and electronic funds transfers. It is important to note that we are not even mentioning her upstream and downstream partners and investors. If we were to revisit Susie in the next 30-second period, we would have to consider her retail operations, a now massive distribution system, just-in-time delivery, her scheduling system, her unified communications system, and perhaps a globalized system of suppliers.

In fact, Susie's rate of change can be plotted as a series of growth decisions along her business expansion that occur (in the commercials) at the rate of roughly one major change every 5 seconds. How many such changes happen in the businesses and organizations where professionals in the field are conducting impact assessments, and at what rate are those changes occurring? Most businesses have no idea. They have multiple growth-oriented projects that come to life and deliver value at different times. This is the most important lesson embedded in the microcosm so wonderfully envisioned by Verizon's commercial—*change enables growth*.

The commercials hold a potent message for the practitioners of business continuity, disaster recovery, and emergency management as well: Growth adds objects and value that can only be captured as a snapshot in time. The postmodern business environment requires change, and with change comes a new dynamic in the impact analysis. If the change rate outpaces our impact analysis (and it always does) the work product of our analysis is only as good for as long as it takes the enterprise to grow. This may be in seconds or it may be in months, but one way or the other, *the enterprise will change*. At its best, an impact analysis can only serve as a snapshot in time unless it is constantly updated and kept relevant. Frankly, very few businesses maintain a real-time view of potential impacts, and in the real world, even the best analysts in our field would have a hard time keeping up with Susie!

15

* * *

Just to be clear, the evolution of impacts demonstrated by Susie's Lemonade Stand could be replaced with the real-world impact of another kind of organization, say, the manufacturer of a life-saving vaccine!

* * *

While Orange County has never suffered from impacts resulting from a lemonade stand disaster, imagine the impacts to America if all of the same technologies used to formulate, package, and deliver the lemonade were instead being used to formulate, package, and deliver a vaccine during a health crisis. Even businesses such as private surveillance organizations, pharmaceutical companies, medical supply organizations, and emergency support provisions providers fit within the evolution of impact model demonstrated by Susie's Lemonade Stand.

1.4.2 A Fundamental Flaw

A flaw results in a damaged product. There are basically two types of flaws:

1. Design flaws
2. Process flaws

With respect to their individual impacts, design flaws trump process flaws by a wide margin; e.g., designing a plane with a fundamental safety flaw is much more serious than having a manufacturing process flaw in the building of the designed plane. There is a fundamental design flaw in the deliverable or work product called the impact assessment currently created in our field.

A **fundamental flaw** in much of what passes for an impact analysis is the tendency to think small, which is contrary to the evolution of impacts based on the booming digital age and postmodernism.

A set of problems and misgivings are embedded in this fundamental flaw:

1. A failure to understand the breadth of suppliers, distributors, and upstream and downstream dependencies that the organization values
2. A failure to align with internal organizational values and external laws and regulations as appropriate to the organization's industry and location

3. A lack of usage of a larger order and taxonomy of impacts, as well
    as their deviations on the part of practitioners

Using Susie's business as an example, we can illustrate these as real problems and better understand the fundamental flaw this textbook will be addressing.

1.4.2.1 Failure to Understand Breadth
First, to consider the breadth of Susie's organization and the impacts she might encounter if faced with a catastrophic disaster, we have to understand that her organization has radically evolved from a single lemonade stand to an empire with multiple stakeholders, vendors, and upstream and downstream systems that have enabled her growth. The scope and breadth of impacts to her business could include the lemonade stand, as well as her friends, her network and computing partners, her community, and her stakeholders. In Susie's example, the business moved from one with a very shallow impact capacity to one with a deep impact capacity in mere seconds.

1.4.2.2 Failure to Align with Internal Organizational Values and External Laws and Regulations
Second, as the lemonade stand business grew, new internal values and external laws and regulations would rapidly come into play. A stand-alone lemonade stand is rarely regulated by anyone other than "Mom." However, in our example above, the Securities and Exchange Commission (SEC) would be involved with Susie's finances. The FDA would be involved with her now mainstream product. Mom and Dad are now replaced with investors and perhaps, unionized employees. Susie's regulatory landscape has shifted with growth driven by information.

1.4.2.3 A Lack of Larger Order and Taxonomy of Impacts as Well as Their Deviations
Finally, the third problem is exhibited in Susie's business by the admixture of knowable, common objects, such as the early stakeholder boy who would ride his bike to Susie to communicate change and her automated response system that tracked inventory and found the nearest truck to replenish it. Here we are confronted with the standard "loyal employee" and the not-so-standard complex of digital and information-driven systems that may or may not be within Susie's control. As these complexities arise in her business, some coexist with one other, some seem redundant,

and to be clear, all of them lack a common taxonomy or language by which we might categorize and enumerate them.

Even as we approach the challenges of conducting meaningful impact assessments with an understanding that most impact analyses are too limited in their scope, if the impact assessment does not address the fundamental issues of the breadth of impact, alignment with values and laws, and a lack of a common taxonomy of impacts, there looms an even larger problem.

1.4.3 A Larger Problem

The fundamental flaw of impact assessments today is manifested in a set of larger symptoms that often accompany radical changes in markets and capital and cost models associated with the work of understanding impacts. With the digital age and globalization have come a host of new challenges and questions. Among them are questions of government policy, corporate stewardship, community, and global citizenry. While often viewed as lofty academic issues, these symptoms of change and change resistance have very real impact assessment influences outside of the sphere of academia.

Most of the transitional periods between ages, such as that from the agrarian age to the industrial age, are accompanied by *revolution*. We had the industrial revolution and we are in the midst of the digital revolution. The larger challenge we face as practitioners conducting impact analyses is that revolutions add turmoil on top of the already ground-shifting changes to the organizations and enterprises we serve. Historically, revolutions embody public, private, and political upheaval as the means of production and the distribution of labor and wealth occur. The digital age is not unique in this manner.

We live in an age of economic, military, and political change. Much of this change is driven by information and a widening global gap in equality as perceived by cultures as a result of these changes. While not all revolutions are in response to changes in monetary policy, political governance, and changes to the relationship between workers and production systems, many are. In 2010 and 2011 alone, the number and scope of revolutions occurring worldwide is dramatic.

As of this writing, there are several revolutions in their early stages, including:

- The Egyptian revolution

- The Libyan revolution
- The Syrian uprising
- The Iraqi protests
- The Jordanian protests
- The Moroccan protests
- The Omani protests
- The Yemeni uprising
- The Occupy Wall Street protests
- The Russian uprising
- The Greek protests
- The Italian protests
- The Spanish protests

The larger problem of extremely fluid global conditions is seen in the Arab Spring, the Eurozone conflicts, the Occupy Wall Street movement, and the recent uprising in Russia. Each of these protests is based on a lack of social confidence in monetary policy and governance. The fundamental flaw of thinking too small in our impact assessments is currently being played out against a backdrop of worldwide radical social uprising and conflicts within new hot spots emerging almost weekly. The outcomes of these protests and revolutions create a dual challenge for the practitioner working on an impact assessment today: One is the massive set of changes brought on by the digital age, and the other, larger challenge is the social and political unrest roiling in the background.

* * *

It is safe to say that the Fundamental Flaw of thinking too small when it comes to impact assessments will be compounded by social, economic, and governance upheavals for the next decade.

* * *

The overarching challenge with revolts and revolutions is that they create geopolitical uncertainty. Historically, such revolts and revolutions result in changes to monetary policy, governance, and the social distribution of wealth and power. There are considerable resources that should be considered outside of this text in regard to these revolutions and revolts. However, one thing should be made clear—none of these revolutions will be short-lived. If history proves anything about revolutions triggered by inequality and worker's rights, it is that the average life span of such transformative movements is 10 years from revolt to resolution (Figure 1.4).

Figure 1.4 Protests and civil unrest are a natural occurrence stemming from changes in economic and political situations.

To place this in context, our earlier example of Susie's Lemonade business is faced with dual challenges for a practitioner conducting an impact assessment. The first set of challenges has to do with her rapid expansion and globalization as captured in her postmodern, digital business construct. The second set of challenges has to do with the broader global reaction to these transformative changes in business and culture, resulting in perceived inequality and revolt—social conflicts that will impact the political, monetary, and governance structures that surround her business.

In a U.S. State Department Overseas Security Advisory Council (OSAC) report issued on July 13–14, 2011, titled *Crisis Management and Evacuation Best Practices*, the new challenges of global revolutions and revolts are extensively discussed. The report was jointly generated by OSAC and ConocoPhillips, the multinational oil and gas company, a testimony in and of itself of the combined interests of the U.S. State Department and multinational organizations doing business abroad in our globalized, digital age. The report was the result of a conference that included 250 participants from academic institutions, nongovernmental organizations (NGOs), multinational companies, and U.S. and foreign government representatives.

One conference member stated, "If you're calling a consulting firm to help you with crisis management plans as tanks are rolling into Tahirir Square, you're too late."[6] Another comment in the report captures the challenge of the times very well: "No plan will fit the bill completely in times of crisis and part of the plan must account for unexpected factors."[7] In this text, revolutions and social changes are not considered "unexpected factors," but rather, a contemporary reality that will be present for at least the next decade.

One of the more profound statements in the OSAC report regarding planning for impacts in the context of recent developments is this: "Your evacuation plan should stand alone from utilizing the resources of your government, building that in as an option of last resort, as opposed to the first or only option."[8] In other words, globalized businesses needing to evacuate personnel from locations abroad should not rely on the U.S. government or their home government as a first-option evacuation plan. This statement alone represents a vast new challenge in a globalized business or organizational impact assessment.

For the purposes of this text, however, the most profound statement in the report has to do with impact assessments in the new era and the need to mix measurable impacts with geopolitical information and localized impact data in order to create a "business case" for crisis management. The report says, "This mix of quantitative data (which can range from analysis of time spent away from business activities due to past crises and revenue lost, dips in market share or stock price as a result of crises, or like assessments) ... and qualitative analysis demonstrate a clear understanding that ... poor or no crisis management can quickly impact the essential elements of an organization."[9]

In review, the core thesis of this book is that there has been an **evolution of impacts** or an increase in the complexity and range of impacts that might be measured both quantitatively and qualitatively, and that those measures lead to a sound impact assessment. Driving this evolution of impacts are the digital revolution and a massive change in production and consumption referred to as **globalization**. These observations lead back to the fundamental flaw with our current approach to impact analysis—a tendency to think too small—composed of three underlying issues manifesting themselves: a misunderstanding of the breadth of the organization and its values to be protected, a misalignment to internal values and external laws, and a lack of a common taxonomy and set of measures to capture potential impacts in a standard manner. While these issues stand in the foreground of our approach to impact assessments today, in the background there is a clear need for mixing quantitative and qualitative impact measures to deal with the geopolitical changes that accompany the digital revolution and the information age with all of its vast complexities.

Now that it is clear *why* we must reconsider our approach to the impact assessment, it is necessary to consider *how* we might critically reexamine our approach to this area of our practice and how we might arrive at significant changes in our methods.

1.5 RECONSIDERING THE IMPACT ANALYSIS AND PROBLEMS OF THE MIND

The challenges embedded in our current approach to impact assessments, as presented in the previous section, will reveal rough ground and unmapped territories as we proceed. However, for now we are going to take a moment to consider *why* the methods of crafting impact assessments should be closely examined and *how* they should be reconsidered. We need to examine what value could come from developing a stronger sense of guiding principles around impact assessments within our profession.

All professional fields are, at one time or another, faced with new realities, new concepts, and new ideas. Approaching "problems of the mind" and knowing how to differentiate between blind criticism and knowledgeable critique is necessary to making well-informed decisions. This section sets out to illuminate the importance of choosing deeper thinking, experimentation, or taking action when faced with new realities, concepts, and ideas. Determining if, how, or when we might choose to give the ideas that are forwarded in this book time for critical thinking, experimentation, and implementation is the question we are exploring. It is very important to note that this is a personal question, not a pedantic notion.

As individual students, practitioners, and professionals we all have free choice regarding the application of the materials presented in this book. This section will provide some clues as to how and when to exercise our personal will toward forward thinking, advancing new ideas, or even taking new action in our approach to impact assessments. As a group, individuals must work together to consider which practices to embrace and which to table for further exploration along the continuum of professional learning.

To help the reader determine his or her ultimate choice in this matter, we will introduce and discuss the history of curating evidence in a body of collected objects, the need to develop taxonomies and thesauri to further ground dialogue, and a willingness to forward a hypothesis or thesis based on logic. This will not be accomplished without the willingness to face the challenge, fail often, and ultimately triumph through trial and error.

The goal of this section is for the reader to establish a means for evaluating the professional need for reconsideration, critical exploration, and to present new guiding principles based on the broader concept of learning, innovation, and invention that has been a key part of scientific and human discovery for hundreds of years.

1.6 OBJECTS AND CRITICAL THINKING: APPLE, CABINETS OF CURIOSITY, AND A DARK NOSTALGIA

Objects can be quantified, enumerated, and accounted for. When objects are in harm's way, they are an important starting point for impact analysis work. Further, objects can be named, placed in orders or taxonomies, and cross-referenced, thereby revealing their relationship to one another and their interdependencies by and between one another. Objects can be architected and have values beyond the signifiers of monetary value or production value. When placed together in a grouping, a set of furniture objects becomes a *house*. Finally, if the furniture and objects are of a period, have a relationship to the owner that span generations, or exhibit other mean-

CATASTROPHIC IMPACT AND LOSS

ingful relationships to the homeowner's values, then those objects can be individually measured by their meaning as objects in a *home*.

According to Jean Baudrillard, in his book, *The System of Objects*, "For children, collecting is a rudimentary way of mastering the outside world, of arranging, classifying and manipulating. The most active time for childhood collecting is apparently between the ages of seven and twelve. ... In later life, it is men over forty who most frequently fall victim to this passion."[10] Mastering the outside world begins as a preferred means of learning in children and reemerges in men through the collection and study of objects. Even as people move into the digital age we find that objects are powerful. Objects still hold an influence over us that is expressed in every attempt to make our anonymity of the digital life more pronounced and tangible.

Evolving into the digital age, interface designers, industrial product designers, and engineers work tirelessly to cross a certain gap in our personal relationship with objects versus those objects rendered in pixels on a flat, high-resolution screen. The design object of our modern age seems to be the secret key between humanity and the digital world, and has almost become the elusive talisman that all designers are desperately trying to find.

If you are reading this book, you are *relating* to an object, even as your laptop is standing by waiting for you to complete a course or write a new paper. The laptop is little more than circuitry, a hard drive, and a monitor. The keyboard is not much changed since the invention of the typewriter in 1868. However, the book remains unchanged with time. Today's book is much like the first book printed hundreds of years ago—timeless. With new book smells, the smudge of graphite from the pencil, and the scent of the highlighter, you are surrounded with objects that make the reading of a book, even *this* book, something more. The book introduces objects into our learning, and objects introduce ritual.

Try as they might, computer engineers cannot reproduce the hard "click" and haptic feedback (sense of touch) once provided by an IBM Selectric II, let alone the noisy chatter of the typewriters, like those made by Remington or Hermes. Nonetheless, even in the digital age, when we introduce objects into the equation they enforce a certain rigor. Rituals and recipes come from objects, and therefore the need to collect and categorize.

Cooking has its rituals, as does yard work and study. Each of us approaches objects in a certain way, with a certain attitude of attack: key placements, methods of holding and storing, grips and touches. These are the rituals *only the object can introduce*. The papers on our desk have a ritualistic order that we simply cannot sense on our computer screen no matter how hard most of us try.

If you are a student that has a ritual, a *way* of learning, you are in a much better place to understand why we are taking a moment to talk about methods of learning, and why sometimes, a profession must reconsider itself, and the professional must decide when to take to deep thought, further experimentation, or real action based on what he or she has studied and learned. Some of this discussion involves considering objects in the context of the digital age. Objects play a role in our ability to make our own choices around discovery, learning, research, and action.

1.6.1 Objects in the Digital Age

The digital age, considered to have begun in the 1970s, is also known as the information age, and is the age in which we are thought to now be living. Steve Jobs' work in technology is worth considering. His passing on October 5, 2011, gave him only 30 short years to imprint his knowledge on an age that will probably never forget him. To understand why, we have to understand what motivated him not only as a businessman and innovator, but also as a learner and thinker.

Steve Jobs was the founder of the company Apple Computers that later evolved (under his guidance) to simply be called Apple. The change of names was an indication from Jobs that he did not see his company as just a computer company, but something less specific—a consumer electronics company. Jobs' main obsession was *how* people interacted with computers at the personal level, unlike his peers working with computers and technology who were interested in the data, programming, and logic embedded into the hardware. This childlike need to explore the distance between all of the objects his company *could* be and what he *wanted* it to be is a testament to his curiosity about the distance and depth of related objects. His focus on all objects digital related to computing narrowed down to our interface and interaction with computers—a focus on *objects* (Figure 1.5).

Jobs became a **curator**. A curator is someone who collects, defines and sorts, and stores objects. It is also someone who will reshape the individual objects of a collection and define a collection for a broader audience. There is no question that working with a computer and other technology devices involves objects—physical objects such as keyboards, mice, and other interfaces.

Figure 1.5 Steve Jobs had a laser-like focus on how technology should work by "standing at the intersection of humanities and sciences." (Used with permission, copyright pressureUA/Shutterstock.com.)

Computing also involves virtual, digital objects, such as programs, data, and storage. The horizon from which Steve Jobs could choose his depth of focus ranged from massive sets of data and the programs that accompanied them, to the point of interaction or interface—the mouse and the keyboard. While all of these objects were related, Jobs ultimately would fashion a depth of field and demonstrate a strong passion for a certain scope of specialization within his field, and while the technology of computing interested him, he became most focused on the computer as an object that was to be interacted with, and exactly how that would be done.

In considering his vision for Apple, Steve Jobs ultimately placed most of his attention on serving the community (the broader audience) by making access to the vast digital space known as the Internet and other data sets more natural through the design of interface objects. Apple, and Jobs specifically, is credited with bringing us the computer mouse, the gesture-based interface (like the iPad or iPod Touch screens), and Siri—the voice-activated small artificial intelligence system embedded in the final device he released to the world, the iPhone 4S.

To say that Steve Jobs was a curator of collected objects and possessed a need to develop thesauri and taxonomies around him would be an understatement. Steve Jobs says in his biography by Walter Isaacson, "I read something that one of my heroes, Edwin Land of Polaroid, said about the importance of people who could stand at the intersection of humanities and sciences, and I decided that's what I wanted to do."[11] Steve Jobs so embodied this ideal that he referenced it several times throughout his life, and even used a visual in his January 2010 keynote (the introduction of the iPad) showing a street sign that illustrated the crossroads between technology and the liberal arts, literally. It was, perhaps, the study of humanities that led Jobs to the focus of his work—the careful curating and creation of technology that now helps the consumer access information in the vast digital age.

In evidence to this commitment to becoming a curator of objects and the need for taxonomies, 1 Infinite Loop (the address of Apple headquarters) had a devotion to design that is broadly considered to be the biggest corporate value at Apple under Jobs' leadership. The Apple design team relentlessly developed, and continues to develop, objects that continually refine the interface between man and machine. They created a deep language and thesaurus of names for the objects they created. Some of these named objects made it to market with the design thesaurus delivering a product called iPad. Others did not, with designed objects such as the Paladin (a PC, fax, scanner, and phone all in one[12]) and the Penlite (a PowerBook Duo and tablet combination[13]) never seeing the light of the consumer marketplace at all.

Guided by Steve Jobs and executed by an amazing design team, there exists within Apple a cultural willingness to try often, fail when needed, and deliver incredibly successful products as a result. Often Apple is characterized by releasing only what it knew would work today in a new product launch, and saving what might work tomorrow based on consensus and market realities for another day.

When we speak of the different ages and the people who influenced them, the term *luminary* is often used. The work that Steve Jobs did while he was at Apple and the culture that he built to outlast him, ultimately manifesting itself in the creation of revolutionary products that have changed the way mankind interacts with the digital age, makes it fair to say that Steve Jobs aptly fits this term as well.

1.6.2 Objects in Japan Today: A Different Worldview

Haruki Murakami writes a poetic utterance in his fictional work *1Q84*: "This may be the most important proposition revealed by history; 'At the moment, no one saw it coming.'"[14] In the traditional culture of Japanese phenomena, Murakami is giving an early nod to the sensibilities of his audience, sensibilities that, even before the 2011 earthquake, included a deeply apocalyptic worldview. Much is said about this in Chapter 7 of the book *Managing Emerging Risk*, including a lengthy discussion of the disaster halo effect of the quake.[15] However, given the discovery of vast and unforeseen impacts from that event, we must revisit the worldview of destruction that is unique to Japan.

In Japan's traditional arts we encounter a particular aesthetic, one so foreign that even its translation to English often defies us. This aesthetic is called *wabi-sabi*. The closest translation for this term is "elegiac." Other writers prefer terms like *impermanent, rustic,* or *crude*. These translations are far from accurate. For generations wabi-sabi has held its place in Japanese formal and popular culture as a reverent longing for that which has failed. It is the object as homage to time, entropy, and the transitional nature of all objects. This aesthetic is directly tied to the predominant religion of Japan, Buddhism, and the view that "we are born to suffer what there is to suffer, enjoy what there is to enjoy and to regard both suffering and joy as facts of life," as taught in the *Lotus Sutra*.

In Japanese culture, wabi-sabi is the visual representation of such suffering. To a certain extent, most Western thinking does not consider the suffering component of this equation, nor does it regard *both suffering and joy* as a fact of life. That being the case, the easiest way to explain wabi-sabi to a Westerner is with this analogy: In America, we visit Washington, D.C., to view the blooming of the cherry trees as a symbol of renewal. In Japan, the blooming of the cherry blossoms, or *Sakura*, is a reflection on the ephemeral nature of objects due to their short-lived beauty. This concept of short-lived perfection is known in Japanese as *mono no aware*, which translates roughly to sensitivity to **ephemera**. *Ephemera* describes objects that are usually tossed away after their use, but are collected for their nostalgic value.

As discussed earlier, the Western mind does not comprehend nostalgia as readily as it does collecting or even learning. Moreover, passing objects are not regarded as objects from which we might learn except in the early tradition of the **cabinets of curiosities**. However, Japan relishes its ephemera, and cherishes the study of the how, when, and most

28

importantly, *why* these objects pass from one state to other. So compulsive is the Japanese need to understand the elegiac beauty of objects once loved but now lost, that this theme permeates nearly all of its culture and to a large degree, its sciences.

* * *

Any good impact assessment is the study of the objects that are *valued* and will be lost. This is not a line of study reflected upon in much of American culture, and much less in our businesses and organizations.

* * *

To further illustrate this concept, a comparison of floral arrangements could be considered. In the West, we consider a flower arrangement based on the freshness and number of new blooms. The Japanese art of flower arrangement is called *ikebana* and is a study in minimalism—wherein special consideration is given to a minimal number of blooms and the inclusion of leaves and stalks. The high public interest in **ikebana** creates demand for educational television shows, and it is taught in Japanese schools (Figure 1.6).

Figure 1.6 A Western flower arrangement opposed to an Eastern, ikebana, arrangement highlights the difference between an obsession with what is new and what is ephemeral.

29

1.6.3 Objects in the Age of Enlightenment

During the age of enlightenment, princes, kings, aristocrats, well-funded botanists, artists, zoologists, and other thinkers kept cabinets of curiosities or *Kunstkammer*, as they were called in German. These were a collection of objects that was typically shown in large rooms that served as a combination of a showcase and physical library. "Princes such as the Medici and the Hapsburgs compiled objects for cabinets that they could command from merchants and explorers to Africa and the New World. The cabinets represent a transformation in knowledge acquisition: new emphasis was placed on gaining information from material objects,"[16] writes Mark Dion, of the University of Minnesota. Gaining information from material objects is a part of the rich history of learning that our profession must begin to consider.

Albertus Seba (1665–1736) was an apothecary, which in today's terms would translate into something akin to a pharmacologist or one working in the pharmaceutical sciences. By the same standard applied to Jobs, Seba could also be called a luminary, but one from an age 400 years earlier. As appropriate to his era of professional practice, he found himself working to create ointments and medicines from plant and animal materials.

Beginning in 1697, one might find Seba down along the harbor of Amsterdam, tending to ailing sailors and seamen with an eager glimmer in his 32-year-old eyes. Each of the mild ailments needing his treatment was really a cause for Seba to bargain. Having many wealthy clients, he was not in desperate need of patients; therefore his treatment of sailors and their meager salaries was not his motivation. Rather, payment for his service was taken from the sailors in the form of natural curiosities—strange objects from foreign lands—something that he could not get from his wealthy clients.

Seba's work required him to seek new treatments and medications for use in the treatment of sickness and disease. Again, with a curiosity that is most aptly compared to that of a child, Seba collected plants and animals from sailors to deepen his understanding of botany, anatomy, and healing. That this notion of collecting objects is a childlike habit is supported by many studies in developmental and social science (as referenced by Baudrillard); collecting and sorting objects during Seba's time was regarded as high thinking, and it garnered him considerable social status.

In the age of enlightenment these collections served many purposes, among them, to convey a sense of knowledge, demonstrate wealth, and principally, to categorize, document, and compare one object to the other.

"The aim was to bring together—at least in representative form—the most complete collection possible of all things knowable and worth knowing, to record them and thus make them easier to grasp,"[17] according to Irmgrad Musch, in his introduction to Albert Seba's *Cabinet of Natural Curiosities.*

The collections became categorized *taxonomies* (the division into ordered groups) that were cross-referenced. These **taxonomies** became illustrations and then copper printing plates. The plates became books, known as *thesauri* (a list of illustrations or words with cross-references and synonyms), and these **thesauri** became the basis for a new level of comparison and hypothesis.

Natural history collections of objects and their books are linked, just as books on anatomy, mechanics, robots, and technologies are often based on collections. For nearly every great book on these topics there is a collection of objects. Seba and his many contemporaries built up vast collections of curiosities and wonder in the 18th century and curated objects, developed taxonomies and thesauri, and forwarded hypotheses based on these collections. "The example set for by Botany was soon followed by medicine, with its plate volumes on anatomy, and biology with richly illustrated books on animals,"[18] writes Musch. Indeed, these collections of objects are the roots of study for most of the modern sciences.

Most learning models, if not all, eventually move beyond the books and letters of their students and return to the roots of the objects—to become tactile, visible, and physical. This is perhaps the most problematic issue with all impact assessments—they are delivered as lengthy reports filled with numbers, tables, and columns of data. These reports are based on theories from other books and studies and often they are far removed from the objects of impact themselves. Few practitioners or professionals have had the fortune (or misfortune, as it might be) to actually *see* the unraveling of the best of impact assessments as a set of crumbled artifacts, destroyed systems, or dead bodies. At the present time, our profession is without its own cabinet of curiosities or collections. A few museums that are well worth visiting exist, but even these have a tendency to be edited with objects inserted or removed in order to convey the view of the curator, such as the Holocaust Survivor Memorial, the USS *Arizona* Memorial, and the National WWII Memorial and Registry.

* * *

Lacking a natural progression from collection, to taxonomy, to thesaurus, to a hypothesis regarding when objects fall apart is both the work of an impact assessment and often a demonstration of the vast gap in knowledge our profession has in conducting them.

* * *

It is important to note that these collections of objects represent the discriminant collecting of objects for study, not the indiscriminate hoarding of objects for collecting "keepsakes." A discriminating collector is gathering objects to inspect problems and search for new solutions.

1.6.4 Applying Seba's Curiosities to Impact Assessments

Sherry Turkle notes in *Evocative Objects*, "Indeed, in the psychoanalytic tradition, both persons and things are tellingly called 'objects' and suggest that we deal with their loss in a similar way."[19] Professionally, an impact assessment is the study of the loss of the object. Yet we lack a reference catalogue or "cabinet" of what stands to be lost. We have not developed our learning in the profession based on knowledge of such objects in the literal sense, and it is in fact questionable if we even could. However, collections and objects are a powerful and proven means of researching a learning model that is well worth exploring.

In order to understand what happens when an organization, city, state, or nation is struck with a disaster or terror attack, that is, to *truly* understand the impacts, we must be able to both build up a knowledge of the objects and systems that have been created by the organization through the study of the organization and then *tear it down*. Yet it turns out that we have some biases regarding *how* objects fall apart. Even if we don't have these biases as professionals, some of our employers certainly do. One major problem humans have is that we are not readily wired to deal with the uncanny realities of imperfection or a strong capacity for deconstruction.

The notion of something being *uncanny* is closely linked to the study of objects. Again, Sherry Turkle, in *Evocative Objects*, writes, the uncanny is "not what seems close, but it is 'off,' distorted enough to be creepy."[20] This is one of the other challenges of conducting accurate impact assessments: When dealing with mass causalities, vast financial impacts, and perhaps the loss of control and systemic failure itself, all data look distorted. Although Seba's work suggests a worthy method to apply to the risk management field, it creates its own set of problems due to the nature of an impact assessment, and requires extraordinary effort to find a manageable application within the field.

32

1.6.5 A Dark Nostalgia

Imagine for a moment, if we had a reference collection of impacts from the last decade's largest disasters and terror attacks—a cabinet of curiosities for emergency managers. For practical purposes the objects in this collection would have to be virtual. What if we could synthesize the great disasters and terror attacks to scale using holographic models that demonstrate how objects came undone? What if each event was rendered accurately, with an unflinching commitment to the facts? It would certainly be a display of dark **nostalgia**, and perhaps, one of the greatest learning tools available to emergency management. The facts of terrible human disasters could be presented to scale, so that abstract details to us, like the scope of the 2004 Indian Ocean tsunami, could be compared to the scope of the Japanese earthquake of 2011.

To bring this concept closer to home, think of September 11, 2001. According to *USA Today*, our imagined collection would have to show at least 200 people falling or jumping to their deaths from Tower 1 on 9/11. "For those who jumped, the fall lasted 10 seconds. They struck the ground at just less than 150 miles per hour—not fast enough to cause unconsciousness while falling, but fast enough to ensure instant death on impact. People jumped from all four sides of the North Tower. They jumped alone, in pairs and in groups."[21] Would each act be annotated with the name, years of service, and contribution to their company for each of those victims? Would documentation of friends, families, and lovers who grieved their loss be readily available for cross-referencing within the virtual disaster model?

* * *

If we had such a collection as a profession, we would have a much greater tool than any book could ever provide for teaching the science and art behind creating an outstanding impact analysis, a study library analogous to a "war college."

* * *

We would be remiss to not also show in our imaginary, virtual collection, by way of objects, the heroic response over time—after the risk had manifested itself. To accurately report on the *unplanned* and *unexpected* waterborne evacuation of Lower Manhattan on that day, one would have to compare it to a sea evacuation "larger than the sea evacuation of Dunkirk [France] in World War II, where 339,000 British and French soldiers were rescued over the course of nine days. On 9/11, nearly 500,000 civilians were rescued from Manhattan by boat. It took less than nine hours."[22]

Of course, this imaginary collection is only a concept today. However, it would be a powerful teaching and learning tool. Two problems present themselves when considering our own virtual cabinet of curiosities. The first is our willingness to explore our dark nostalgia. Public reaction to the Holocaust Museum in Washington, D.C., suggests that collections of terrible events and their related objects do not bode well with the general public. Our suggested collection would represent a view of some of the worst events in the last decade. Consider the etymology of the word *nostalgia* itself. In modern use, it has positive associations, but the historical use of the word is tied directly to loss and trauma. The Civil War period use of nostalgia is what we now call post-traumatic stress disorder, and was directly associated with the trauma and loss experienced by veterans of that war. All collections of objects, by their nature, are nostalgic (Figure 1.7).

The second problem is one of curation. Who would be an appropriate curator for such a dark collection? What might he or she edit out or choose to keep? The second challenge with our proposed collection is the core

Figure 1.7 During the Civil War, nostalgia was a diagnosis for what we now know as post-traumatic stress disorder.

question of how curating such emotional objects results in distortions, whether intentional or not.

While curating objects into meaningful architectures, taxonomies, and thesauri, and applying values to them, we are moving forward the idea that an impact assessment starts with object identification and evaluation. By curating such objects and considering their worth, we are also considering their loss, something that requires a willingness to look beyond the emotional distortions we enforce upon such edits, and to lay out the true impacts that will come from the loss of the objects, as systems, architectures, processes, people, and the qualified measures of relationship, trust, confidence, and public perception we might attach to such objects.

History is rich with sciences that have used objects as a starting point, collecting and evaluating them along the way. It is the building of rich taxonomies and thesauri to accompany them, and ultimately, creating standard naming conventions, values, and measures that are within norms based on hypotheses and experiments that have forwarded other sciences.

* * *

It is this basic notion that is most needed in the critical reexamination of our approach to impact assessments—how we curate objects and understand their names, relationships, and values.

* * *

1.7 CONCLUSION

A risk assessment expresses *what will bring our clients harm*. Impact assessments inform us about *what is in harm's way and what is at risk of being damaged or lost*. While risks may or may not come to be, once they do, the reality of the impacts (however we have calculated them in an impact analysis) becomes very real. By their nature, impact assessments capture the unimaginable by the orderly, logical categorization of systems and organizations, and then project what will happen when those well-ordered and logical objects fall apart, become chaotic, lose their relationship to each other and their environment, and then finally succumb to entropy.

In order to better understand the modern impact assessment, we must consider the context in which many enterprises, both public and private, now operate. This context is referred to as the digital age or the information age, which is the notion that we now operate in a period in which the primary output of the enterprise or organization is information and services. This complex system of management, design, and output is rapidly becoming the norm in U.S. organizations—and not only in business. Much of the public sector now relies on foreign computer chips, internationally networked systems, and even celestial information from satellites to operate and deliver public safety and counterterrorism capabilities. This highlights the primary condition of the economy of the digital age, which is that every piece of the factory is now a globalized point of service, not a localized process. The digital age is often referred to as a culture condition known as postmodern. To be postmodern is to be less tethered to location and more attached to time, context, and conditions that are fluid.

We conclude that a fundamental flaw with much of what passes for an impact analysis is the tendency to think small, which is contrary to the evolution of impacts based on the booming digital age and postmodernism.

We suggest that a set of larger problems and misgivings is embedded in this fundamental flaw:

1. A failure to understand the breadth of suppliers, distributors, and upstream and downstream dependencies that the organization values
2. A failure to align with internal organizational values and external laws and regulations as appropriate to the organization's industry and location
3. A lack of a larger order and taxonomy of impacts, as well as their deviations as practitioners

With the digital age and globalization have come a host of new challenges and questions. Among them are questions of government policy, corporate stewardship, community, and global citizenry. While often viewed as lofty academic questions, these symptoms of change and change resistance have very real impact assessment influences. The larger challenge we face as practitioners conducting impact analyses is that revolutions add turmoil on top of the ground-shifting changes to the organizations and enterprises we serve. As the means of production and the distribution of labor and wealth occur, revolutions and civil unrest often arise.

It is safe to say that the fundamental flaw of thinking too small when it comes to impact assessments will be compounded by social, economic, and governance upheavals for the next decade. The overarching challenge with revolts and revolutions is that they create geopolitical uncertainty. Historically, such revolts and revolutions result in changes to monetary policy, governance, and the social distribution of wealth and power. The challenges embedded in our current approach to impact assessments, as presented in this chapter, will reveal rough ground and unmapped territories as we proceed.

Critical exploration and new guiding principles based on the broader concept of learning, innovation, and invention that has been a key part of scientific and human discovery for hundreds of years is now needed in our professional field. Objects can be quantified, enumerated, and accounted for. When objects are in harm's way, they are an important starting point for impact analysis work. Further, objects can be named, placed in orders or taxonomies, and cross-referenced, revealing their relationship to one another and their interdependencies by and between one another. Finally, objects can be architected and have values beyond the signifiers of monetary value or production value.

A natural progression from collection, to taxonomy, to thesaurus, to a hypothesis regarding when objects fall apart is both the work of an impact assessment and the vast gap in knowledge our profession has in conducting them. In order to understand what happens when an organization, city, state, or nation is struck with a disaster or terror attack, that is, to *truly understand impacts*, we must be able to both build up a knowledge of the objects and systems that been have created through the study of the organization that was built up of objects and then *tear it down*. It is the building of rich taxonomies and thesauri to accompany them, and ultimately, creating standard naming conventions, values, and measures that are within norms based on hypotheses and experiments that have forwarded other sciences. It is this basic notion that is most needed in the critical reexamination of our approach to impact assessments—how we curate objects and understand their names, relationships, and values.

1.8 QUESTIONS

1. How would you describe the difference between a risk assessment and an impact assessment?

2. How does the current period in which we practice give rise to a new set of challenges in the area of impact assessments? What are the unique challenges these changes present?
3. Illustrate an understanding of the fundamental flaw to our current approach to impact assessments and provide examples of specific factors that qualify and quantify the underlying problem.
4. Provide an example of the evolution of impacts as they have manifested themselves in today's practice of impact assessments.
5. Discuss how looking back at similar times of change in history can yield clues for critical thinking and exploration to the way in which impact assessments are conducted.

ENDNOTES

1. *Merriam-Webster*. ND. Risk. http://www.merriam-webster.com/dictionary/risk (accessed July 6, 2011).
2. Burton, Kevin. 2011. *Managing Emerging Risk*. New York: CRC Press, p. 37.
3. Ibid., p. 36.
4. You can view the eBay page at http://www.ebay.com/itm/Susies-Lemonade-Charity-/180678461171#ht_500wt_1140.
5. Chapman, Mike. 2011. Ad of the Day: Verizon Wireless, "Lemonade." http://www.adweek.com/news/advertising-branding/ad-day-verizon-wireless-lemonade-129362 (accessed December 7, 2011).
6. U.S. State Department Overseas Security Advisory Council. 2011. *Best Practices for Crisis Management/Evacuation Whitepaper*, p. 3.
7. Ibid., p. 3.
8. Ibid., p. 6.
9. Ibid., p. 10.
10. Baudrillard, Jean. 2005. *The System of Objects*. London: Verso.
11. Isaacson, Walter. 2011. *Steve Jobs*. New York: Simon & Schuster.
12. Wikipedia. 2010. Apple Paladin. http://en.wikipedia.org/wiki/Apple_Paladin (accessed November 21, 2011).
13. The Apple Museum. Prototypes. http://www.theapplemuseum.com/index.php?id=45# (accessed November 21, 2011).
14. Murakami, Haruki. 2011. *1Q84*. 1st ed. New York: Knopf.
15. Burton. *Managing Emerging Risk*, p. 196.
16. Dion, Mark. 2006. *Cabinet of Curiosities*. Minneapolis: University of Minnesota Press.
17. Musch, Irmgard. 2008. *The Collection of Specimens and Its Pictorial Inventory, an Introduction to Cabinet of Natural Curiosities by Albert Seba*. 25th anniversary ed. London: Taschen, p. 8.
18. Ibid.

19. Turkle, Sherry. 2011. *Evocative Objects: Things We Think With*. Cambridge: MIT Press, p. 9.
20. Ibid.
21. Cauchon, Dennis, and Moore, Martha. 2011, September 9. Desperation Forced a Horrific Decision. http://www.usatoday.com/news/sept11/2002-09-02-jumper_x.htm (accessed November 5, 2011).
22. WoodenBoat Forum. 2011. Boatlift: An Untold Tale of September 11 Resilience. http://forum.woodenboat.com/showthread.php?136581-BoatLift-An-Untold-tale-of-September-11-Resilience (accessed November 5, 2011).

2

Five Guiding Principles for Postmodern Impact Assessments

2.1 KEY TERMS

2.2 OBJECTIVES

After reading this chapter you will be able to:

1. Describe the meaning of a negative public perception impact.
2. Discuss how postmodernism has created new challenges for public sector emergency managers.
3. Discuss why all impacts should be presented as potential impacts in an impact assessment.
4. Use the example of the BP oil spill to illustrate postmodern business values.
5. Choose one of the five guiding principles to impact assessments and apply it to a fictional organization.

2.3 OVERVIEW: A FUNDAMENTAL FLAW AND THE FIVE GUIDING PRINCIPLES

As discussed in Chapter 1, a fundamental flaw with much of what passes for an impact analysis is the tendency to think small. This kind of thinking is contrary to the evolution of impacts based on the arrival of the digital age and postmodernism.

By way of review, it is important to recall that a set of problems and misgivings are embedded in this fundamental flaw:

1. A failure to understand the breadth of suppliers, distributors, and upstream and downstream dependencies that the organization values
2. A failure to align with internal organizational values and external laws and regulations as appropriate to the organization's industry and location
3. A lack of usage of a larger order and taxonomy of impacts, as well as their deviations on the part of practitioners (Figure 2.1)

We also established that the digital age and globalization have presented a larger challenge for impact assessments—that of revolutions, which embody public, private, and political upheaval as the means of production, and the distribution of labor that accompanies changes in production, consumption, and the distribution of wealth.

In this chapter we further explore the symptoms of the development of the digital age and postmodernism in order to establish a deeper view of the fundamental flaw and its accompanying misgivings. We also further explore the evolution of impacts, providing a disconcerting view of the postmodern business model when in crisis, discussing key stakeholders in the impact assessment process, and finally outlining the five guiding principles that will frame the discussions in chapters to follow and serve as a method to meet the new challenges faced by practitioners in conducting impact assessments.

2.4 LOOKING DEEPER AT THE EVOLUTION OF IMPACTS

As we discussed in Chapter 1, the nature of impact has evolved. While this evolution is attributed to postmodernism and the digital age, there is no question that we have progressed with uncertainty from simply measuring potential financial, brand, or compliance impacts, injury and loss of life, and property damage impacts. Critical thinking, applied studies, and innovation are required in this area of our practice to truly overcome the challenges and assumptions that undermine the impact assessment as a valued tool in our professional toolkit.

Figure 2.1 Key concepts in this chapter include understanding a fundamental flaw of impact analysis, the five guiding principles of modern impact assessments, and the evolution of impacts.

Not understanding potential impacts creates a gap in the response planning process that can quickly lead to **systemic failure**. Systemic failure occurs when a single event causes system-wide impacts, including impacts to other organizations outside of the scope of the original response plan. As we said in Chapter 1, ignoring that impacts have evolved is to put our head in the sand and ignore that the world has changed around us, and that our practice must evolve with this evolution (Figure 2.2).

* * *

When we accept that the impact assessment captures our objectives, we must then confront that our objectives may be very different now than they were 20 years, or even 2 years, ago.

* * *

Here we consider some of the evolutionary changes we have seen in impacts and the driving factors behind them. First, we consider the impact of modernity on both the private and the public sector and what those sectors value.

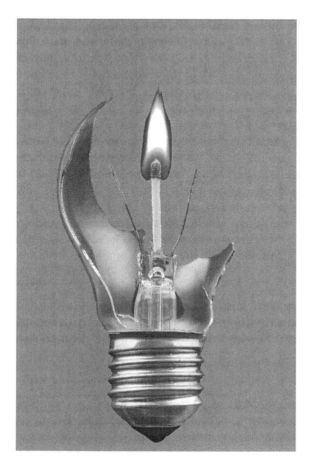

Figure 2.2 A systemic failure occurs when a single failure causes system-wide impacts.

2.4.1 Postmodernism and the Evolution of Impacts

The term *modernity* refers to a post-traditional/postmedieval historical period and the move toward capitalism, industrialization, and the nation-state with its constituent institutions. Late **modernity**, widely considered to have ended in the late 1970s, may have been replaced, as some sociologists would contend, with postmodernism. To be *postmodern* is to be beyond the modern tendencies of classification and authoritarian cultural values based on objective truth, and to consider a world in which many, if not all, apparent realities are not only social constructs (as they are subject to change), but also highly suspect based on time and place. Postmodernism is concerned with principles such as identity, unity, authority, a certain plurality, and skepticism. All of these attributes are exhibited in our postmodern culture through the media, the Internet, and even in the need for varied (and often skeptical) points of view in American and international political discourse.

Assuming that this evolution away from objective truth to subjective realities has not influenced value at the corporate or nation-state level is naïve at best. Consider the impacts of postmodernism on corporate culture, a rapid 20-year change in which those things we now place value in (and on) are completely different. Diversity now trumps authority. Just-in-time fulfillment now trumps simple delivery and craftsmanship. Partnership now trumps private, in-house research, development, delivery, and even, in some cases, the creation of goods.

* * *

Many postmodern businesses are simply pass-through organizations in which the only thing "sold" is a network of partners that offer supply chain logistics, sales support, delivery, and the manufacturing of the goods we buy.

* * *

Amazon, Wal-Mart, and Costco are all prime examples of this phenomenon. Around these focal points of purchase are massive organizational partnerships and networks comprised of many companies that sell discrete and highly specialized third-party services.

These services can take the form of advertising, sales, manufacturing, packaging, fulfillment, logistics, and customer service. It can safely be said that the postmodern corporation is more likely to be a specialized firm selling business-to-business support systems than it is to be a one-stop shop for all of the services or goods they offer. Even banking is supported by a wide array of such support operations and is highly dependent on partners and networks to stay in operation. A simple cup of coffee from a local donut shop is the endpoint of a complex, global, and convoluted goods creation and supply chain system so far removed from the point of sale that the transfer of one cup of coffee from a person behind the counter into our hands is a mere period in pages of far-flung manufacture and logistics management design.

2.4.2 Other Problems Surrounding Impact Assessments

Impacts are a fluid thing. As surely as production and revenue waxes and wanes, so too do impacts. This is perhaps the biggest challenge of all; however we measure impact—from revenue, to loss of life, to property damage—the valuations of these objects are changing all the time. Populations increase and decrease seasonally, as do the revenues of companies, and the value of properties. While impact assessments are often regarded as a static picture of what might be damaged or lost in a catastrophe, the reality is that a "one-off" impact assessment can only capture **potential impacts**. An impact assessment only points out *potential* impacts, and it is subject to change at the time of a disaster. Any private or public sector impact assessment that fails to point out this critical fact is not only misrepresenting the impacts themselves, but also undermining solid response planning for the future, and ultimately eliminating the effectiveness of the work that was done.

* * *

Potential impacts are the true deliverables found in an impact assessment. They are subject to change, and are based on the fluid nature of business, human life, culture, and the perceptions of value to the organizations we serve.

* * *

Embedded in these serious questions about our current approach to impact assessments is that our treatment of data gathered for, and reported in, them speaks to our ethics as private and public sector emergency managers.

The importance of impact assessments across the disciplines is that they inform our objectives, the stated goals of our programs. As such, impact assessments have a huge influence over funding and stakeholder buy-in. The objectives and goals of our response programs may not necessarily be aligned with the organizations we serve, as we will discuss in Chapter 4. An impact assessment that is not conducted with a high degree of accuracy and currency can create multiple, ill-informed response-related challenges and issues for emergency managers and the organizations we serve.

What this postmodern context suggests is that while impacts to revenue, brand, and shareholder value may be good to measure, there are many other impacts, such as impacts to partners and the potential for unraveling the true owner of the business during a disaster. To emphasize this point, consider the BP oil spill of 2010.

2.5 THE BP OIL SPILL OF 2010: A POSTMODERN FAILURE

The BP oil spill in the Gulf of Mexico was the largest accidental marine oil spill in the history of the petroleum industry. British Petroleum, known as BP, operated the *Deepwater Horizon* rig, but when things failed, questions around the operation and ownership of this rig were spotlighted in a manner that did not keep with the official desires of BP. The handling of the failure also brought to light how difficult it can be for any governmental agency to assign accountability, and how easy it can be for a postmodern organization to avoid responsibility. Take a look at the following public and private organizations that had a hand in the operation of the *Deepwater Horizon*.

Hyundai Heavy Industries manufactured the rig. Transocean Ltd., one of the world's largest offshore drilling contractors, owned it. It operated under a Marshallese flag of convenience, a practice in which the maritime rig was registered under a sovereign state different than that of its owners, which in this case happened to be the Marshall Islands. Halliburton Energy Services was installing a production casing and cementing the rig's drill tunnel at the time of the incident. BP was the stated operator and principal developer of the Macondo prospect lease, owning a 65% share of the oil field. However, Anadarko Petroleum Corporation owned 25%, and MOEX Offshore, a unit of Mitsui, owned 10%. Cameron International Corporation built the blowout preventer that failed. Thus there were at least eight players involved with the accidental spill.

Beyond addressing the true owner of the rig and the impacts caused by the spill, postmodern insurance constructs further complicated the picture. Jupiter Insurance Ltd. was BP's key insurance company. In fact, BP owns Jupiter, and it operates out of Guernsey, an offshore UK tax haven. The firm does not reinsure the liabilities to BP by selling them to other insurers, a practice called **reinsurance**, but BP did not have loss of property and liability claims insurance that may have been carried through Lloyds of London.

Other companies involved in the operation of the *Deepwater Horizon* rig were insured or reinsured by three large firms: PartnerRE Ltd., which reinsures Paris Re (*Re* stands for reinsurance) Holdings Ltd., faced claims of $60 million or more. Montpelier Re Holdings Ltd., a Bermuda-based reinsurer, may have had losses tied to the explosion that reached $20 million. Hanover Re estimated its losses from the accident at $53 million. These same reinsurers had been slammed just 1 month earlier by the Chilean 8.8 earthquake—the world's fifth strongest earthquake in a century (prior to the Japan quake of 2011).

What this massive complex of companies within companies that partnered with companies to drill oil created, when disaster struck, was a situation in which the impacts rippled across all partners and suppliers involved, including loss of life, loss of jobs, loss of revenue, impacts to perception and brand recognition, as well as myriad legal and compliance impacts. BP, as a postmodern company, did not exist as a single entity responsible for the event (although the U.S. administration and Homeland Security Secretary Janet Napolitano laid the responsibility of the cost of cleanup squarely on BP). Postmodern BP's operation of the *Deepwater Horizon* rig was completely constructed through agreements, based on needs, time, and place, and in a sense, it was a strategic organizational construct of BP's making.

Understanding the risk to the rig might have been an easy task from a planning perspective. Should a catastrophic failure occur, understanding the impacts to all of those responsible for the rig, as well as to the public, would be a highly complicated task. In fact, the response to the disaster during the first several weeks had partners publicly blaming one another rather than taking action, and in many people's opinion, they were wasting valuable time.

* * *

This type of hypercomplex, intertwined, role-specific organization of industry is much more common than one might suspect. It is the rule in a postmodern society, not the exception.

* * *

The *Deepwater Horizon* rig was a postmodern operation, beyond the modern tendencies of classification and authoritarian cultural values, and *not* based on objective operational truth. The operation was constructed for a world in which many, if not all, apparent realities were only business arrangements that were subject to change and highly influenced by time and place. Without the highest level of organizational confidence in the practitioners responsible for planning for a potential event at the site, not all of the partners could know, let alone imagine, the sheer magnitude of the impacts a prolonged failure would generate.

This is not an indictment of globalization or postmodern business ethics. We will leave those judgments to sociologists and economists.

* * *

What the BP example highlights is that there is a strong organizational tendency in the postmodern era for context-specific partnerships and networks, not only in the Fortune 500 companies or with the BPs of the world, but even in small businesses.

* * *

Private sector planners need to look closely at how out-sourcing, in-sourcing, and supply chain complexities influence their consideration of what might be impacted and what they should be assessing during their business impact assessments.

While a tendency for abstract, context-specific business models is strongly exhibited in today's businesses, the people who run them may not have full command over another postmodern reality: **cultural relevancy**.

Consider the BP oil spill once more. BP's chief executive at the time, Tony Hayward, made the surprising and disappointing comment "I'd like my life back" during a television interview in the midst of the crisis. He clearly lacked any perspective into the cultural relevancy of his comments and did not consider that in a postmodern era he would be expected to be accountable to the context of time and space incumbent to the issue at hand. In short, he had no idea how poorly his comments would be taken in the context of an America that was in the midst of a recession. The end result was that he was quickly replaced with an American BP employee named Robert Dudley, who hailed from Mississippi. Dudley became BP's first non-British chief executive. He was culturally relevant for the crisis at hand, and would end up doing a better job of managing the **negative public perception impact** to BP's image through the crisis. Negative public perception impacts arise often, shaping public opinion and causing a negative reaction to the responding agency or organization.

One of the dual challenges of postmodern business models is that operations may be global, while corporate operators themselves may be very local in terms of their worldview, and therefore lack the international context and local consideration that is required of them during a local event. This dual challenge increases the risk of negative public perception impact: Does a global company, or even a local company with global distribution, manufacturing, or other partners, have the human capital required to lessen the severity of the negative public perception impact locally based on context? One component of this question has to do with the stakeholders included in an impact assessment.

2.6 STAKEHOLDERS IN AN IMPACT ASSESSMENT

Today, the fields of business continuity, emergency management, and counterterrorism include **stakeholders** such as Homeland Security professionals and consultants, emergency management students (graduate and undergraduate) and professionals, security managers, city, state, and federal officials, corporate executives, contingency planners, disaster recovery and business continuity experts, and others who are interested in the current state of emergency preparedness in both the private and public sector, including stakeholders from the FBI and other intelligence agencies that interact with these groups.

One last group of stakeholders is perhaps the most interesting—the laypersons that seek to understand emergency preparedness for personal or business reasons. The breadth of fields in which the interested layperson works and his or her depth of influence in the discipline cannot be overlooked, as it is often a business analyst or a sharp observer of current events that is the most deeply invested in emergency planning for both the public and private sectors. For brevity within this text, the term *emergency manager* applies to *all* of these stakeholders. To a large extent, any interested and informed person who cares about the future and his or her ability to survive an event is an emergency manager in his or her own right.

Former Homeland Security chief Tom Ridge said at a speech in Miami Dade County, "We cannot let anything impede the ability of brave men and women to save the lives of citizens as well as their own."[1] Later, the head of the Department of Homeland Security (DHS), Janet Napolitano, made similar comments on cyber security and other terror threats. She said this about the H1N1 virus: "The government cannot solve this alone. We need everybody in the United States to take some responsibility. If you are sick, stay home. Wash your hands. Take all of those reasonable measures that will help us militate and contain how many people actually get sick."[2]

Given this broader view of impacts and the stakeholders in an impact assessment, it is important to start considering a framework for how to capture impacts that allows for postmodernism and the digital age. In fact, the evolution of impacts is so pronounced that five guiding principles are being suggested in this volume to create a baseline of essential knowledge that will serve practitioners now and in the future. These five guiding principles serve as a framework for capturing impacts within the digital age and postmodernism.

2.7 FIVE GUIDING PRINCIPLES FOR POSTMODERN IMPACT ASSESSMENTS

We have explored some of the negative outcomes that result from poorly rendered impact assessments and have hinted at the need for more accurate and quantifiable means of conducting impact analyses. It is important to transform critical thinking about these concepts into actionable ideas. The analogy of a box will be used to illustrate our succession of the five guiding principles for postmodern impact assessments.

2.7.1 Understanding the Second Phase in an Emergency Management Program: Conducting a Potential Impact Assessment

Emergency management professionals work in phases. The first phase of an emergency management program is often a risk assessment. This is the first process step in an emergency management program (covered in the book *Managing Emerging Risk*). From a process point of view, if we understand this first phase is about risk, we can then understand the second phase is about impact. The second phase in an emergency management program is the assignment of criticalities to objects by conducting a potential impact assessment. The challenge with this second phase, this process of conducting a potential impact assessment, is that it is completely different from the first phase, the process of conducting a risk assessment. The potential impact phase is the subject of much debate based on varying points of view and the distortion of facts (accidentally or intentionally). The second phase of the program (a potential impact assessment) is also of great importance to the quality and perhaps the funding of mitigation and planning activities that take place in the remaining phases of most emergency response programs.

* * *

Five guiding principles for postmodern impact assessments are designed to help us address a fundamental design flaw in the deliverable called the potential impact assessment, through the application of new processes and controls.

* * *

A risk assessment is a Pandora's box of possibilities. We open it only to find ourselves confronted with varied data sources, biased views, probability, and possibility. We work that box with the intent of moving beyond what is expected in risk to what is not expected. As we discuss in *Managing Emerging Risk*, we are looking for, and often at, that which we have not seen before. Just like Pandora's box, one possible horror leads to the next, in what we refer to as the disaster halo effect. What the author recommends in *Managing Emerging Risk* is that we take all of these halo effects under consideration and evaluate the probable and the possible with a sense of cunning intelligence, or *metis*, thereby applying our expertise to the challenge of creative foresight and learning to expect the unexpected. As discussed in Chapter 1, our collection or thesaurus of past events would be very helpful in this regard.

Like Pandora's box, we open the lid of a risk assessment out of a professional need to understand all of the threats and hazards we may encounter as emergency management professionals. As pointed out in *Managing Emerging Risk*, when all the threats and hazards inside of that box are poured out and considered, we are no longer fearful of them; maybe we are even amazed by learning all of the things that may bring us harm, but ultimately, we now view these potential events with an informed risk assessment of the possible and the probable. Most importantly, however, what should be left in Pandora's box of myth is not very different than what is left within the risk assessment deliverable—hope. Only after every threat and hazard is reviewed and considered, as it is implied both by the mythical analogy and in *Managing Emerging Risk*, can we look forward with hope in our planning and response efforts.

2.7.2 The Second Phase—Five Guiding Principles for Postmodern Impact Assessments

Fortunately, the phase being considered in this volume is *not* Pandora's box. This phase is more like the fabled Chinese box, a box of nested boxes, each measured to fit within the other and each containing a principle that makes the nesting of ideas possible, yielding containers within containers. The Chinese box of potential impact assessment is used here as a figurative example of the nested and recursive arrangements that guide the expert in the crafting of an expert potential impact assessment through the application of these suggested **five guiding principles**.

* * *

Five guiding principles for postmodern impact assessments have been created specifically to codify and manage the challenges of the digital age and postmodernism.

* * *

Specifically, it has been derived to ensure that potential impact assessments can be conducted within a simple and consistent framework. This foundation gives emergency management professionals a cornerstone for designing their emergency management programs, enabling actionable steps for consideration; it also provides students with material needed for critical examination and future study. Table 2.1 provides an overview.

The five guiding principles are designed to address the fundamental flaw concept presented in Chapter 1 and its underlying problems—the tendency to think small. Thinking small is contrary to the evolution of impacts based on the booming digital age and postmodernism. When applied, the five guiding principles align with the fundamental flaw to meet this challenge.

The set of larger problems and misgivings that are embedded in the fundamental flaw are addressed by the five guiding principles of impact assessments as follows:

1. A failure to understand the depth of impact is addressed by the first principle, which is to create an impact horizon.
2. A failure to align with internal organizational values and external laws and regulations is addressed by the second and third principles, and results in an initial weighted score that can be applied to objects.
3. The fourth principle brings all of these elements together through (a) the creation of a range of criticality values, the scoring of objects based on the weighted score, creating a weighted object; (b) the placement of a weighted object into this range of criticality values; and (c) the establishment of a logical order and a common taxonomy that are required in completing an impact assessment.

54

Table 2.1   Five Guiding Principles of Potential Impacts

Guiding Principle	Deliverables
1. Establish the impact horizon	An impact horizon statement
2. Align impact measures to core values	The initial development of a weighted score that reflects the core values of an organization and can be applied to each object evaluated in the impact assessment so that each of the core values is represented, with the most important value holding the most weight, and the least of these holding the least weight
3. Consider and align national and state laws and industry regulations	The further development of a weighted score with the enumeration, recital, and clarification of national and state laws and industry regulations that have been considered and are either addressed or not addressed by the potential impact assessment
4. Apply rigorous data analysis	(1) The creation of a range of criticality values, the scoring of objects based on the weighted score, creating a weighted object (2) The placement of a weighted object into this range of criticality values (3) The establishment of a logical order and a common taxonomy that are required in completing an impact assessment
5. Document deviations and overrides	The documentation of any changes to our final range of criticality values, or the weighted objects within them, based on overrides or deviations to our analysis

4. The fifth principle addresses any deviations through executive overrides or other considerations (Figure 2.3).

To summarize this point, conducting a risk assessment is likened to taking hold of Pandora's box. This box, frightening in its containment of possibility and probability, when it has run its course and is thoroughly examined, leaves us only with hope. Conducting a potential impact assessment is very different from Pandora's box and more similar to the Chinese box of measures. When a sound potential impact assessment is

Figure 2.3 The five guiding principles of modern impact assessments address the fundamental flaw concept presented in Chapter 1.

completed we are left with a recursive, nested set of boxes demonstrating exacting measure, accountability, and useful motivation. This moves us beyond the ideal of hope and into measurable action in the form of the innermost box—response tactics and operations.

2.7.2.1 The First Box—Establish the Impact Horizon
Upon initiating a potential impact assessment, the first principle is in the outermost box; this box should fit and integrate with many other boxes. The principle is simple: *The potential impact assessments should reflect potential impacts both inside and outside the organization as deemed appropriate by an established impact horizon.*

This is the first measure: How large is the **impact horizon** (what is in scope and what is not), and how does it integrate and overlap with that of suppliers, partners, and other stakeholders? In order to meet the conditions of the first principle the practitioner would take a wide-angle view of impacts and achieve consensus within the organization and communications outside of the organization about how to achieve this fit.

The practitioner will have to take measure of this principle and organize an impact horizon matrix that considers upstream and downstream impacts. These would then be organized into a **responsibility assignment matrix** (RAM or RACI: responsible, accountable, consulted, and informed) that concludes with a detailed impact horizon statement that includes all in-scope and out-of-scope assets and locations for the potential impact assessment.

2.7.2.2 The Second Box—Align Measures to Core Values
After the first principle, the next box is opened and its contents are revealed—a smaller box. This is a recursive exercise, and each box will

reveal a new box containing a new principle. This new principle, like the one before it, is a simple statement: *The potential impact assessment should align to the organization's core values.* The second principle is keener on a basic alignment of **key potential impacts** (a set of key measures that relate to impacts) to the narrow and specific core values of the organization, company, or community. State, national, and industry values will be covered in Chapter 3, followed by a discussion on federal laws and regulations in Chapter 4.

This is the second measure: alignment to core values. How does the set of key potential impacts align with the company, community, or state core values? In order to meet the condition of the second principle, one must take into consideration the core values of the organization and align them with key potential impacts. The goal is to achieve a fit between the inner edges of the impact horizon and the outer edges of the company, community, or state's core values. As illustrated in the following examples, this may be harder than it seems.

If the organization holds the idea that "We will be the safest place to work," then human death and injuries are key potential impacts aligned to core values. If the organization holds the idea that "We will protect shareholder value and deliver strong returns," then revenue and financial impacts are key potential impacts aligned to core values. If the organization says, "We will protect the environment in our operations," then environmental impacts are key potential impacts that align to core values. The challenge is that most companies, communities, and states have more than one core value.

Core values are expressed as an admixture of value statements that drive the organization forward. They can range from "being the safest," to being the "best quality," to "being the most secret." Given that there is more than one core value, the practitioner will have to use weighted scores to establish the exact level of importance for each of these factors as they are aligned to our core values. A weighted score is the only way to ensure that the second measure is done correctly. To accomplish this, the practitioner must include three or more core values and assign them percentages within the weighted score to organize core values based on importance.

The result of this measure is an informed potential impact assessment that aligns score values to a specific weight, and then places them in a weighted score. Values can range from the most important, like "being a safe place to work," to the least important value statement, which might be "protect the environment." The final deliverable for the second box is the development of a weighted score that reflects the core values of an organization and can be applied to each object evaluated in the impact assessment so that each of the core values is represented, with the most important value holding the most weight, and the least of these holding the least weight. From here, it is time to open the next box.

2.7.2.3 The Third Box—Consider and Align National and State Laws and Industry Regulations

With the impact horizon set and organizational core values reflected in the weighted score, it is time to look at the third box. The third box is no different than the first or second box; it is equally proportioned, stepping down in size to nest perfectly within the second box. The tolerances are ever so thin, with the margins between the boxes exacting and well fitted.

As expected, the third box reveals a new principle. This new principle, like those before it, is simple and self-evident. It says, "The potential impact assessment should reflect due consideration and appropriate alignment as an organization, community, or state to state or national laws and industry-specific regulations." This principle refers to the wider policies of the nation or state in which the organization does business. They can take the form of guidance or general policy statements and come from a variety of sources. This third principle can either be very easy to achieve or prove very difficult.

This is the third measure: alignment of core values to state or national law and industry regulations. How does the set of key potential impacts based on the core values of the organization align with national or state law and industry regulations? A practitioner can meet conditions of the third principle by considering national or state laws and industry-specific regulations and including them and further developing the weighted score. To achieve this fit between the refined weighted score and national or state laws and industry regulations the professional must consider which policy statements, if any, apply to the organization and whether or not the approach has already been captured in the weighted scoring of key potential impacts. This principle helps to ensure that the program prioritizes and places value on the impacts that matter to the state or nation in which we are conducting the potential impact assessment. However, it does not guarantee the organization will abide by them; ergo the professional should capture any laws or regulations that are met along with those that are not, and document them.

For example, if the organization is a utility company that has been identified as critical infrastructure or a key resource under the National

Infrastructure Protection Plan (NIPP), the practitioner will have to ensure that he or she adjusts the weighted score around being "a trusted provider of power" (a core value statement) in the national policy, and that the highest value on continuing operations is placed. This readjustment of the weighted score for key potential impacts often pits private sector interests with public safety interests. However, upon a review of the second box in which one weighted the core values, it should be found that there already is a core value that supports national policy well enough. If not, it is time to reassess the core values and consider changing one of two things: Either the professional advocates change to the core value statements and updates the weighted score, or he or she changes the internal policy around emergency management to reflect national or state policy. It is not an option for the practitioner to challenge the interpretation of laws and regulations; however, it is the role of the professional to inform the client of the existence of laws and regulations and to recommend changes in policy as appropriate.

The challenge is that most companies, communities, and states may wish to differentiate themselves by having unique core values. Core values are often "soft" values and the stuff of dreams. As strong emergency managers, we can accommodate this by arranging an internal policy to reflect and give weight to national or state policy in our potential impact assessments. To accomplish this, the practitioner may need to advise the organization to adjust the weighted score to reflect the core values that represent a commitment to national security. The argument here is purely one of patriotism, goodwill, and also good public relations.

We must be mindful that the national policy and laws we are working under will vary from nation to nation. The third box is highly nuanced if the practitioner is working in a multinational setting. In some cases, not aligning the potential impact assessments will result in negligence that amounts to a lack of information and a slap on the wrist. In other cases, not aligning to national policy will land our leadership in jail. We will consider international policy later in this volume; for now, we must contend with the realities of the third principle. We should align our weighted score for the key potential impact assessments to national and state laws and industry regulations.

While we realize this may be challenging in some organizations, our recommendation is that if the privately held organization we work for does not want to align itself to national policy, find a new job! This holds true for local, municipal, or state agencies as well. We do not wish to place ourselves in the role of being complicit with any organization that is convinced that it will "go it alone" or place the values and goods it is protecting over those of the greater good as represented in national policy. None of us have entered the field of emergency management to solely protect the interest of a few at the cost of many. None of us would place a high value on a job that ignores national policy at its own peril, or the peril of our families and communities.

The final deliverable for the third box is the further development of a weighted score with the enumeration, recital, and clarification of national and state laws and industry regulations that have been considered and are either addressed or not addressed by the potential impact assessment.

2.7.2.4 The Fourth Box—Apply Rigorous Data Analysis

Upon fulfilling the principle of the third box, there is now a single, weighted score that can be used for all objects that reflects the core values of our clients, and the laws of our nation or state along with industry-specific regulations. The fourth box reveals a principle about the weighted scores created and how to use them. The principle of the fourth box is a logic concept: (1) the creation of a range of criticality values, the scoring of objects based on the weighted score, creating a weighted object; (2) the placement of a weighted object into this range of criticality values; and (3) the establishment of a logical order and a common taxonomy that are required in completing an impact assessment.

First, the range of criticality values created is an abstract notion based on the client's risk appetite. It is relative to the needs of each organization and may be broken down into any range of values from one business to the next. With this understanding, it must be informed, consistent, and portable across the set of weighted objects being placed within that range of criticality values. For discussion purposes, we will use the score of 100 being the highest impact, and therefore the highest value to protect, and the score of 1 being the lowest impact and the lowest value to protect.

From 1–100 we need to create a range of values so that we come up with four or five **ranges of criticality** values. A range of four criticality values, for example, would be called quartiles. A range of five criticality values would be called quintiles. This range of criticality values informs us of two things. First, it determines the appetite of risk for an organization and how it wishes to arrange weighted objects across the range of criticality values. Second, it infers a scale of potential tactics based on expense and effort that might be applied to each range of criticality values. For example, we can establish some basic quartile values in the range of a 1–100 scale.

* * *

When arranged in a quartile, a value in the range of 1–25 will mean that the thing we are measuring is desirable to protect. A value in the range of 26–50 will mean it is important to protect. A value in the range of 51–75 will mean that it is essential to protect. Finally, a value in the range of 76–100 will mean the thing is critical to protect.

* * *

The weighted score that has been developed by applying the second and third principles can now be applied to an object to create a weighted object that can be placed within the range of criticality values. The total makeup of organizational values and legal and regulatory concerns has been incorporated into the weighted score, and is reflected in the weighted object. Now the weighted object can be placed into the range of criticality values. Keep in mind that the second and third principles state that the objects measured can be anything—from employee safety to profit protection. Given that there is now a range of criticality values, we must consider this principle: How does our weighted score apply to any object?

Take this under consideration and apply it to the specific objects being measured based on principles 2 and 3. If human safety objects score 80, placing them high in the range of criticality values, and this seems reasonable, then the principles are working. Does the same logic work for technology objects? Of course! If a technology object is very important it should score in the range of 76–100. What about other infrastructure objects? Absolutely!

There are not separate ranges of criticality values for humans and for machines. This is also true for water and gas. Whatever key potential impact object is being measured, as long as it is weighted by the second and third principles and will result in a weighted object, it can then be placed within the range of criticality values. With the first half of the principle out of the way (which is understanding that the range of criticality values and the weighted score can apply to any object), the practitioner should suspect what he or she is measuring to ensure it has a logical hierarchy that will help determine *what* to measure, and a common taxonomy that will help ensure that there are not different names for the same objects.

At the highest level, one measure might be to "protect revenue," but revenue is generated by various means and we want to limit the number of variables we measure in order to keep things manageable. Here is the logic of the corporate world of revenues: Processes generate revenue, people do processes, and people need computers to aid with processes.

61

Therefore if we score an object as "critical" within the range of criticality values based on a high revenue impact in the weighted score, then the people and technologies that support that object *inherit the criticality*. This is called **inherited criticality**, which means criticality is given because of the highest-order measure variable, which in this case was the first object.

Here is another example of the fourth principle at work. The "ensure public safety score" logic train might work like this: First responders ensure public safety. First responders need to be safe to ensure public safety. To be safe, first responders need working equipment, including vehicles, active communications, and running water. Therefore if we score public safety as "critical," all of the objects that make up a solid first response capability are also "critical" based on the inherited public safety score. Finding the highest-order measure for each category in the potential impact assessment will ease the scoring of variables into a manageable number as long as we link the core object score to its metadata. The **core object** is the highest object in the logical order of what we are trying to protect. The **metadata** (that is, all of that object's related information) are the objects that enable the core object to function. The weighted score placed on the core object (the weighted object) informs the criticality of all of its dependent metadata, and other objects that support the core object are weighted at the same level, based on inherited criticality.

In order to fulfill the fourth principle, we must identify a range of criticality values that is applicable to any set of objects, view the set of weighted objects based on their individual weighted scores, and then array the objects within the range of criticality values. Finally, there must be a common taxonomy in place. This is what the application of rigorous data looks like. The range of criticality values and the weighted object score are important, but they are not the end all, be all of the fourth principle. We explore this in detail in Chapter 7.

The result of the fourth principle is simple and elegant. Once we have applied it, we will have identified our core weighted objects, their interdependencies and inherited criticality, and finally, and most importantly, how they will be arrayed across the range of criticality values. A detailed description of the mathematics and assumptions used to create a range of criticality values, a weighted object score, a logical order, and a common taxonomy is found in Chapter 7. It is time to open the fifth box.

2.7.2.5 The Fifth Box—Document Deviations and Overrides

Now that we have a range of criticality values and we know what we are measuring, we can open the fifth box, which of course reveals a new and final principle. This principle is so basic it often eludes us. It says, "All deviations, including nonactuarial findings, opinion-based scores, and executive overrides to the process, should be documented."

This is the fifth measure: If the total additive impacts measured in each weighted object score do not exceed the current realities (unless the potential impact assessment is for a special event in which projections are required) we must document the discrepancy as a matter of professionalism. In private practice this means that the function of human resources cannot contribute to 100% of a company's revenue, or claim the total company revenue as its weighted object score. We cannot allow individual departments or functions to posit that their contribution is the only contribution that constitutes 100% of the revenue picture in any single weighted object score. Using the weighted score approach, a total 100% impact to an organization would require the combinatorial consideration of multiple weighted objects and would never result in an impact to the organization exceeding 100%. Many of us have experienced such phenomenal claims, in which a business impact analysis breaks down processes and assigns financial impacts that when taken together, equal 800%—or more than the total earnings of the company!

This is also true of the public sector. Overstated or overestimated single weighted object scores for critical infrastructure, key resources, first responders, hospital capacity, or any of the measures used to justify programs must be documented and disclosed. Professionals must capture accurate and verifiable information to support every single weighted object score. In cases where total accuracy is not possible, we must apply reasonable assumptions based on clean data and expert stakeholder interviews, and disclose these assumptions.

The fifth principle exists to ensure credibility. Unless we can accurately verify a weighted score based on the interviews and data presented to us, practitioners should not continue with the inclusion of that weighted score in the weighted object score without stating clearly that there have been deviations or overrides. The fifth principle exists to ensure that when deviations or overrides occur they are documented.

Regardless of the numerical or formulaic output of the potential impact assessment, overrides will occur in situations under which there are regulatory or legal considerations. In most cases, these overrides will result in a measured impact becoming mission critical, regardless of its formulaic score on the criticality scale.

The **executive override** is often used to forward agendas other than those that are prudent, principle based, and aligned to stated organizational or communal values. Executive overrides must be done by a committee and signed off by the CEO or highest power of authority within the organization. To allow this approach to go unchallenged is akin to letting a patient tell a doctor how to proceed with his or her clinical care. While in medicine patient advocacy has allowed for a person to choose his or her treatment (to some degree), this practice of allowing executive overrides (to lower the cost of the recovery solution, or to upgrade or downgrade the single weighted object score for a given person, process, or technology) has run amok within our industry.

Some consultancies in the private sector even offer executive business impact analyses as a cheaper and more user-friendly alternative to the five principles just outlined. The author believes that there needs to be much more accountability and accuracy in potential impact assessments. To affect meaningful practice of the fifth principle, it should be embedded in internal program policy as well as our emergency management culture.

2.7.3 Summary of the Five Principles of Potential Impacts Analysis

When we are given the assignment of conducting a potential impact assessment, we are given a Chinese box of principles measured, managed, and integrated into smaller boxes. This box requires a downward application of logic and accuracy, along with care and attention to detail. A constant pressure ensures a tight fit when care is given to every principle. Yet when we look on the bottom of that fifth and final box, a small note will be found. It says: "All of this is potential impact. In a real event return to the first box and assess your situation."

It is true. This is the hard fact of even the best potential impact assessment. It only captures potential impacts as we can see them at the time of consultation. It does not capture the true impacts we will encounter tomorrow, or the next day, or the next year. Disasters and terror attacks happen on a calm Tuesday morning, deep in the autumn, when our potential impact assessments have long ago been completed and are now collecting dust. There is nothing sensible to do but revisit these original assessments and adjust them to the current realities when disaster strikes. This is why seasoned professionals in the field refer to a pre-event impact assessment as a *potential impact assessment that must be revisited and periodically updated.*

2.8 REVISITING: POSTMODERNISM, REVOLUTION, AND THE PUBLIC SECTOR

In the public sector, emergency managers are dealing with a new type of impact as well—an impact from the contemporary political landscape—a fear of FEMA and DHS. Over the past 5 years this fear has risen to hysteria and *conspiracy* as people have blamed FEMA and DHS for all manner of ill will toward the people of the United States. However, it is not just the conspiracy theorists that have taken up this worldview; it is also politicians vying for a certain voting base. It can be said that the origins of a conspiracy theory surrounding FEMA and DHS began with the events of 9/11. As hard as it may be for emergency management and counterterrorism professionals to accept, a very vocal fringe group within American culture has speculated that the terrible events of that day were somehow a conspiracy related to the U.S. government. Today, the potential for negative public perception impacts abounds (Figure 2.4).

Figure 2.4 In today's world, conspiracy theorists have a loud enough voice to cause a negative impact for many government activities.

Hurricane Katrina in 2005 and the H1N1 pandemic scare in 2010 seemed to accelerate the narrative. Soon, claims came out that were both wild and frightening. Among them claims were made by fringe groups that:

1. FEMA "death camps" were being built for mass killings.
2. There was a set of covert government plans to forcibly evacuate 50 million people from the Gulf Coast.
3. H1N1 was disseminated by DHS.
4. The H1N1 vaccine was a "death shot" created by the Centers for Disease Control (CDC).

Beyond the conspiracy theories and armchair quarterbacking of FEMA and DHS activities by "watchdog groups" (who are protected by the First Amendment and have a right to question authority), there is the potential for serious negative public sector perception impacts. First is the possibility that after an original risk manifests itself, a potential impact may be a public unwilling to cooperate with first responders. Second is that some politicians will use disasters and terror attacks, as well as the FEMA and DHS budgets, to their political advantage. This is a key component of the skepticism that accompanies postmodernism.

* * *

The polarizing argument and conspiracies around American emergency management, both at the grassroots level and within political parties, are why negative public perception impacts are more important than ever and could further feed the revolutionary rhetoric of the Occupy Wall Street movement or other such revolts.

* * *

After Katrina, a Senate report entitled "Hurricane Katrina: A Nation Still Unprepared" recommended that FEMA be dismantled.[3] "We have concluded that FEMA is in shambles and beyond repair, and that it should be abolished," Sen. Susan Collins, R-Maine, said in a written statement released by the Senate Homeland Security and Governmental Affairs Committee, which she chairs. Senator Collins is not part of any lunatic fringe; she is a politician plying for attention, which is a clear indication of the scope of this challenge. This political move to raise questions about the response to Katrina and the capabilities of FEMA itself gave credibility to the radical conspiracies in which the public itself could be threatened by FEMA. After all, in the eyes of most conspiracy theorists, if a Senate report recommended dismantling the agency, the conspiracy theories must have some credibility.

Now with a national budget crisis at hand in 2011, DHS is under scrutiny and has already taken budget cuts: "On January 24, 2011, Rep. Jim Jordon (R-OH), Chair of the Republican Study Committee (RSC) introduced H.R.408, the 'Spending Reduction Act of 2011.'" This bill, according to the RSC, if passed, "would reduce Federal spending by $2.5 trillion over ten years." According to projections by the Democratic Staff of the House Committee on Homeland Security, the proposed cuts would transform the Department of Homeland Security into the Department of "Homeland Insecurity."

Under the plan, the TSA "takes a big hit under H.R.408. As aviation terrorist attack potential remains significant, the bill proposes a $500 Million cut in security operations, a $75 Million cut in surface transportation operations, and a cut of $174 Million for federal air marshals."

In the run-up to the 2012 presidential election, the funding of DHS continues to be a political issue. Ron Paul, a past presidential candidate, went so far as to say in a 2007 Republican debate in South Carolina, "DHS is a monstrous type of bureaucracy. It was supposed to be streamlining our security and it's unmanageable. I mean, just think of the efficiency of FEMA in its efforts to take care of the floods and the hurricanes…. We should not go to more bureaucracy. It didn't work. We were spending $40 Billion on security prior to 9/11, and they had all the information they needed there to deal with the threat, and it was inefficient. So what do we do? We add a gigantic bureaucracy, which they're still working on trying to put it together, and a tremendous amount of increase in funding."[4]

* * *

Two new impacts have manifested themselves in public sector potential impact analyses: One is a negative public reaction or even civil disturbance if the trend toward government distrust continues. The other is the possibility of a political backlash and budget cuts if public sector emergency managers fail to fully understand and reevaluate potential impacts as they occur based on the current political climate.

* * *

A negative impact to the public perceptions of our emergency management and counterterrorism agencies at the local, state, or federal level should now be a part of any potential impact assessment for public sector emergency managers. The negative public perception threat to our own agencies is a very real impact—even for the top U.S. emergency manager, the Department of Homeland Security secretary. A May 17, 2011, poll showed that only one out of every five American voters approved of Secretary Napolitano.[5]

In the public sector, the new impacts of public distrust and budget cuts loom larger than ever before, as our nation struggles to prepare for, and be proactive to, new risks and to understand the impacts of real disasters as they strike.

With postmodernism and public distrust facing both private and public sector emergency managers, it becomes clear that impacts have changed to require at least the inclusion of protecting the responding organization or agency during an event. This deep understanding of the local perception of first responders, or the corporate body, will be explored in the global context further in this text. However, for now, the point has been made that the act of responding to an event itself creates a negative public perception impact, and that potential impact must be measured to successfully respond to an event (Figure 2.5).

The evolution of impacts suggests that both public and private organizations now face more complex and distributed impacts than before, and that the miscalculation of those impacts can threaten emergency managers. Simply stated, the stakes now include the careers of emergency managers and counterterrorism professionals themselves. The evolution of impacts has reached a point in which accountability to impacts can have a positive or negative impact on the emergency management program itself, stripping it of leadership and budget dollars, or if well conducted, accelerating it forward. Whether we work in the private sector or the public sector, understanding impacts is to understand our objectives, and those objectives are informed by the values we protect and the impacts for which we prepare.

2.9 SUMMARY

The evolution of impacts suggests that both public and private organizations face more complex and distributed impacts today than ever before, and that the miscalculation of those impacts can threaten emergency managers. Simply stated, the stakes now include the careers of emergency managers and counterterrorism professionals themselves. To meet these stakes, they must be acknowledged and faced as the new realities of the digital age and the postmodern worldview that accompanies it, combined with the fundamental flaw of thinking too small. We covered negative public perception impacts, postmodernism, cultural relevancy, and the

Figure 2.5 As impacts have evolved with the advent of postmodernism and public distrust, new, deeper impacts present themselves that are impossible to discern without new tools.

true nature of an impact assessment. We also addressed the solution to these problems by introducing the five guiding principles.

Negative public perception impacts shape public opinion and cause negative reaction to the responding agency or organization. The potential for negative public perception impacts abounds. As hard as it may be for emergency management and counterterrorism professionals to accept, a very vocal fringe group within American culture has speculated that the terrible events of September 11, 2001, were somehow a conspiracy related to the U.S. government. Considering this, the polarizing arguments and conspiracies around American emergency management in general, both at the grassroots level and within political parties, are why negative public perception impacts are more important than ever and could further feed the revolutionary rhetoric of the Occupy Wall Street movement or other such revolts.

Postmodernism has introduced new levels of never before seen complexity to today's businesses. Many postmodern businesses are simply pass-through organizations in which the only thing sold is a network of partners that supply chain logistics, sales support, delivery, and the manufacturing of the goods we buy. Around these focal points of purchase are massive organizational partnerships and networks comprised of many companies that sell discrete and highly specialized third-party services. It can safely be said that the postmodern corporation is more likely to be a specialized firm selling business-to-business support systems than it is to be a one-stop shop for all the services or goods they offer. Private sector planners need to look closely at how outsourcing, insourcing, and supply chain complexities influence their consideration of what might be impacted and what they should be assessing during their business impact assessments.

Cultural relevancy is also a dominating factor in impact assessments. While a tendency for abstract, context-specific business models is strongly exhibited in today's businesses, the people who run them may not have full command over this postmodern reality. Simply put, this means that while there may be processes in place to address and solve the problems caused by an impact, the people in place to oversee them may not be the best suited for leadership because of their inability to see a complex, multifaceted business as one that has a global impact outside of their limited cultural experience or worldview.

While impact assessments are often regarded as a static picture of what might be damaged or lost in a catastrophe, the reality is that a one-off impact assessment can *only capture potential impacts at a specific moment in time.* Any private or public sector impact assessment that fails to point out that all impacts are *potential* impacts and subject to change at the time of a disaster is misrepresenting the impacts themselves and undermining solid response planning for the future. The importance of the impact assessment across the disciplines is that it informs our objectives, the stated goals of our programs, and they have a huge influence over funding and stakeholder buy-in.

Finally, we introduced the five guiding principles, which are composed of:

1. Establish the impact horizon.
2. Align impact measures to core values.
3. Consider national and state laws and industry regulation.
4. Apply rigorous data analysis.
5. Document deviations and overrides.

Looking back at the fundamental flaw presented in Chapter 1, we can see how the five guiding principles align to meet the challenge of the flaw and its underlying fundamentals. To review, the fundamental flaw with much of what passes for an impact analysis is the tendency to think small, which is contrary to the evolution of impacts based on the booming digital age and postmodernism. This can be addressed by applying the five principles.

A set of larger problems and misgivings is embedded in this fundamental flaw:

1. A failure to understand the depth of impact is addressed by the first principle, which is to create an impact horizon.
2. A failure to align with internal organizational values and external laws and regulations is addressed by the second and third principles, and results in a weighted score that can be applied to objects.
3. The fourth principle brings all of these elements together through (a) the creation of a range of criticality values, the scoring of objects based on the weighted score, creating a weighted object; (b) the placement of a weighted object into this range of criticality values; and (c) the establishment of a logical order and a common taxonomy that are required in completing an impact assessment.
4. The fifth principle addresses any deviations through executive overrides or other considerations.

In the next five chapters we are going to address each of the five guiding principles and highlight how they address the problems and misgivings that stem from the fundamental flaw of thinking too small in a postmodern world. Specifically, we are going to discuss the problems of depth of impact, failure to align with internal and external values, and understanding the larger order and taxonomy of impacts, as well as their deviations.

2.10 QUESTIONS

1. What is the meaning of a negative public perception impact?
2. Discuss how postmodernism has created new challenges for public sector emergency managers.
3. Are there other examples that can be used to illustrate postmodern business constructs other than BP? Describe one.
4. Discuss why all impacts should be presented as *potential impacts* in an impact assessment.
5. Choose one of the five guiding principles to impact assessments and apply it to a fictional organization.

ENDNOTES

1. Ridge, Tom. 2004, July 30. Interview by Miami-Dade Office of Emergency Management. Secretary of Homeland Security.
2. U.S. Department of Homeland Security. 2009. Remarks by Secretary Napolitano at Today's Media Briefing on the H1N1 Flu Outbreak. http://www.dhs.gov/ynews/releases/pr_1241530553980.shtm (accessed July 7, 2011).
3. Hsu, Spencer S. 2006. Senate Report: Dismantle FEMA. http://seattletimes.nwsource.com/html/nationworld/2002955813_fema27.html (accessed August 19, 2011).
4. On the Issues. 2009. Ron Paul on Homeland Security. http://www.ontheissues.org/2012/Ron_Paul_Homeland_Security.htm (accessed July 30, 2011).
5. World News. 2011. Poll: Only 23 Percent of US Voters Approve of DHS Secretary Janet Napolitano. http://article.wn.com/view/2011/05/17/Poll_Only_23_percent_of_US_voters_approve_of_DHS_Secretary_J/ (accessed August 19, 2011).

3

The First Principle
Establish the Impact Horizon

3.1 KEY TERMS

3.2 OBJECTIVES

After reading this chapter you will be able to:

1. Describe the meaning of the term *market state* and how it reflects postmodern and globalization activities in the public and private sector.
2. Differentiate between business continuity and disaster recovery.
3. Provide an example of an impact horizon for a public or private sector organization.

4. Discuss the meaning and importance of disclosures in terms of professional ethics.
5. Generate an RACI chart to illustrate an impact horizon for a sample organization.

3.3 OVERVIEW: A FUNDAMENTAL FLAW AND THE IMPACT HORIZON

As discussed in Chapter 1, a fundamental flaw with much of what passes for an impact analysis is the tendency to think small, which is contrary to the evolution of impacts based on the arrival of the digital age and postmodernism. In the book *Managing Emerging Risk*, we explore the concept of two key drivers that are transforming postmodern emergency management practice. These two drivers are described as:

1. The disaster halo effect, the recognition that modern threats exhibit more than one event and multiple outcomes that can be viewed as being **emergent** (or evolving)
2. The worldview of the nation as a **market state** in which nationalism is replaced with a globalized approach focused on the trading of goods, services, and ideas between nation-states

Understanding the influence of these two drivers as well as the concept of an **impact horizon** (the notion that impacts measured within one enterprise or organizational impact assessment will be comingled with the impacts to other enterprises or nations, states, or municipalities), and this is the leading principle in the five guiding principles of postmodern impact assessments because it addresses the fundamental flaw of "thinking too small" by establishing the boundaries and **scope** (what is to be considered and what is not) of any given potential impact assessment. Since one of the misgivings embedded in the fundamental flaw of thinking too small when it comes to impact assessments is a failure to understand the depth of impact, an important step in managing this challenge is establishing an impact horizon (Figure 3.1).

In prior chapters we established that the postmodern corporation is more likely to be a specialized firm selling business-to-business support systems than it is to be a one-stop shop for all the services or goods it offers. This concept is closely tied to the notions of postmodernism and

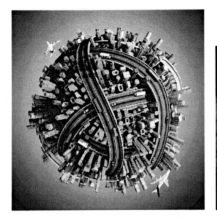

Figure 3.1 Key concepts in this chapter are understanding the impact horizon based on the market state, criticality, and stakeholder input.

globalization presented in this book. The concept is also very much linked to ideas presented in *Managing Emerging Risk*.

One of the key ideas presented in *Managing Emerging Risk* is that disasters and terror attacks exhibit a disaster halo effect. The disaster halo effect is the recognition that modern threats exhibit more than one event, and that multiple events can be viewed as being emergent (evolving). Often multiple events are manifested from a single trigger event, the event we call the **first event scenario**. These multiple events can be more dangerous, more costly, and ultimately even more catastrophic than the trigger event itself. The disaster halo effect is based on the notion of emergence, which is studied in the fields of social science and computer science to explain complex and novel systems.

The disaster halo effect is increasingly pertinent and useful *because of the complexity of our planet and the interaction of our postmodern technologies and social structures*, yet many emergency management practitioners are unaware of the disaster halo effect and do not incorporate it into their recovery planning. Specifically:

1. Emergency management professionals are often surprised by the radical novelty of the natural disasters or terror attacks they face, mostly due to previous expectations created by hindsight bias. Hindsight bias is the tendency to say, "I've never seen it that way before, so it couldn't be that way now." For example, the fact that the earthquake in Chile that occurred February 27, 2010, did not create a tsunami that struck Hawaii was novel because it did not match emergency managers' expectations of what should happen based on previous events.

2. Emergency management professionals are often surprised by the coherence or correlations that catastrophes exhibit. Thinking that water scarcity and civil unrest events are the unexpected outcomes of a large-scale event versus expecting there will be multiple coherent outcomes as a result of the first event scenario is one example. The on-the-ground reality is that the availability of petrol will impact the giving of aid, which will increase the likelihood of a civil unrest event. Notions like these seem to evade the typical emergency manager. Often, emergency managers do not see these correlations and bring them together into a single view of catastrophes or attacks. Yet time and again, the correlations exist.

3. Emergency management professionals are often surprised by the global or macro-level impacts of the events they plan for and respond to. However, if the first 10 years of the new millennium has proven anything to the emergency management community, it is that the world is more connected, more integrated, and more reliant on other nations' attitudes, approaches, and support, or lack thereof, during these events. In addition, natural hazards are being tracked globally now more than ever, and there is a globalized, worldwide scientific review of these events that suggests that few, if any, are truly localized.

4. Emergency management professionals see the evolution of disasters and terror attacks as the product of a dynamic process, but

are wary of approaching catastrophe with a wide-angle view that considers that most, if not all, events exhibit the disaster halo effect in which more than one catastrophic event can manifest itself.

5. Emergency management professionals do perceive that the complexity of modern attacks and disasters is demonstrable and obvious, but seem confounded by this observation and continue to deal with events as one-off issues, as opposed to one major event with multiple emergent events embedded within.

* * *

Often, the scope of emergency management risk scenarios is minimized, budgets are restricted, and myopic views of "what would really happen" hamstring efforts to plan for and mitigate what has happened time and again—the disaster halo effect in natural catastrophes and terror attacks.

* * *

The second key concept from *Managing Emerging Risk* that requires further investigation is the notion of the market state. The market state is a worldview of the geopolitical environment in which nationalism is replaced with a globalized approach focused on the trading of goods, services, and ideas between nation-states. The market state is defined as nation-states that "are becoming increasingly skillful in enlisting the support of market forces to achieve their own objectives."[1] The market state concept is reflected in the writings of many knowledgeable authors and discussed extensively in *Managing Emerging Risk*—it is also the cornerstone concept in this volume, as these ideas are linked to postmodernism and globalization (Figure 3.2).

This notion that the state is a market, and therefore is measured by the goods, services, ideas, and ideologies it transfers to and from other nations, has created some of the most thought-provoking books of our generation. The notion that a "flat" world creates a more interactive, competitive, and data-rich information-sharing environment as a clear by-product of the market state can be witnessed today by anyone. A shift to the market state era means that the interplay between nations and their leaders is based in market thinking and informs decisions and the distribution of aid. It also means that stateless actors can "market" their ideologies and tactics across borders more readily.

Nationalism, values, religion, and messaging play a role in predicting and responding to both natural and man-made disasters in a market state world. When emergency managers consider the term *marketing*, they may

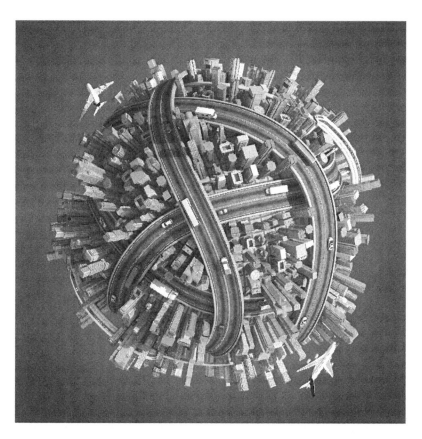

Figure 3.2 The market state is a worldview of the geopolitical environment in which nationalism is replaced with a globalized approach focused on the trading of goods, services, and ideas between nation-states.

have a hard time reconciling it with their daily practice in the field. You may ask yourself, "How do **marketing** concepts and this idea of a market state affect me?"

Marketing consists of the commercial functions involved in transferring goods, whether products or ideals, from the producer to the consumer. That said, the market state worldview is not about selling hot dogs or sneakers. It is not about simply advertising or "hawking" goods. Marketing plays a role to be sure, but not in the simple sense of selling. The market state worldview hinges on the idea, for example, that the past World Wars look nothing like the prolonged war on terror. However,

WWII certainly serves as a key early indicator as the world shifted toward the postmillennial, 9/11 era. WWII began September 1, 1939, when Nazi Germany engaged in a campaign of war against Poland, and eventually all of Europe and Russia, based on the nation-state concepts of territory and ideology. However, Japan did not join WWII until over 2 years later on December 7, 1941, for completely different reasons—market state reasons. Japan joined WWII to protect its interest in trade routes and its access to Indonesian oil.

Today, ideologies and politics are traded across borders just like goods and services. With the understanding that this is the key to winning the war on terror, and has a direct impact on international aid and disaster response, mankind is now moving on a long road away from stand-alone nation-states to integrated market states, in which there are huge stakes at play in planning to be a good neighbor, partner, and protector of the people.

When first encountering the notion of a market state world, we might assume it is purely a geopolitical view and merely impacts the work of emergency managers in the public sector. Certainly, our national stance on terrorism and disasters worldwide is impacted by this new development in geopolitical thinking, but there is also an influence deep within private sector companies that has already had a vast impact on how they conduct their emergency management programs (as exhibited in Chapters 1 and 2).

Consider large multinational companies that emergency managers might serve, such as BP in Chapter 2. The market state environment encourages international trade and opens international markets. The term *globalization* is directly linked to the concept of the market state. We are encountering more and more organizations, especially those in the Fortune 1000, which rely on foreign markets for the manufacture and sale of goods and services. The term *emerging market* is often used to describe far-off consumer and business-to-business markets that were not previously within the scope of the private sector emergency manager's work— today they are.

Market state policies have been crafted to encourage trade and therefore increase the globalized supply and demand chain of companies across multiple nation-states. Large enterprises often refer to markets in four geographic categories: the United States, EMEA, ASIA-PAC, and CANLA. These markets constitute the United States; Europe, the Middle East, and Africa (EMEA); and East Asia, Southeast Asia, and Oceania (ASIA-PAC). Sometimes this area will also include Russia. Finally, CANLA is optional (as the United States can be replaced with the term *the Americas*), which includes Canada and Latin America. Many U.S.-based companies have interests in all of these market sectors, and trade agreements come into play for each.

Realizing that the U.S.-based companies that employ us and serve our needs as citizens most likely have foreign assets, and therefore foreign risk, significantly changes the role of the private sector emergency manager. Events half a world away can, and will, have an impact on the U.S. companies we serve, and designing programs for globalized companies here has a much broader scope than designing programs for "U.S. only" companies.

* * *

The transnational agreements and arrangements that now extend to enterprises around the world are the domain of wise emergency managers who are managing risk for U.S. companies. Transoceanic events can have very real consequences in those regions, or here in the United States. In addition, the shape, scope, and approach to public sector emergency management planning may be very different abroad than it is here in the United States, not only in terms of risk, but also in terms of *impact*.

* * *

The disaster halo effect and the market state have forced a change in how private and public sector organizations perceive preparedness. International law, local laws and customs, and the intertwined nature of business today demand a global view and command over the practice of emergency management, unlike any other time in the history of our discipline. Today's emergency manager is faced with global realities and, as we will explore later in this text, the threats, opportunities, and impacts that come with this new, much broader field.

Within the five guiding principles of postmodern impact assessments presented in Chapter 2, establishing the impact horizon allows the practitioner to address the potential for misgivings and errors when conducting a potential impact assessment.

* * *

Specifically, establishing an impact horizon is a policy view that says: "The potential impact assessments should reflect potential impacts both inside and outside the organization as deemed appropriate by an established impact horizon."

* * *

In this chapter we are going to take a hard look at what it means to establish an impact horizon and how to affect an outcome of a clear scope statement that indicates all in-scope and out-of-scope assets and locations, as called for in the five guiding principles of postmodern impact assessments.

3.4 TAKING A WIDE-ANGLE VIEW OF POTENTIAL IMPACTS

Given that the disaster halo effect will convey downward and additional events that are varied from the first event, and that such events will increasingly cause complex and systemic impacts, it is important to reflect on the concept of postmodern business practices as discussed in Chapter 2, and to apply this wide-angle view to the common practice of the business impact analysis that informs much of our thinking about impact assessments in both the private and the public sector. The outcome of critical thinking about these underlying changes in the world is a realization that, unlike impacts captured in traditional business impact analyses, manifested postmodern risks exhibit a potential for a much broader impact horizon. As you will recall from the introduction of this chapter, the impact horizon is the notion that impacts measured within one enterprise or organizational impact assessment will be comingled with other enterprises or nations, states, or municipalities.

Taking this wide-angle view of impacts, we must consider how the traditional impact assessment would evolve to account for transnational operations, market state realities, and the expected impact horizon. Some financial institutions may plan for systemic risk, or risk that, when manifested, would impact the whole financial system. However, few financial institutions truly have an integrated potential impact assessment that accounts for such a broad impact horizon, and fewer private companies and public sector organizations conduct impact assessments that account for the reality of a wider breadth of impacts that would be manifested in an event that had multiple upstream and downstream supply chain impacts that were catastrophic. The reason for this lack of application in our professional practice is our keen reliance on the traditional model for conducting a business impact analysis.

As stated in Chapter 2, the traditional private sector business impact analysis accounts for potential impacts to finances, brand, customer satisfaction, and sometimes, regulatory compliance. In the public sector, traditional business impact assessments account for impacts to human life, human injury, real property, economies, and in some cases, the environment. These impacts are measured over time in the form of daily, weekly, and monthly projected losses. The resulting impacts are attached to assets, such as people, processes, property, and technological systems, and thus inform our planning objectives by means of creating a list of assets and their potential loss and associated criticality.

This approach to impact assessments is very much influenced by the modern industry of **business continuity** and **disaster recovery** (BC/DR). While the definitions of business continuity and disaster recovery vary, for the purposes of this book we set forth the following definitions: *Business continuity* should be understood to mean the acquisition and organization of tasks and materials needed to work around a business interruption in the absence of technology and computing systems. *Disaster recovery* is the focal area of disaster response that deals with technology and business computing systems recovery. The two practices rely on one another, but may have completely different needs and require different approaches.

3.4.1 Impacts and Criticality

Criticality can be expressed in a number of ways; *mission critical, essential,* and *desirable* are some of the terms used in Chapter 2 to infer criticality. In some traditional impact assessments, these terms are replaced with tiers of three or four levels and demarked alphanumerically. A tier A person, process, or technology may be mission critical, with a tier B criticality ranking indicating a lesser or essential descriptor. Whatever name or moniker ascribed to the assets at risk, or to convey their importance to the organization, the ranking of the assets is based on the measured potential loss that will occur if those assets are damaged or catastrophically impacted by an event (Figure 3.3).

These criticality rankings are traditionally tied directly to the timeliness of planned response actions. This is the direct link we will explore when we discuss how impact assessments inform our policies and objectives developed by our work method. For now, it is sufficient to understand that the proposed potential impacts to a given asset result in a tier, or criticality rating, that is linked to a response action and typically, a **recovery time objective** or **recovery point objective**. The typical recovery time objective (RTO) expresses the desired time to recover an asset's functionality after an event and is expressed in minutes, hours, days, or weeks. The recovery point objective (RPO) is also a time calculation related to the

Figure 3.3 Much like chess pieces, business assets have different levels of value and impact.

criticality of the asset and refers to the acceptable point at which the last backup of the asset was made, or the last transaction was processed and captured prior to the event.

To better understand the RTO and RPO relationship, consider this example: A computer is processing real-time surveillance monitoring of a bank. The bank requires such monitoring to maintain its insurance in the event of a robbery. The expected loss of the surveillance data is deemed critical due to its regulatory and legal nature, and that it will exhibit a high degree of financial impact if such data are not available to the bank for insurance purposes. The recovery time objective for the bank's surveillance system data is expressed as 1 hour, the time in which it would like to reopen a functional and compliant bank. The recovery point objective for the bank's surveillance system is 1 minute, as it would like to have data from the system as current as possible prior to the event. Therefore, the criticality of the system based on the potential impact is mission critical with an RTO of 1 hour and an RPO of 1 minute.

Criticality can vary widely within the traditional business continuity and disaster recovery fields, as well as within emergency management and counterterrorism, with some high-transaction, mission-critical systems and processes allowing for mere seconds of downtime and data loss, or an RTO/RPO of less than 1 second. These highly critical systems may be associated with theater of war operations systems, flight controls, safety systems, or even simple online credit card transaction systems. It all depends on the potential impact.

3.4.2 The Impact Horizon and Public Perception

Traditionally, these impacts are based on interviews with business stakeholders or on data gathered during the impact analysis process. Usually, they are not validated and not evidenced by business realities, but rather rely solely on personal opinion. The same is true of projected loss of life, injury, and economic impacts. The problem with the current approaches to impact assessments, as mentioned before, is that they do not consider the impacts measured as *potentials*, often do not have an actuarial basis, and finally, do not account for change. Nonetheless, beyond the obvious constraints of our current practice and the challenge of capturing expert opinion or real data prior to an event, the traditional view of impact assessments does not have linkages to the wider stakeholders and range of other organizations (either internal or external to the organization for which we are working) that would be impacted by the same event, as is required in the establishment of an impact horizon.

* * *

The impact horizon is not often considered or discussed within our culture or by and between the emergency manager and the stakeholders in the impact analysis, *but it should be.*

* * *

Establishing an impact horizon is a means for informing how much of the supply chain we will consider, whether or not to include suppliers and customers in the process, what cultural boundaries should be considered both locally and globally, and how the impact measures we are about to take will be interpreted by many worldviews—including sensitivities to varied perspectives on public perception.

As discussed in Chapter 2, a negative public perception impact is both relative and subjective, based on the region in which it is being applied. Here is an important example to demonstrate this principle. A multinational effort, led by an American team, could use impact measures such as financial, brand, and customer satisfaction to generate aggressive tiers or criticality rankings for their business. Once this work effort is completed within the United States, the organization tries to use the same criticality rankings in Japan, where it has major operations. However, it learns that the cultural values of that country consider it bad form to place profits over community assistance in a catastrophic event, and that sub-24-hour criticalities do not make sense in that country's context. This has created a situation in which the multinational organization now has a dependency to meet the RPOs and RTOs of a supplier who was not consulted prior to conducting the impact assessment and cannot support the RTOs/RPOs of North American operations, let alone sustain or advocate for them in Japan. These varied local worldviews and cultural criticalities play a paramount role in both private and public sector planning.

The American approach to criticality is culturally biased, and to believe that these same criticalities based on American impacts inform the same mission objectives in China, India, Mexico, or Europe is just naive. In China, for example, any effort to privately recover your business after a catastrophic failure that includes the release of information to the public, which downplays the People's Republic of China's role in keeping your company safe, could be construed as spreading "rumors during a disaster" and will land you in jail! Later in this volume, we will take a close look at various cultural worldviews about impact and response. For now, it is important to understand that lacking a view of impacts that does not include globalized operations, cultural boundaries, and varied local and national worldviews is setting up an impact assessment that is doomed to fail from the start.

Some would argue that emergency managers should not consider globalization and not reconsider their impact horizon because they operate in highly localized event areas in which impacts would only be registered within a small community. To this, we offer two simple facts:

1. Any large-scale catastrophe will garner worldwide media in this postmodern age.
2. The nature of the market state is such that whoever your customers are at the end of the day, be it the general public or business-to-business relationships, the impact of a catastrophe to your "local" organization will have a much broader impact horizon than your stakeholders may realize.

A failure to consider the impact horizon and to scope the potential impact assessment as appropriate to the organization or region, as well as the organization's and region's dependent neighbors, is a failure in imagination—the same type of intelligence failure that was the root problem in the 9/11 attacks. Not foreseeing a potential risk is one thing, as it is hard to imagine all the possible threats and hazards that make up the disaster halo effect and to plan for all conceivable scenarios. However, not knowing the interrelationships between one organization and another, or between one municipality and another, or between one state and another, is much less excusable. The relationships are *knowable*—not imagined threats or scenarios, but the true conditions under which the organization or municipality operates.

In simple terms, if the impact assessment is designed to measure potential impacts, it is a bit like a diagnosis for a potential disease. You may not have cancer yet, but your chances greatly increase if you keep smoking. The next obvious question in this line of diagnosis is, "Does anyone else in your family have cancer?" Then, "Are there children in your home?" These questions push the impact horizon *out* to better understand not only the potential impact smoking has on you, but also the potential impact you can have on others as a smoker. Emergency managers who fail to fully diagnose the potentials across a wide-angle impact horizon might find themselves caught off guard when the patient dies of cancer at 49 and it turns out that both of his parents smoked and died at an early age of cancer, and that the child in the patient's home has asthma!

Our own expectations of care are not met when physicians fail to consider all the potential impacts across a broad impact horizon for a given risk. The same standard should be applied in *our* practice. Consider this question: If businesses want a strong potential impact assessment completed, then why not include the cost of lost intellectual capital and human life as associated with years of service for the company and an employee's education level? Are not the employees a valued, mission-critical asset? Certainly they are, but often they are not ranked by criticality to the organization by function or skill level, and their protection is not the responsibility of the emergency planner, but that of security or human resources personnel.

Now that we have forwarded the idea of measuring the human impact in business, let's put forward the idea that in public practice, environmental impacts and long-range economic impacts are often missed, and that whole generations of income-creating trades and work-craft have been impacted by disasters like Katrina and the BP oil spill. The first responders to 9/11 were severely impacted by the event, and it took years of study and legal wrangling, *after the fact*, to come to terms with the idea that first responders need to have their own **response impact assessments** for various scenarios in order to lower long-term health impacts. A response impact assessment considers the impact to first responders and the environment during response *and* recovery efforts. Yet, even today, many such studies have not been conducted in the public sector.

There is not a single answer for the myriad issues just raised by our review of the traditional impact analysis approach. However, it is clear that not considering the impact horizon prior to conducting an impact assessment is a recipe for failure. The linkage between established criticality from the impact analysis to response plans is simply too important to not fully consider the impact horizon. The current impact measures in both private and public practice could, and probably should, be revisited with a wide-angle lens so that new guidance can be established that is more aligned with our postmodern, market state world. Finally, understanding that the impact horizon includes supply chain, business partners, other towns, states, or nations, and that decisions made in the impact analysis phase can either include those linkages or not, should no longer be up for debate (Figure 3.4).

* * *

When we lose sight of the importance of the impact horizon, we fail to understand our response objectives, fall off message, and fail to align our resources to the appropriate impacts at the time of disaster.

* * *

Establishing an impact horizon requires the practitioner to identify upstream and downstream impacts that will occur after a risk becomes a real disaster and to determine the impacts, criticalities, and objectives that will be informed based on the established scope, or impact horizon that is established. In practice, this includes giving due consideration to public perception and the integration points between upstream suppliers and downstream consumers of the outputs of the organization being served.

As an example of private sector impact assessments failing to realize the downstream impacts to customers, a look at the Amazon cloud computing outage of 2011 is a good place to start.

Figure 3.4 Considering impact horizons with a wide-angle lens gives us valuable information on relationships and impacts that go beyond our front doors and extend to our global supply chain.

3.5 THE AMAZON CLOUD COMPUTING OUTAGE OF 2011

On April 20, 2011, the Amazon cloud computing service known as Amazon Web Services, a shared access computing service offered by the company Amazon, took a hard outage. **Cloud computing** is a service that utilizes large, fault-tolerant, and scalable data centers to host private sector websites and ecommerce sites. Amazon Web Services is a subscription-based service that allows companies to run large websites and web-based services without incurring the cost of owning their own data centers. The Amazon outage was caused by technical problems with a specific service known as **Elastic Block Storage** (EBS). EBS is designed to provide scalable or "elastic" data storage based on a website's traffic and demand needs. The technical problem occurred when several customer accounts were affected by "stuck" data in the EBS service.[2]

A couple of known websites impacted included Reddit (which is a popular discussion site among technologists) and Qoura, a group sourcing website that lets people ask and answer questions from other users. Reportedly, a company providing cardiac monitoring services

89

was impacted, and a user posted to the Amazon Web Services discussion forum the following (the true account addresses and IDs have been marked with xxxxx by the author to protect the firm involved):

> Life of our patients is at stake—I am desperately asking you to contact.
> Sorry, I could not get through in any other way
> We are a monitoring company and are monitoring hundreds of cardiac patients at home.
> We were unable to see their ECG signals since 21st of April
> Could you please contact us?
> Our account number is: xxxx-xxxx-xxxx
> Our servers IDs:
>
> > i-xxxxxxxx
> > i-xxxxxxxx
> > i-xxxxxxxx
>
> Or please let me know how can I contact you more directly.
> Thank you[3]

While some claim that the post to the forum was a hoax, Amazon has not taken the discussion off its message board, suggesting that it may be true. Amazon's Web Service is HIPPA compliant, suggesting that it is an appropriate location for storing patients' medical information. While nondisclosure agreements and the need for companies to minimize damage to their reputation by not publicly announcing that the Amazon outage impacted them makes it difficult to understand the totality of the crisis, we do know some of the organizations that could have been affected by this crisis. Amazon hosts a long list of customers' websites, including:

- Arcus Global: A company that builds solutions for UK government bodies on Amazon Web Services.
- The Guardian News and Media: The publisher of the national United Kingdom newspapers the *Guardian* and the *Observer*.
- Nextpoint: A website that provides trial preparation and evidence management for Fortune 100 corporations.
- Nimbus Health: Helps doctors and hospitals share medical information with patients.

- Synectics for Management Decisions: A total solution IT provider that offers federal and state government agencies, nonprofits, and commercial clients a full range of planning, design, development, and operational support services. It uses Amazon Web Services to implement an unspecified "tracking system" used by federal agencies as an element of their software-as-a-service offering.[4]

A business impact assessment of Amazon's Web Services cloud computing data center business would be a moving target as new companies adopted the service rather than built their own data centers, bringing with them a host of new economic impact potentials, regulatory impacts related to privacy, and even the potential impact to the continuity of government.

***

As the world becomes more technologically advanced, it is easier and easier for companies to conjoin or comingle their operations such that a disaster at one provider could well be a catastrophe for many.

***

The use of third-party computing services and data centers is a growing trend in business, with many companies choosing to outsource their data centers and computer services to third-party "hosting" companies. The real impact of a catastrophe bringing one or more of these data centers down is the stuff of nightmare scenarios and risk assessments. Multiple companies and services across the United States could be impacted, not only financially, but also in terms of communications, life and health services, brand, and customer impacts. The reality is that data center and computer services outsourcing is a confidence game. More importantly, there is very little publicly available knowledge of the real cost of a catastrophe in this business sector, as the upstream vendors of services and components are often protected by nondisclosure agreements.

If we are practicing in the private sector or in the public sector, there are nondisclosure agreements or need-to-know sets of data regarding upstream producers and downstream consumers of the outputs of our organizations that may or may not be discussed with us as practitioners seeking to develop a sound potential impact assessment with a clear impact horizon. A degree of healthy paranoia on our part is thus justified.

* * *

The prudent impact horizon is arrived at based on consensus with financial, security, geopolitical, and leadership expertise and input and is not the sole responsibility of the emergency manager. The responsibility of the emergency manager in forwarding an impact horizon for the impact assessment is to establish a clear scope of impacts to be considered based on accurate and complete input from these other stakeholders.

* * *

3.6 THE IMPORTANCE OF STAKEHOLDERS AND ESTABLISHING THE IMPACT HORIZON

3.6.1 The Business Continuity Perspective

In the field of business continuity, Kelley Okolita, in her book *Building an Enterprise-Wide Business Continuity Program*, says, "The BIA [business impact analysis] is invaluable for identifying what is at stake following a disaster and for justifying spending on protection and recovery capability."[5] Most, if not all, practitioners of private and public sector business continuity link the potential for impact directly to the justification of spending and investment in planning that follows this critical step in the overall management of a business continuity program.

In the book *Business Continuity Planning: Protecting Your Organization's Life*, by Ken Doughty, a chapter by Carl B. Jackson on the business impact assessment process says: "The reason that the business impact assessment (BIA) element of the business continuity planning (BCP) methodology takes on such significance is that it sets the stage for shaping a business-oriented judgment concerning the appropriation of resources for recovery planning efforts."[6] This orientation of impact assessments toward framing our judgment and even our funding decisions can also be found in the field of emergency management.

3.6.2 The Emergency Management Perspective

The Federal Emergency Management Agency (FEMA), a division of the Department of Homeland Security (DHS), uses many impact assessment types to clarify and frame the decision-making process for national preparedness. The use of software packages such as the geographic information system (GIS)-based HAZUS-MH program "continues to play an important role in advancing one of FEMA's priorities in 2007—planning for catastrophic earthquakes and hurricanes in the United States."[7] **HAZMUS-MH** uses historical data to plot critical infrastructure and key resources on maps and is used with "other tools at FEMA headquarters for supporting impact assessments." FEMA and other federal and state emergency managers tend to link impact assessments to risk assessments, including the impact of a catastrophic event, in the same documents that explore scenarios that create the risk for a catastrophic event. This approach, usually called an **all-hazards risk assessment**, is a key component of the Robert T. Stafford Disaster Relief and Emergency Assistance Act (42 USC 5131 et seq.), commonly known as the **Stafford Act**. **All-hazards planning** means considering *all threats and scenarios equally* and preparing for *any possibility*, as well as including *potential* impacts.

3.6.2.1 The Stafford Act and Emergency Management

The Stafford Act is a 1998 amended version of the Disaster Relief Act of 1974. The act has been updated with the passing of the **Disaster Mitigation Act** (DMA) of 2000, and again in 2006 with the Pets Evacuation and Transportation Standards Act. At its core the Stafford Act outlines the requirements and roles for federal aid during a disaster at the national, state, and local levels. The act calls for a form of impact assessment, as it requires the creation of a national disaster hazard mitigation program to "reduce the loss of life and property, human suffering, economic disruption, and the disaster assistance cost resulting from natural disasters."[8] The findings of an all-hazards risk assessment usually include forward-looking statements regarding impacts to life, property, and economic damages.

These work products, created at the federal, state, city, and tribal levels, are integral to funding and grant programs managed by FEMA and the Department of Homeland Security. The outcome of an all-hazards risk assessment for state and local governments according to the Stafford Act is "to provide sources of pre-disaster hazard mitigation funding that will assist states and local governments (including Native American tribes) in implementing effective hazard mitigation measures that are designed to ensure the continued functionality of critical services and facilities after a natural disaster." In this manner, FEMA ties the all-hazards risk assessment (and impact data therein) directly to funding at the state and local government levels.

3.6.3 The Counterterrorism Perspective

In a similar fashion, there is a link to the protection of critical infrastructure and key resources (CI/KR) and counterterrorism. The Department of Homeland Security has identified 18 areas considered to be **critical infrastructure and key resources** under the **National Infrastructure Protection Plan** (NIPP). The Department of Homeland Security (DHS) first published the NIPP in 2009. "The overarching goal of the NIPP is to build a safer, more secure, and more resilient America."[9] Critical infrastructures are "the assets, systems, and networks, whether physical or virtual, so vital to the United States that their incapacitation or destruction would have a debilitating effect on security, national economic security, public health or safety, or any combination thereof." Key resources are "publicly or privately controlled resources essential to the minimal operations of the economy and government."[10] The 18 areas considered to be critical infrastructures under NIPP are (in alphabetical order):

1. Agriculture and food
2. Banking and finance
3. Chemical
4. Commercial facilities
5. Communications
6. Critical manufacturing
7. Dams
8. Defense industrial base
9. Emergency services
10. Energy
11. Government facilities
12. Healthcare and public health
13. Information technology
14. National monuments and icons
15. Nuclear reactors, materials, and waste
16. Postal and shipping
17. Transportation systems
18. Water

Key resources under NIPP "are publicly or privately controlled resources essential to the minimal operations of the economy and government." Neither NIPP nor the Department of Homeland Security Act of 2002 actually lists specific key resources such as the Hoover Dam. However, the identification of critical infrastructure and key resources is directly tied under the Stafford Act to obtaining federal disaster aid and funding, including funds for emergency management and counterterrorism programs at the state level.

Elsa Lee, in her book *Homeland Security and Private Sector Business*, discusses the unique relationship between privately controlled critical infrastructure and key resources and counterterrorism:

> Government officials approximate that 85 percent of U.S. infrastructures are owned by the private sector. This puts our country in a vulnerable position because the private sector does not have its own armies, fortresses, or intelligence resources like the federal government. The federal government has an assumption that given the guidance published by DHS, private sector security professionals know exactly what they need to do to help protect infrastructures.... We are a young nation compared to European countries that have been dealing with terrorism for decades.[11]

To underscore this point, recent attacks on basic critical infrastructure and key resources have become a serious concern in 2011. According to the BBC, on December 13, 2011, the infrastructure systems of three U.S. cities had been attacked according to the FBI. Michael Welch, the deputy assistant director of the FBI, told a Flemings Cyber Security conference: "We just had a circumstance where we had three cities, one of them a major city within the US, where you had several hackers that had made their way into SCADA systems within the city."[12] **SCADA** systems are supervisory control and data acquisition systems that control much of the water, gas, oil, and electrical grids in the United States. The BBC report went on to say, "The hackers had access to crucial water and power services."[13]

Professionals in counterterrorism and emergency management are approaching the gap outlined by Lee's observations with concern and alarm. While most impact assessments (like those found in private sector business continuity planning or public sector all-hazards planning) are directly tied to funding and executive sponsorship, the relationship between critical assets and infrastructure in harm's way and counterterrorism funding is a lot less direct. One reason for this is DHS's dependence on private sector industries to self-monitor the people, process, and assets that make up their critical infrastructure and key resources.

Another outcome of this indirect relationship between critical infrastructure and key resources and counterterrorism professionals is much more alarming. According to Gary Ackerman and Jeremy Tamsett in their book *Jihadists and Weapons of Mass Destruction,*

> In recent years, jihadists have chosen targets largely related to public transportation (subways, commuter trains, airports, ferries, and airlines), commerce (hotels, office buildings, cafes, nightclubs, etc.), and civil authority (government offices, police stations, etc.).... The primary objective of the network has a direct relevance for the question of targeting: to "bleed" (exhaust) the United States economically and militarily both by directly causing inordinate economic losses and forcing the United States to spend excessive amounts of money to protect its vast infrastructure.[14]

This soft targeting approach, now favored by many terrorist and lone-wolf actors, is generating a clear and present danger to assets and individuals outside the scope of public sector counterterrorism and emergency management planners, and placing much greater stress on private sector businesses to plan for and protect against such attacks. Many public sector targets are hard, or have been hardened by the federal government. However, many private sector targets remain relatively unsecure, with many dangerous opportunities for attack yet to be remediated.

In the counterterrorism profession, there are **hard targets** (usually government-run, noncivilian properties or resources protected with countermeasures and prepared for attack) and **soft targets** (such as malls, schools, and other areas of civilian activity) that are not prepared or expected to be attacked. The recent dual attacks carried out by Anders Behring Breivik in Norway on July 22, 2011, are a stunning example of both hard and soft targeting. This lone-wolf extremist not only chose to attack the government center in Oslo called the Einar Genhardsen plaza, a secure and critical target, but then he went on to a much softer target—a Labor Party youth camp on the small island of Utoya, killing 74 young people.

* * *

This stunning example of a modern lone-wolf terror attack in Oslo, Norway, highlights the blurring of the lines between public spaces and private spaces, and emphasizes the need to protect both.

* * *

The "targeting calculus" used by terrorists is not much different than the impact assessments we conduct in our professional fields. Looking for those locations or networks with the highest impact to lives, our economy, and our ability to defend our country is every bit as important to our impact assessments as it is to building better response plans. To quote Malcolm W. Nance, the author of the *Terrorist Recognition Handbook*, "High-value targets (HVT) will, if damaged or destroyed, contribute to the degradation of the victim society's ability to respond militarily or sustain itself economically."[15] Nance is a 20-year veteran of the U.S. intelligence community and an expert on counterterrorism, with firsthand knowledge of the field. His view of high-value targets, based on his experience, focuses on how we can better understand what is in harm's way, in order to better fund programs that protect, plan for, and even thwart future attacks.

Another important distinction between private sector impact analyses and counterterrorism impact analyses is that in counterterrorism, we often calculate the potential impact caused by the action of persons of interest, terror cells, and specific terrorist devices, or plots executed. In this sense, the distinction between emergency management and counterterrorism could be viewed as being very different, as the potential impact in emergency management may be caused by human error or a natural hazard, whereas in counterterrorism the potential impact is caused by human determination and man-made threats. Nonetheless, the concepts set forth in this book apply across both of these fields as both emergency managers and counterterrorism professionals are challenged in the same manner when conducting impact assessments.

Across the board, from private sector business continuity planning to counterterrorism, the primary importance of the impact analysis is to clearly understand what is in harm's way: the people, processes, property, and perceptions that might be damaged or lost in the event of a catastrophic event. In all three disciplines (business continuity, emergency management, and counterterrorism), this understanding is the basis for ongoing funding and the clarification of program and mission objectives to key stakeholders and decision makers. In fact, the private sector and the public sector are unavoidably linked through the notion of critical infrastructure and key resources by impact assessments: *A failure to understand this link is a failure to understand the impact horizon.*

* * *

The policies of the Department of Homeland Security rely on the private sector to understand the people, processes, and property it controls to better protect our national security, and a failure to understand this link is a failure to understand the impact horizon.

* * *

One of the results of our postmodern world is that the private and public sectors have overlapped and, in some cases, become highly interdependent upon one another. An example of this can be found in how (as previously outlined) monetary policy can generate impacts for private sector businesses as well as emergency managers in the public sector. Consider the financial crisis of 2008 through 2011.

3.7 THE PUBLIC/PRIVATE IMPACT HORIZON—MIXED IMPACTS FROM THE 2008 FINANCIAL CRISIS

Of course everyone has heard of the financial crisis and the resulting TARP legislation that bailed out big investment banks in 2007 and 2008, but few people truly understand the impact that was looming shortly after the bailout of Fannie Mae and Freddie Mac on September 7, 2008. On September 15, the investment bank Lehman Brothers collapsed, causing a meltdown and the need for swift action by Federal Chairman Ben Bernanke and Treasury Secretary Henry Paulson. On that day, panic set in and investors pulled out of other investment banks around the globe. According to the *New York Times*, General Electric (GE) had difficulty securing the ongoing credit it needed to keep its day-to-day operations running.[16] However, it was not just the big banks or GE that was impacted by the catastrophe that hit the banking sector.

Bank of America prevented McDonald's from acquiring the credit to build in-store coffee bars due to the resulting "credit crunch." Companies as diverse as General Electric and the small household cleaning company Method were also hit with credit restrictions that impacted their ability to operate their businesses as usual.[17] Even after coming right to the edge of a systemic financial impact, very few impact assessments of these events conducted by financial risk managers or governmental agencies considered that they might be looking at a domino in a supply chain that had the potential to create systemic impacts to other businesses that went well beyond financial, brand, or customer impacts.

It seems that our ability to plan for and respond to catastrophes without understanding the interdependencies between large corporations and other critical infrastructure and key resources should have been made clear by the financial crisis. Yet we still have limited understanding of what is in harm's way should catastrophe strike again and go unabated. On October 3, 2008, TARP was passed into law, allowing the U.S. Department of Treasury to purchase or insure up to $700 billion in "troubled assets." The U.S. economy was still recovering in 2011—much in part due to a misunderstanding regarding the breadth of austerity and credibility across global financial markets, and though the law and actions taken by the federal government were controversial back in 2008, what should not be controversial is that systemic economic failure is a real potential impact if multiple financial institutions fail for any reason—thereby putting our national and personal security, as well as global financial trade markets, in harm's way.

Admittedly, even the most seasoned practitioner of emergency management, disaster recovery, business continuity, or counterterrorism would not feel qualified venturing onto the rough ground of high finance and fiscal policy; however, these events have directly impacted our profession. Some practitioners may choose to ignore financial and policy-related risks and their associated impacts for now, and some might choose to integrate their programs more closely with financial risk managers. In either instance, the 2008 and 2009 financial crisis has become a manifested risk that is now impacting emergency managers and other practitioners across America. We should all be willing to understand these phenomena better. Just consider that in spite of its humble origins, the Occupy Wall Street movement continues to evolve around the nation, and there are similar economically rooted protests occurring worldwide.

This broad range of impacts, from the need to remedy an immediate financial crisis to the resulting feedback loop of public unrest manifesting itself, not only in America by Occupy Wall Street protesters, but also around the world as the European Union adopted similar measures, is a testament to just how wide an impact simple legislation can have. Again, it becomes immediately clear that establishing an impact horizon requires multiple inputs from key stakeholders both inside and outside the organization. These may include financial advisors, security advisors, sociologists, suppliers, consumers, and the responders themselves (Figure 3.5).

* * *

When an impact horizon is set without the input of other stakeholders, or is established without exploring both long-range and broad potential impacts, full disclosure must be made by the responsible emergency manager as to who was consulted and who was not.

* * *

Establishing an impact horizon is as much about choosing how deeply we will investigate impacts both inside and outside the organizations we serve as it is about ethically providing the appropriate disclosures regarding what is in scope and what is not in the potential impact assessment.

Figure 3.5 Stockholders are a critical component for establishing the impact horizon. Their varied information and experiences provide a valuable, wide-angle perspective of the whole enterprise.

Too many impact assessments assume that the reader will understand that all possible impacts have been considered, and that there are some impacts that are simply out of scope and "too far out" to consider. This is a poor assumption. The best practice in this area is to clearly identify the impact horizon and to fully disclose whom the practitioner consulted to reach the impact horizon definition.

3.8 DELIVERING THE IMPACT HORIZON

The principle of an impact horizon says, "The potential impact assessments should reflect potential impacts both inside and outside the organization as deemed appropriate by an established impact horizon."

Disclosures are needed as part of any impact horizon. A disclosure is a fact that is made known. It informs the reader of the impact assessment as to whom has been consulted and who has not, as well as what is in scope and what is not. **Assumptions** in impact assessments are very different than disclosures. An assumption is taking something for granted as truth, but there are no facts supporting this truth. For instance, assuming that the reader of an impact assessment will understand the phrase "considers impacts to the whole enterprise" is very dangerous. What constitutes the "whole enterprise"? What does not? A sound set of disclosures is as important to the delivery of the impact horizon as the impact horizon itself. Disclosures demonstrate diligence and professionalism in *any* field. Assumptions are an invitation for further mayhem in the wake of a disaster or terror event.

To be clear, making disclosures while establishing an impact horizon introduces the concept of professional ethics into our work by asking questions such as, "Which truths about this impact assessment should be told and which should not?" Disclosure is different than so-called transparency. Disclosure is the willful telling of fact and the willful withholding of information. There will be some instances in which a professional may only be able to say: "A private firm was not consulted for this impact assessment due to legal constraints." Or, "Due to national security concerns, certain key stakeholders are not divulged in this report." On the other hand, it is important to recognize that disclosure is an act of choosing who and what to discuss openly, and is best completed with the aid of key stakeholders and clear communications. It will take time and money to determine what to disclose regarding the impact assessment and what to withhold. That investment of time into the construction of a sound impact horizon speaks volumes about the professional ethics of the practitioner. To choose assumptions over disclosures is to take a shortcut that results in poor outcomes and misunderstandings.

To determine the impact horizon (what is in scope and what is not), key stakeholders should be consulted and agreements should be made as to how the potential impact assessment integrates and overlaps with that of suppliers, partners, and other stakeholders.

The key deliverable of the first principle is *deliver an impact horizon statement*.

The seasoned practitioner will take a wide-angle view of impacts and then achieve consensus within the organization and communications outside of the organization to determine which impacts will be measured and which will not, also indicating those stakeholders that were not consulted.

The practitioner must organize an impact horizon matrix that considers upstream and downstream impacts, and then organize these into a **RACI matrix** (a RACI matrix illustrates who is responsible, accountable, consulted, and informed). It is a document that concludes with a detailed impact horizon statement that includes all in-scope and out-of-scope stakeholders, assets, and locations for the potential impact assessment.

Two key work products will come out of the impact horizon work effort:

1. A set of disclosures for stakeholders that were consulted and those that were not
2. A RACI chart for all potential impacts

Sample disclosures:

- The following impact assessment does not consider financial impacts based on line of business, as the finance department did not provide discrete line of business impacts. Rather, aggregated impacts are considered across all shared systems and processes on a regional basis.
- The following impact assessment does not include regulatory impacts, as the legal department considered such impacts to be out of scope for this effort.
- The following impact assessment does not include customer impacts beyond 1 month, as it has been stated by the board of directors that such impacts are incalculable.
- The local FEMA Regional Office was not consulted with regards to customer impacts or the organization's impact to the community should a risk manifest itself.
- Upstream providers of goods and services were not engaged in the impact assessment process, as the CEO did not wish to raise concerns with his suppliers regarding a potential business interruption.
- Some internal impacts cannot be discussed in this report due to national security issues. Please see the organization's compliance officer for additional information.
- Income that cannot be repatriated without deep taxation is not considered in this report, as such losses are outside the scope of U.S. operations.

3.9 SUMMARY

The fundamental flaw with much of what passes for an impact analysis is the tendency to think small, which is contrary to the evolution of impacts based on the arrival of the digital age and postmodernism. In the book *Managing Emerging Risk*, the author explores the concept of two key drivers that are transforming postmodern emergency management practice. These two drivers are described as:

1. The disaster halo effect, the recognition that modern threats exhibit more than one event and multiple outcomes that can be viewed as being emergent (or evolving)
2. The worldview of the nation as a market state in which nationalism is replaced with a globalized approach focused on the trading of goods, services, and ideas between nation-states

Understanding the influence of these two drivers as well as the concept of an impact horizon (the notion that impacts measured within one enterprise or organizational impact assessment will be comingled with the impacts to other enterprises or nations, states, or municipalities), and this is the leading principle in the five guiding principles of postmodern impact assessments because it addresses the fundamental flaw of thinking too small by establishing the boundaries and scope (what is to be considered and what is not) of any given potential impact assessment.

Taking a wide-angle view of impacts, we must consider how the traditional impact assessment would evolve to account for transnational operations, market state realities, and the expected impact horizon. Some financial institutions may plan for systemic risk, or risk that, when manifested, would impact the whole financial system. However, few financial institutions truly have an integrated potential impact assessment that accounts for such a broad impact horizon, and fewer private companies and public sector organizations conduct impact assessments that account for the reality of a wider breadth of impacts that would be manifested in an event that had multiple upstream and downstream supply chain impacts that were catastrophic. The reason for this lack of application in our professional practice is our keen reliance on the traditional model for conducting a business impact analysis.

The traditional private sector business impact analysis accounts for potential impacts to finances, brand, customer satisfaction, and sometimes regulatory compliance. In the public sector, traditional business impact assessments account for impacts to human life, human injury, real property, economies, and in some cases, the environment. These impacts are measured over time in the form of projected daily, weekly, and monthly losses. The resulting impacts are attached to assets, such as people, processes, property, and technological systems, and thus inform our planning objectives by means of creating a list of assets and their potential loss and associated criticality.

This approach to impact assessments is very much influenced by the modern industry of business continuity and disaster recovery (BC/DR). While the definitions of business continuity and disaster recovery vary, for the purposes of this book we set forth the following: Business continuity should be understood to mean the acquisition and organization of tasks and materials needed to work around a business interruption in the *absence of technology and computing systems*. Disaster recovery is the focal area of disaster response that deals with technology and business computing systems recovery. The two practices rely on one another, but may require completely different needs and approaches.

Establishing an impact horizon is as much about choosing how deeply we will investigate impacts both inside and outside the organizations we serve as it is about ethically providing the appropriate disclosures regarding what is in scope and what is not in the potential impact assessment.

The seasoned practitioner will take a wide-angle view of impacts and then achieve consensus within the organization and communications outside of the organization to determine which impacts will be measured and which will not, also indicating those stakeholders that were not consulted.

The practitioner can organize an impact horizon matrix that considers upstream and downstream impacts, and then organize these into a responsibility assignment matrix (RAM or RACI: responsible, accountable, consulted, and informed) that concludes with a detailed impact horizon statement that includes all in-scope and out-of-scope stakeholders, assets, and locations for the potential impact assessment.

Two key work products will come out of the impact horizon work effort:

1. A set of disclosures of the stakeholders who were consulted and those who were not
2. A RACI chart for all potential impacts

By establishing an impact horizon the practitioner actively addresses the fundamental flaw of thinking too small with regards to impacts by establishing the scope of an impact assessment and disclosing the stakeholders who were and were not consulted as part of the effort.

3.10 QUESTIONS

1. Describe the meaning of the term *market state* and how it reflects postmodern and globalization activities in the public and the private sector.
2. What differentiates business continuity and disaster recovery?
3. Provide an example of an impact horizon for a public or a private sector organization.
4. Discuss the meaning and importance of disclosures in terms of professional ethics.
5. Generate a RACI chart to illustrate an impact horizon for a sample organization.

ENDNOTES

1. Royal Dutch Shell Group. 2005, November 5. Executive Summary of the Shell Global Scenarios to 2025. http://www.static.shell.com/static/about-shell/downloads/our_ strategy/shell_global_scenarios/exsum_23052005.pdf (accessed July 7, 2011).
2. Miller, Rich. 2011. The Aftermath of Amazon's Cloud Outage. http://www.datacenterknowledge.com/archives/2011/04/25/the-aftermath-of-amazons-cloud-outage/ (accessed July 7, 2011).
3. Amazon Web Services. 2011. Discussion Forums: Life of Our Patients Is at Stake—I Am Desperately Asking You to Contact. https://forums.aws.amazon.com/thread.jspa?threadID=65649&tstart=0 (accessed July 7, 2011).
4. For a partial list of Amazon Web Services customers see http://aws.amazon.com/solutions/case-studies/.
5. Okolita, Kelley. 2009. *Building an Enterprise-Wide Business Continuity Program*. Auerbach.
6. Doughty, Ken. 2000. *Business Continuity Planning: Protecting Your Organization's Life (Best Practices)*. Auerbach.
7. FEMA. ND. Resource Record Details GIS and HAZUS-MH: HAZUS Applications for Catastrophic Planning. http://www.fema.gov/library/viewRecord.do?id=2932 (accessed July 7, 2011).
8. FEMA. 2000. The Stafford Act, Title 1, Section 101. http://www.fema.gov/library/viewRecord.do?id=1935 (accessed July 6, 2011).
9. U.S. Department of Homeland Security. 2009. The 2009 National Infrastructure Protection Plan. http://www.dhs.gov/files/programs/editorial_0827.shtm#0 (accessed July 6, 2011).

10. U.S. Department of Homeland Security. 2008. Homeland Security Presidential Directive 7: Critical Infrastructure, Identification, Prioritization, and Protection. http://www.dhs.gov/xabout/laws/gc_1214597989952.shtm (accessed July 6, 2011).
11. Lee, Elsa. 2008. *Homeland Security and Private Sector Business: Corporations' Role in Critical Infrastructure Protection.* Auerbach.
12. BBC. 2011. FBI Says Hackers Hit Key Services in Three US Cities. http://www.bbc.co.uk/news/technology-16157883 (accessed December 17, 2011).
13. Ibid.
14. Ackerman, Gary, and Jeremy Tamsett. 2009. *Jihadists and Weapons of Mass Destruction.* Boca Raton, FL: CRC Press.
15. Nance, Malcolm W. 2008. *Terrorist Recognition Handbook: A Practitioner's Manual for Predicting and Identifying Terrorist Activities.* 2nd ed. Boca Raton, FL: CRC Press.
16. *New York Times.* 2008. 10 Weeks of Financial Turmoil. http://www.nytimes.com/interactive/2008/09/27/business/economy/20080927_WEEKS_TIMELINE.html (accessed July 8, 2011).
17. Tippett, Mike. 2008. McDonald's Loans Halted Because of Credit Crisis. http://www.nowpublic.com/tech-biz/mcdonalds-loans-halted-because-credit-crisis (accessed July 7, 2011).

4

The Second Principle
Align Impact Measures to Core Values

4.1 KEY TERMS

4.2 OBJECTIVES

After reading this chapter you will be able to:

1. Describe how aligning the core values of an organization to the impact assessment can reduce negative public perception impacts.
2. Describe what it means to be on mission and on message.
3. Provide an example of a weighted score based on core values for a public or private sector organization.
4. Discuss the meaning and importance of aligning core values to the impact assessment in the private and the public sector.
5. Generate a weighted score pie chart to illustrate an alignment to core values for a sample organization.

4.3 OVERVIEW: AN UNDERLYING PROBLEM AND THE ALIGNMENT TO CORE VALUES

As discussed in Chapter 1, a fundamental flaw with much of what passes for an impact analysis is the tendency to think small, and one of the misgivings or problems that quantify this fundamental flaw is that impact assessments are often misaligned with the core values of the organizations they serve. In Chapter 2, we introduced five guiding principles of postmodern impact assessments as a considered means for addressing a fundamental flaw and other problems and misgivings that are embedded in the current approach to impact assessments (Figure 4.1).

Figure 4.1 The proper alignment to core values makes the difference between response and messaging that can be helpful or harmful and should be determined by the impact assessment. (Top left photograph used with permission, copyright Bruce C. Murray/Shutterstock.com; bottom photograph used with permission, copyright Melissa Brandes/Shutterstock.com.)

* * *

A failure to align with internal organizational values causes the impact assessment to *underestimate* the negative public perception impacts to the organization and *misinform* key messaging and communication tactics that are rooted in the study of impacts.

* * *

109

In this chapter, we will be looking directly at the problems that occur when we do not create impact assessments that align with internal organizational values, and how we can use the second principle of the five guiding principles to address this problem. Before we proceed, however, it is important to reflect on the ideas presented in Chapter 3 regarding the impact horizon; specifically that a properly completed impact horizon generates two key work products:

1. A set of clearly stated disclosures about the impact assessment
2. A RACI matrix that indicates who was responsible, accountable, consulted, and informed regarding the total scope of the impact assessment

Establishing an impact horizon helps to frame the scope of the impact assessment, but it *does not* address the underlying problem of misalignment to core values that many impact assessments exhibit. In prior chapters we established that the conditions of postmodernism, market state economies, and globalization are exerting an influence on organizations of all types. One of the challenges that this influence creates is to the **core values** of the organization. Core values are principles that guide an organization's internal conduct as well as its external relationships with the community and other partners. These are usually found in a mission or vision statement for the organization. *Once written, these mission and vision statements are often filed away to collect dust. The use of these statements in the creation of a good impact assessment should take the applicability of these documents under consideration.*

We have also discussed the idea of negative public perception impacts and how multinational corporations and public sector emergency managers must be aware of messaging during an event. On a world stage all disasters and terror attacks are transmitted and viewed instantaneously around the planet. As you'll recall, BP's then-CEO, Tony Hayward, made several gaffes in the midst of BP's response to the 2010 Gulf Coast oil spill, one of which was, "I want my life back." As you'll also recall, this comment, among other insensitivities he displayed, did not fare well for BP during its management of the worst oil spill in U.S. history.

Some of these earlier concerns were addressed with actionable steps that can be taken by applying the impact horizon principle as presented in Chapter 3. However, there are two principles of impact alignment that can vastly improve the prioritization of messaging and response capabilities. One of the principles is focused on the internal core values of the organization, and the other is focused on external laws and regulations that affect the organization. These principles can ensure appropriate key potential impacts are measured, that response tactics and key messages are prioritized, in order to provide a better overall understanding of the impact data and the resulting response tactic options we consider based on those data.

While establishing the impact horizon addresses the outer edges and boundaries of the scope of impacts to be assessed, the second principle, that is, aligning the impact measures to core values, addresses the need for an alignment of impacts (and the response tactics informed by them) to the core values of the organization. In other words, the second principle enforces a certain rigor with an eye toward improving the proposed impact measures *before* conducting an impact assessment, so that what is measured in terms of impact is aligned to the organization's core values.

* * *

Specifically, the second principle of alignment to core values will generate an initial weighted score, which will diminish one of the problems with impact assessments—a failure to align with internal organizational values.

* * *

To review, the second principle creates an output that *aligns core values to a specific weight, and then places them in a weighted score* (Figure 4.2).

We will take a look at three seminal events—Hurricane Katrina, the Joplin tornado, and the Oslo terror attack—as examples of how an alignment with core values assists or disrupts messaging and can create or avoid negative public perception impacts. We will critically examine how the tactics and messaging deployed during these events either aligned to the core values of the public organizations affected or did not.

The key lesson of this chapter is that some emergency managers and their leadership have fared better than others at aligning their tactics and messaging to core values during a crisis. Tragically, the true cost of misalignment can be more than political—it can be very practical, with the ministration of budgets and the narrowing of a program's scope being the rough reaction to poor management and messaging. The value of this chapter is to best understand the importance of culture and messaging on impact in the context of establishing an alignment to core values.

Figure 4.2 Alignment to organizational core values provides a better overall understanding of impact data and the resulting response tactic options.

4.4 POSTMODERN CULTURE AND THE IMPORTANCE OF MESSAGING FROM THE CORE DURING A CRISIS

We want to take a moment to reflect on what **public messaging** can look like and point to some examples of poor messaging, as well as some examples of fantastic messaging delivered by informed leadership during fearful events. At its best, public messaging is a set of specific communication tactics employed by the **public information officer** (PIO) identified in a response plan and informed by *pre-established tactics* based on impact. Unfortunately, the public information officer is often not involved with the impact assessment process. We believe that clear, concise, and positive messaging is the product of extremely skilled professional emergency managers who understand the importance of perception impacts and who have considered how to manage those impacts through communication. By applying the second principle of aligning the impact assessment to core values, the emergency manager can convey core values into messaging tactics for the PIO.

The second principle, "align to core values," informs the degree to which the fifth (and final) principle is adhered. The fifth principle, you should recall, is the principle of deviations and overrides. If the second principle delivers an accurate weighted score that reflects the core values of an organization, there should be no need for deviations or overrides, and we should be well in alignment with our overall impact analysis approach and the goals and expectations of the executive in charge. Whether he or she is a president, prime minister, state governor, administrative director, or chief executive officer, we can ensure well-aligned public messaging tactics if we do the tough work of framing the impact assessment within the second principle. In doing so, we guarantee that there is clear alignment to the organization's core values and need only to use the final principle to validate that we have reflected the appropriate internal values.

Using the five guiding principles of postmodern impact assessments drives toward an executive understanding of the impact assessment process *concisely* by establishing an impact horizon, aligning the impact assessment to core values, then aligning the impact assessment to national or state policy and law, and finally, ensuring that executives buy in or opt out. This applied sequence to impact assessments deeply prioritizes the response options and tactics that may be communicated before, during, and after an event.

There have been some inspiring examples and fantastic developments in 2011 that are wonderful tributes to leaders who are messaging on impact in a direct and positive way. The application of the five guiding principles of postmodern impact assessments has been forwarded here with the hopes of seeing more of these successes in the future. There are some contemporary examples of messaging on impact that have gone terribly wrong as well, and these are used as illustrations in this chapter to deepen our appreciation of what it means to be truly aligned with an organization's core values.

* * *

When impact messaging is done right, we see communications that are hopeful in the face of fear, triumphant in the presence of failure, and controlled in the context of chaos. We believe these are not accidental occurrences, but the results of careful practice and engaged partnership with leadership by emergency managers, who are applying the notion of a perception impact to their practice by extension of their experience.

* * *

113

The five guiding principles of postmodern impact assessments serve to forward a process based on principles by which such experience can be communicated and applied in the lives of all of those who practice in the field and have not yet benefited from such experience. Hurricane Katrina and the Joplin tornado provide case studies of *not* aligning to core values and falling off message. The Oslo terror attack is a case study in being on message and on mission, with deep alignment to core values.

4.5 HURRICANE KATRINA, AUGUST 2005:
OFF MESSAGE AND OFF MISSION

The events of Hurricane Katrina are almost completely framed by the messaging that occurred during the event. The tactics used during the event, while discussed at length in other texts, pale in comparison to the loud messaging and contrarian positions taken by a mayor, a governor, and a commander in chief who did not seem to understand how to interact with one another under the National Response Framework and did not share a common messaging approach based on shared core values. While great credit is due to those who performed under impossible conditions, the poor and inconsistent messaging that occurred during the event unfortunately drowned out the good works of military and civilian responders. In this case, the words spoke louder than the actions (Figure 4.3).

Prior to Katrina, Hurricane Ivan had previously threatened the Gulf of Mexico in September 2004. The mayor of New Orleans, Clarence Ray Nagin, urged the people of New Orleans to be ready for the storm, preferably to evacuate with some "Benjamins" ($100 bills) handy, and urged any who planned to stay to not only stock up on food and water, but also make sure they had "an axe in the attic," which was a reference to the many people trapped in their attics by rising floodwaters when Hurricane Betsy hit the city in 1965. Mayor Nagin issued a call for a voluntary evacuation of the city at 6 p.m. on September 13. Some 600,000 New Orleanians left.

Thousands were stuck in highway traffic for 12 or even 24 hours. Meanwhile, the eye of the hurricane missed the city! The events surrounding Hurricane Ivan created a negative public perception impact that would not be felt until the next year when the public's trust in

Figure 4.3 As this image of a protest in Hawaii shows, the U.S. government's lack of unified messaging based on shared core values had a negative public perception impact surrounding Hurricane Katrina that spanned the nation. (Used with permission, copyright Bruce C. Murray/Shutterstock.com.)

Mayor Nagin would be needed most. While this negative impact was unintended by Mayor Nagin, much care should be taken to combat public apathy with positive messaging, education, and honest ownership of "false alarms."

* * *

Emergency managers or the public officials they support cannot afford to become "the boy who cried wolf," by denying that evacuations are sometimes necessary even when a risk does not manifest, and reinforcing that the public servants are responsible for the public's well-being and should be taken seriously *at all times.*

* * *

Returning to the subject of Katrina, Kathleen Babineaux Blanco is the former Democratic governor of Louisiana, having served from January 2004 until January 2008. She was the first woman to be elected to the office of governor of Louisiana. Blanco had a difficult working relationship with New Orleans' mayor Ray Nagin. Despite having joined the Democratic Party in 2001, Nagin endorsed the Republican gubernatorial candidate Bobby Jindal for governor (rather than Blanco) in 2003. Thus Nagin and Blanco were at odds with one another.

Less than 2 years into her term, Hurricane Katrina, the most devastating hurricane ever to make landfall in the United States, struck New Orleans and greater Louisiana and Governor Blanco was criticized for an inadequate response to the disaster.

On the morning of Friday, August 26, 2005, at 10 a.m. CDT, Katrina had strengthened to a category 3 storm in the Gulf of Mexico. Later that afternoon, the **National Hurricane Center** (NHC) realized that Katrina had yet to make the turn toward the Florida Panhandle and ended up revising the predicted track of the storm from the Panhandle to the Mississippi coast. The NHC issued a hurricane watch for southeastern Louisiana, including the New Orleans area, at 10 a.m. CDT, Saturday, August 27. That afternoon, the NHC extended the watch to cover the Alabama to Mississippi coastlines, as well as the Louisiana coast westward to Intracoastal City.

The U.S. Coast Guard began prepositioning resources beyond the expected impact zone starting on August 26, and activated more than 400 reservists. Aircrews from the Aviation Training Center in Mobile, Alabama, staged rescue aircraft from Texas to Florida. All aircraft were returning back toward the Gulf of Mexico by the afternoon of August 29. Aircrews, many of whom lost their homes during the hurricane, began a round-the-clock rescue effort in New Orleans and along the Mississippi and Alabama coastlines.

On August 27, 2005, Governor Blanco, speaking about Hurricane Katrina, told the media in Jefferson Parish, "I believe we are prepared.

That's the one thing that I've always been able to brag about."[1] Later that day she issued a request to President George W. Bush for federal assistance and U.S.$9 million in aid, which stated:

> I have determined that this incident is of such severity and magnitude that effective response is beyond the capabilities of the State and affected local governments, and that supplementary Federal assistance is necessary to save lives, protect property, public health, and safety, or to lessen or avert the threat of a disaster. I am specifically requesting emergency protective measures, direct Federal Assistance, Individual and Household Program (IHP) assistance, Special Needs Program assistance, and debris removal.

Also in the requesting letter, the governor stated:

> In response to the situation I have taken appropriate action under State law and directed the execution of the State Emergency Plan on August 26, 2005 in accordance with Section 501(a) of the Stafford Act. A State of Emergency has been issued for the State in order to support the evacuations of the coastal areas in accordance with our State Evacuation Plan.[2]

That same day, Mayor Nagin advised New Orleanians to keep a close eye on the storm and prepare for evacuation. He made various statements encouraging people to leave without officially calling for an evacuation that day. It wasn't until the evening before formally issuing a call for voluntary evacuation. He stressed the potential danger posed by Katrina by saying, "This is not a test. This is the real deal."[3] He was hesitant to order a mandatory evacuation because of concerns about the city's liability for closing hotels and other businesses. Nagin continued to announce that the city attorney was reviewing the information regarding this issue and once he had the city attorney's opinion in hand he would make a decision regarding a mandatory evacuation of New Orleans.

Then-President George W. Bush declared a state of emergency in selected regions of Louisiana, Alabama, and Mississippi on Saturday, August 27—two days before the hurricane made landfall and in keeping with Governor Blanco's request. However, the president's declaration did not include any of Louisiana's coastal parishes, a fact that would be addressed in congressional hearings held in the wake of the eventual disaster. That same evening, the NHC upgraded the storm alert status from hurricane watch to hurricane warning over the stretch of coastline between Morgan City, Louisiana, and the Alabama-Florida border. Twelve hours after the watch alert had been issued, a tropical storm warning for the westernmost Florida Panhandle was also issued.

117

During videoconferences involving the president on August 28 and 29, the director of the NHC at the time, Max Mayfield, expressed concern that Katrina might push its storm surge over the city of New Orleans' levees and flood walls. In one conference, he stated, "I do not think anyone can tell you with confidence right now whether the levees will be topped or not, but that's obviously a very, very great concern."

On Sunday morning, August 28, Katrina became a category 4 hurricane, and with fewer than 24 hours left before the storm's landfall, Nagin declared a mandatory evacuation of New Orleans, the first in the city's history, and the first for a U.S. city of this size since the American Civil War.

Beginning at dawn on Sunday morning, New Orleans radio and television repeatedly broadcast Mayor Nagin's pleas for everybody to leave town as quickly and safely as possible. He declared the Superdome as a shelter of last resort for those who couldn't leave. Nagin and Blanco urged the citizens who sought shelter at the Superdome to bring enough food and water for at least 3 days. The two leaders also urged the people to treat their stay in the Dome as a "camping trip." State governor-controlled National Guard troops were stationed inside the Superdome to screen evacuees for weapons and feed the citizens gathered there, yet the situation within the Superdome became very difficult for evacuees.

On Sunday, August 28, as the sheer size of Katrina became clear, the NHC extended the tropical storm warning zone to cover most of the Louisiana coastline and a larger portion of the Florida Panhandle. The National Weather Service's New Orleans/Baton Rouge office issued a vividly worded bulletin predicting that the area would be "uninhabitable for weeks" after "devastating damage" caused by Katrina, which at that time rivaled the intensity of Hurricane Camille. On the same day, President Bush spoke with Governor Blanco to encourage her to order a mandatory evacuation of New Orleans; she did not issue her evacuation orders for the city until August 28 (per page 235 of Special Report of the Committee on Homeland Security and Governmental Affairs).

Voluntary and mandatory evacuations were issued for large areas of southeast Louisiana as well as coastal Mississippi and Alabama. About 1.2 million residents of the Gulf Coast were placed under a voluntary or mandatory evacuation order.

In the aftermath of the disaster, during a September 26, 2005, hearing, former FEMA chief Michael Brown testified before a U.S. House subcommittee about FEMA's response. During that hearing, Representative Stephen Buyer (R-IN) inquired as to why President Bush's declaration of a state of emergency on August 28 had not included the coastal parishes of Orleans, Jefferson, and Plaquemines. (In fact, the declaration did not include any of Louisiana's coastal parishes, whereas the coastal counties were included in the declarations for Mississippi and Alabama.) Brown testified that this was because Louisiana Governor Blanco had not included those parishes in her initial request for aid, a decision that he found "shocking." After the hearing, Blanco released a copy of her letter, which showed she had requested assistance for "all the southeastern parishes including the New Orleans Metropolitan area and the mid-state Interstate I-49 corridor and northern parishes along the I-20 corridor that are accepting [evacuated citizens]."

Many private caregiving facilities that relied on bus companies and ambulance services for evacuation were unable to evacuate their patients. Rental cars were in short supply, and many forms of public transportation had been shut down well before the storm arrived. Some estimates claimed that 80% of the 1.3 million residents of the greater New Orleans metropolitan area evacuated, leaving behind substantially fewer people than remained in the city during the Hurricane Ivan evacuation.

By August 26, the possibility of an unprecedented cataclysm was already being considered. Many of the computer models for the hurricane had shifted the potential path of Katrina 150 miles (240 km) westward from the Florida Panhandle, putting the city of New Orleans directly in the center of their track probabilities; the chances of a direct hit were forecast at 17%, with strike probability rising to 29% by August 28.

This scenario was considered a potential catastrophe because some parts of New Orleans and the metro area are below sea level. Since the storm surge produced by the hurricane's right-front quadrant (containing the strongest winds) was forecast to be 28 feet (8.5 meters), emergency management officials in New Orleans feared that the storm surge could go over the tops of levees protecting the city, causing major flooding.

By Sunday, August 28, most infrastructures along the Gulf Coast had been shut down, including all Canadian National Railway and Amtrak rail traffic into the evacuation areas as well as the Waterford Nuclear Generating Station. The NHC maintained the coastal warnings until late on August 29, by which time Hurricane Katrina was over central Mississippi.

At a news conference at 10 a.m. on August 28, shortly after Katrina was upgraded to a category 5 hurricane, New Orleans Mayor Ray Nagin ordered the first-ever mandatory evacuation of the city, calling Katrina "a storm that most of us have long feared." The city government also established several "refuges of last resort" for citizens who could not leave the city, including the massive Louisiana Superdome, which sheltered approximately 26,000 people and provided them with food and water for several days as the storm came ashore.

On August 29, Katrina's storm surge caused 53 different levee breaches in greater New Orleans, submerging 80% of the city. A June 2007 report by the American Society of Civil Engineers indicated that two-thirds of the flooding was caused by the multiple failures of the city's flood walls. The storm surge also devastated the coasts of Mississippi and Alabama, making Katrina the most destructive and costly natural disaster in the history of the United States, and the deadliest hurricane since the 1928 Okeechobee hurricane. The total damage from Katrina was estimated at $81.2 billion (2005 U.S. dollars when adjusted for inflation), nearly double the cost of the previously most expensive storm, Hurricane Andrew.

On September 1, 2005, Governor Blanco made several statements regarding the deployment of 300 National Guard troops to supplement local police forces. Ultimately, she made threatening statements relaying expectations about these supporting forces, which many interpreted as orders to "shoot and kill" looters:

> Three hundred of the Arkansas National Guard have landed in the city of New Orleans. These troops are fresh back from Iraq, well trained, experienced, battle-tested and under my orders to restore order in the streets. They have M-16s and they are locked and loaded. These troops know how to shoot and kill and they are more than willing to do so if necessary and I expect they will.[4]

These statements failed in three primary ways:

1. They failed to present any kind of message of support and hope to the community at large.
2. They portrayed an official state position as having expectations for National Guards forces to shoot and kill its own citizens.
3. They painted war veterans as bloodthirsty killers waiting for the opportunity to shoot and kill their own kinsmen over a stolen TV.

All in all, Governor Blanco failed to show any positive support of those suffering from thefts, and failed to present herself professionally when dealing with a natural symptom of a natural catastrophe.

On September 1, 2005, Mayor Nagin held a high-profile interview on the relief situation with Garland Robinette on radio station WWL in which he bluntly criticized the delays in aid to the city. He expressed anger with what he saw as the slow federal and state response, imploring citizens to request that President Bush and Louisiana governor Blanco send the required resources. "I don't want to see anybody do any more goddamn press conferences," he said. "Put a moratorium on press conferences. Don't do another press conference until the resources are in this city." He compared the reaction to Hurricane Katrina with the swift national reaction to 9/11 and the war in Iraq. He concluded the interview by telling President Bush and the federal government, "Now get off your asses and let's do something, and let's fix the biggest goddamn crisis in the history of this country."[5]

As part of what was apparently a larger effort to assign responsibility for the inadequate response, Michael Chertoff, the secretary of Homeland Security at the time, explained on September 4, "The way that emergency operations act under the law is, the responsibility and the power, the authority, to order an evacuation rests with state and local officials. The Federal Government comes in and supports those officials."[6]

On September 3, President Bush responded to Nagin's criticism by focusing on the failings of state and local authorities, stating that the disaster's magnitude "created tremendous problems that have strained state and local capabilities. The result is that many of our citizens simply are not getting the help they need, especially in New Orleans. And that is unacceptable."[7]

As of May 19, 2006, the confirmed death toll (total of direct and indirect deaths) stood at 1,836, mainly from Louisiana (1,577) and Mississippi (238). However, 705 people remain categorized as missing in Louisiana. Many of the deaths were indirect, and it is almost impossible to determine the exact cause of some of the fatalities.

Federal disaster declarations covered 90,000 square miles (233,000 km^2) of the United States, an area almost as large as the United Kingdom. The hurricane left an estimated 3 million people without electricity. On September 3, 2005, Homeland Security Secretary Michael Chertoff described the aftermath of Hurricane Katrina as "probably the worst catastrophe, or set of catastrophes," in the country's history, referring to the hurricane itself plus the flooding of New Orleans.

It is impossible to know the core values of Kathleen Blanco, the former governor of Louisiana, or Mayor Nagin, the mayor of New Orleans, or the president at the time. Each of them had taken an oath in which they swore to uphold the Constitution of the United States as well as (in Blanco and Nagin's case) the state's constitution. Nagin and Blanco made various speeches on their inaugurations into office that hinted at better justice systems, a better business environment, and deeper community relations.

What is clear from the events of Katrina is that *all three leaders did not rely on the core values of their office while messaging to the public regarding Katrina.*

If the core values of these public officials included the notion that they would *serve the people* of their city, state, and country, they appear to have failed in that regard. To serve the public is perhaps the most fundamental core value of any public official. With this core value in mind, reconsider some of the public messages delivered by the mayor, the governor, and the president during Katrina (Table 4.1).

* * *

Despite the legal complexities of declaring a disaster at the state and federal levels, and confusion surrounding the impacts of the hurricane, the victims of New Orleans were not well served by messages and tactics that were not aligned to the core values their leaders shared.

* * *

The negative public perception impact looms large in the story of Katrina. Michael D. Brown, undersecretary of the Department of Homeland Security Emergency Preparedness and Response and director of the Federal Emergency Management Agency, left his office 2 weeks after Katrina under pressure from Chertoff, who had pulled him from his incident commander role on Friday, September 9, in an effort to regain control of New Orleans. He was replaced by Thad Allen, a Coast Guard vice admiral.

In Chapter 2 we spoke about cultural relevancy and negative public perception impacts. In the case study above, the messaging did not have cultural relevancy for the victims on the ground, and the negative public perception impacts directly affected FEMA, the Department of Homeland Security, and its leadership. Katrina put the alignment of the core values of local, state, and federal government response messaging and tactics to the test with negative public perception impacts being the result.

4.6 THE JOPLIN, MISSOURI, TORNADO OF 2011: OFF MESSAGE AND OFF MISSION

The tornado that hit Joplin, Missouri, on May 22, 2011, killed 158 people, injured hundreds, and was one of the deadliest tornadoes in American history (Figure 4.4). The Glazier-Higgens-Woodward tornado cluster of

Table 4.1   Core Value: To Serve the Public

Date	Mayor Nagin	Governor Blanco	President Bush
August 27, 2005	"This is not a test. This is the real deal."	"I believe we are prepared. That's one thing I've always been able to brag about."	
August 28, 2005	"This is a storm that most of us have long feared."		"We will do everything in our power to help the people in the communities affected by this storm."
August 29, 2005		"Mr. President, we need your help. We need everything you've got."	"For those of you who are concerned about whether or not we're prepared to help, don't be. We are. We're in place. We've got equipment in place, supplies in place."
August 30, 2005		"I wouldn't think it would be toxic soup right now. I think it's just water from the lake, water from the canals. It's, you know, water."	"We're beginning to move in the help that people need."
August 31, 2005			"Buses are on the way to take those people from New Orleans to Houston."

(continued)

123

Table 4.1   Core Value: To Serve the Public (continued)

Date	Mayor Nagin	Governor Blanco	President Bush
September 1, 2005	"Now get off your asses and do something, and let's fix the biggest goddamn crisis in the history of this country."	"Shoot to kill."	"Again, my attitude is, if it's not going exactly right, we're going to make it go exactly right. If there's problems, we're going to address the problems."

Figure 4.4   With two letters from *Joplin* that survived the EF-5 tornado, a person who used duct tape to add an *H* and *E* to spell *HOPE* gave a more personal message than FEMA and DMORT were able to provide at the time of the event. (Used with permission, copyright Melissa Brandes/Shutterstock.com.)

1947 that swept across Texas, Oklahoma, and Kansas is the only known deadlier tornado event. During that event, in Woodward, Texas, alone, 152 were killed.

Joplin was not the mega-city tornado of a St. Louis or Dallas–Ft. Worth FEMA scenario and was probably never estimated to be. Here's why: From an impact perspective, the population of Joplin is only around 50,000 people, which may well have been the number used by emergency managers to plan for a potential catastrophe in the city. However, the day-time population swells to over 200,000 people as individuals from the surrounding areas commute to the location for work, education, and medical services. At question is which number was the right impact number to work from—the 50,000- or the 200,000-person population?

The cost of not getting this right is the difference between planning for a catastrophic loss of life that impacts potentially 400% more human lives than the actual population of the town!

Beyond the challenge of understanding the impact of an active, flexing population, responders were faced with a more daunting problem; some of the remains of those killed in the tornado were not identifiable and Missouri state officials were left with 142 body parts in a morgue. Families with missing loved ones expressed their anger and frustration on national television, even as authorities seemed to be scrambling for a policy position on how to deal with identifying victims.

Officials wrangled with the list of missing persons reports after the event, and Andrea Spillars, from the Missouri Department of Public Safety, held a news conference in which she stated, "We will provide today, a list of 232 individuals, that we have actual reports … that individuals have come in and said that they were missing and unaccounted for."[8] When the list was given to the media, they immediately honed in on duplication on the list. Lance Hare, a missing Joplin teen, was on the list twice. He was listed once as Caley Hare, and on the next page as Caley Lance Hare—both with the same address and age and only one page apart on the two-page list.

Other families expressed frustration at not being able to enter the morgue to identify their missing loved ones. When asked by CNN about this, Spillars struggled to articulate a policy position on the matter, saying, "The Disaster Federal Mortuary Team has several mechanisms to positively identify individuals. That is the most important thing. In a catastrophic event—we want to make sure we don't make mistakes—that we positively identify these individuals … so fingerprints, DNA, medical records, whatever we need to do to positively identify so that those family members can get some solace." Another federal responder told CNN that often "families make mistakes" when trying to identify loved ones in a morgue.[9]

The Disaster Federal Mortuary Team (DMORT), which was deployed to Joplin, had been part of DHS up until 2007, when it was repositioned under the Department of Health and Human Services under the control of the assistant secretary for Preparedness and Response. DMORT uses multiple sophisticated methods of forensic techniques, such as DNA sampling and matching, fingerprint matching, and information gathered from family members to gather unique characteristics to assist with identification for bodies, or body parts that defied visual identification. It was activated for the World Trade Center disaster as well as Hurricanes Rita and Katrina. DMORT maintains a Mobile Mortuary Container at Sky Harbor Airport in Phoenix, Arizona. The Mobile Mortuary Container is a depository of equipment and supplies for deployment to a disaster site. It contains a complete morgue with designated workstations for the processing of body parts and deceased persons who have been damaged beyond visual recognition.

According to DMORT their responsibilities include:

- Temporary morgue facilities
- Victim identification using latent fingerprint, forensic dental, pathologist, and forensic anthropology methods
- Processing
- Preparation
- Disposition of remains[10]

It is unclear if these responsibilities are the mission of DMORT. However, what is clear is that to the families who were missing loved ones in Joplin after the tornado struck, the technical jargon of *forensics* and *positive identification* of individuals used as talking points during the press conference and afterward in interviews with CNN and other news outlets left many outraged. In Spillars' comment to CNN, the terms *victims* and *families* were used almost as an afterthought.

Whether it was intentional or not, the lack of a clear message based on a high death toll by DMORT or the Missouri Department of Public Safety is stunning. DMORT has been deployed to some of America's worst disasters, disasters involving the highest impacts of all, a large loss of life. Disasters during which a consoling, family-facing, sympathetic message should have *at least* been developed, adopted, and delivered. The impact of those disasters and others DMORT would plan for surely must have required preparation to deal with the impact of the amount of fatalities and an ability to explain the challenges of identification in a consoling way to families.

In addition, Spillars, working as a Missouri Department of Public Safety employee, could have started her statements based on the mission of her department, which is "to use its resources to safeguard the people who live, work, do business and visit the city. The staffs of the various divisions are hardworking and committed to improving their level of performance as well as developing policy and procedures that are transparent, understandable and streamlined. Together, we strive to be the premier municipal public safety department."[11] The sad reality is that the response to the Joplin families' missing loved ones did not appear to be focused on safeguarding people, or transparent and understandable. The message around the use of DMORT at Joplin added a public perception impact that is rarely factored into impact assessments in the public sector once again. A negative public perception impact is an impact that harms the reputation of first responders and emergency management officials.

The messy nature of interagency cooperation and messaging is not unique to the events at Joplin or to Ms. Spillars. This is not an indictment of the handling of this event or any of the important public servants who were performing their duties in the days that followed. What this section asks is how we are dealing with these types of messaging errors. Clearly, they are symptomatic of the broad challenge all practitioners face when working in large-scale events with multiple agencies. They are also reflective of the need for more work in our profession on how such communications should be managed. Depending on our level of practice, some professionals may choose to work on this issue now, and others may choose to examine the issue with a critical eye for improvement in the future. The option to be proactive regarding messaging with an alignment to organizational goals is offered as the second principle.

The real cost of the Joplin catastrophe, beyond property damage and human lives, may be an increased distrust for FEMA and further anti-federal sentiments based on a lack of clarity regarding the impact and response to the disaster. Beyond the normal measures of the loss of life, injury, and property damage, we must include the loss of public trust. And this is the area where it appears we slipped up and did not clearly define our mission, administer compassion to the living, or treat the dead with the respect and honor they deserved. Thus the first responders to this event and their leaders unintentionally created a negative public perception impact that reflected poorly on the emergency management profession.

Again in Joplin, just as in New Orleans, the complex network of responders and a lack of clarity around the core values impacted by the event led to a negative public perception impact. This is the main problem embedded in a fundamental flaw of thinking too small about impact assessments. When we consider the alignment of core values to the impacts, we are better prepared to avoid these thorny challenges and build better messaging and tactics into our response plans.

4.7 THE OSLO TERROR ATTACKS: ON MESSAGE AND ON MISSION

July 22, 2011, was the day of the well-known dual terror attacks in Oslo, Norway. The impact most felt from this event was the incredible loss of life at the hands of one "lone wolf" perpetrator. Considering the potential for negative perception impacts after this horrible event, consider the messaging from leaders and others during and after the event.

During the event, first responders and leaders alike were incredibly honest about what they knew and what they did not know. As the events unfolded on the island, police inspector Bjoerne Erik Sem-Jacobsen told Reuters, "We don't know how many people were on the island, and therefore we have to search further."[12] This is an amazingly frank assessment of the response—without speculation or guesses about the real-time impact. It is an honest statement about procedure that speaks volumes about the care with which the police inspector's department was carrying out its duty.

Prime Minister Jens Stoltenberg shared his shock from the attacks openly with his constituents saying, "A paradise island has been transformed into a hell."[13] Later that night, while touring the damaged public buildings he said, "There are still people missing ... one cannot rule out anything. This is evil, pure evil" (Figure 4.5).[14]

Later, Stoltenberg gave a press conference at Sundvollen and said he had just spoken to many of the survivors. He said many of them had been "heroes" and had saved the lives of their friends. He stated, "They are deeply affected and a lot of them said that the best way of honoring those who lost their lives is to carry on being active ... and those who try to scare us will not succeed."[15]

At a church service merely days after the attack, Jens Stoltenberg related, "In the middle of all the tragedy, I am proud to live in a country

Figure 4.5 The response of Oslo's government was so honest and aligned to the core values of the public they served that its messaging aligned with the public's response. (Used with permission, copyright Robert Rozbora/Shutterstock.com.)

which has managed to stand tall in a critical time." He continued, "Our response is more democracy, more openness, more humanity, but never naïveté."[16] Even in the face of an election coming in November in which his response and the perception impact of his messaging might hurt his candidacy, Stoltenberg candidly advised, "I believe everyone understands that we have to discuss the form of the debate … to avoid a conflict between the political debate and the need to show dignity and compassion."[17]

This messaging alignment to the core values of a country that values its openness and democratic freedoms gave Stoltenberg's opponents in the opposition Conservative Party pause, with the leader of the opposition party saying, "We have to agree to the rules of the (political) game." This unification in messaging around the terrible impacts of loss and of innocent life, and a renewed focus on "democracy, openness, and humanity" without "naiveté" is honorable and profound. It exhibits a true command on the second principle—to align core values with impacts. When deftly executed, the message resonates with the public in such a manner that locals enter the conversation letting go of fear, and taking hold of hope.

Consider these quotes from the Norwegian public. In an email to the BBC, a citizen from Oslo identified as Maria wrote, "In the past few hours we've found a face to attach to the gruesome acts. As it turns out, this is the face of a blonde, blue-eyed Caucasian man. A description that could match many a Norwegian. However, what needs to be the focus now is not this madman and his mad cause or he'll get exactly the attention that he wanted. What needs to be our focus is rebuilding our city and assisting those in need."[18]

Perhaps the most telling messaging came from the young people who were there on that island on that horrible day. They have taken their cultural cues from the reactions of the leadership around them.

* * *

The victims of this tragic event display very little fear or political ranting; instead, in the face of strong leadership and messaging during the event, we find victims who are resilient—almost defiant.

* * *

Sixteen-year-old Ivan Bengamin Ostebo lost five friends to the attack perpetrated by Breivik on July 22. He wrote the following statement on his Facebook page, and rather than seeing someone defeated, you saw a young man that refused to be a victim and who faced the threat directly: "You might think that you have won. You might think that you have ruined something for the Labour Party and for people around the world who stand for a multicultural society by killing my friends and fellow Party members. Know that you have failed."[19] To paraphrase, this young man articulated Norway's true core values: We stand for a multicultural society.

Much of the world could only sympathize and honor the bravery, compassion, and steadfast resolve with which the leaders and people of Norway managed the perception impact during this terrible event.

Political "thinkers" *did* arrive on the scene later, calling for an inspection into Christian fundamentalism and the neo-Nazi terrorist threat. However, the core messaging during and immediately after the event was nothing less than commendable. The political leadership, first responders, and even a majority of the victims seemed to stand unified against this affronting attack on their core values.

Unfortunately, only a stilted and jaded American "journalist" could offer his shameful commentary, but it fell on deaf ears in Norway. Glenn Beck, an American right-wing talk show host, compared the victims of the shooting at the Labor Party camp to Hitler Youths. Beck described the brutal incident "as a shooting at a political camp, which sounds a little like the Hitler Youth. I mean who sends their kids to a political camp?"[20] Torbjørn Eriksen, a former press secretary to Jens Stoltenberg, Norway's prime minister, called Beck's comments "a new low" and continued with, "Young political activists have gathered at Utoya for over 60 years to learn about and be part of democracy, the very opposite of what the Hitler Youth was about," he told the *Daily Telegraph*. "Glenn Beck's comments are ignorant, incorrect and extremely hurtful."[21]

Perhaps the messaging around the Oslo attacks shows that, at our best, we can frame the dialogue around negative public perception impacts through the sound application of the second principle and with careful attention to the alignment of impacts to our core values. The messaging also sadly demonstrates that there is often no way of avoiding the ignorant statements of commentators seeking the limelight.

* * *

Here is how the first responders, emergency managers, and leaders during the attacks on Oslo came out on top: They managed the message and pushed the rhetoric of politics and opinion out of the spotlight and into the darkness of the shadows—where they belonged.

* * *

4.8 IN THE PRIVATE SECTOR—CORE VALUES AND MEASURABLE IMPACTS

In the private sector, companies create vision and mission statements to reflect their core values. They often reflect corporate policy and are designed to inform the leadership, employees, shareholders, customers, and sometimes even the community about what the organization values. As you will recall from Chapter 1, to conduct an impact assessment is to study the loss of what we value. If the core values of private organizations are *truly* reflections of the organization's core values, they can assist us in better preparing the impact assessment with alignment to the core values of the organization as required in the second principle.

Vision and mission statements often provide valuable and important clues to what the organization values and how we can include those in framing our impact assessments. Some examples of core values would include:

- Providing the best customer experience in the industry
- Being the most trusted provider of service in our business
- Being the best place to work by protecting our employees' well-being
- Increasing shareholder value through consistent quality improvement
- Putting people first in everything we do

This is just a small sampling. Whatever the mission or vision statement for a private organization says, it is important to consider how the values embedded in that statement align to the impact assessment. This is how we inspect and align the core values of the organization to the impact assessment.

Consider the statement "Providing the best customer experience in the industry." If this is the top-line mission, then *anything* that impacts the customer experience should have a high value and be ranked as critical to the organization. Likewise, "being a trusted provider of service" places a considerable value and criticality on security, availability, and a low tolerance for service outages. "Protecting our employees' well-being" places an emphasis on health and safety, an important component of any emergency management plan.

"Increasing shareholder value" adds criticality to revenue-generating systems and processes—including the employees who deliver value to the organization. "Putting people first in everything we do" places value on health and safety planning and lessens the criticality of systems and processes that only generate revenue by some degree.

* * *

When pressed, many private organizations will say that their vision and mission statements are just marketing fluff, but many will work closely with the emergency management practitioner to consider their core values and achieve the best alignment.

* * *

The rhetorical question of what comes first, "people, processes, or technologies?" is best responded to by this approach. First, emergency response planning is a three-legged stool and requires that people, processes, and technologies all be recovered and restored after an event. Second, which people, processes, and technologies should be given the highest criticality is framed by the core values of the organization. If customers come first, then customer-facing people, processes, and systems are given a high criticality. If revenues are the core value, then those people, processes, and systems that drive revenues come first.

* * *

Often, there is more than one core value at play in the private sector, and an effort to align impacts to each core value from the highest-order impact to lower-order impacts is an important exercise that informs the impact assessment and the resulting tactics and messaging approaches that will come out of this effort.

* * *

If an organization does not wish to align its core values to the impact assessment, the practitioner is *strongly* advised to disclose this disconnect in the impact horizon RACI matrix. As a professional ethic, we would strongly recommend that when an executive chooses values for the organization under duress that are different from the core values the organization holds during normal operations, there has been a considerable deviation and it is incumbent upon the emergency management professional to disclose such a discrepancy.

Organizations that do align their core values to the impact assessment find that the resulting ranking of criticality for people, processes, and systems is much more affable to the organization at large, normally achieves earlier executive buy in, and lays the foundation for much more effective messaging and response tactics in the planning phase.

4.9 DELIVERING ALIGNMENT TO CORE VALUES

If the organization holds the idea "We will be the safest place to work," then human death and injuries are a factor of the key potential impacts aligned to core values. If the organization holds the idea "We will protect shareholder value and deliver strong returns," then revenue and financial impacts are key potential impacts aligned to core values. If our

133

organization says, "We will protect the environment in our operations," then environmental impacts are a key potential impact that aligns to core values. The challenge is that most companies, communities, and states have more than one core value, or do not operate under their vision and mission statements at all.

Core values are expressed as an admixture of value statements that drive the organization forward. They can range from "being the safest," to having the "best quality," to "being the most secret." Given that there is more than one core value, the practitioner will have to use weighted scores to establish the exact level of importance for each of these key potential impacts as they are aligned to the organization's core values. A weighted score is the only way to ensure that the second principle is right. The total score of all key potential impacts cannot exceed 100% for any single impact measure, but must reflect the whole capacity of the organization from a profit, capacity, or output perspective. To accomplish this, the practitioner must spread out three or more core values and assign them percentages of the total impact to organize the core values based on priority.

The principle of aligning impact measures to core values says: "The potential impact assessment should align to the organization's core values."

The key deliverable of applying the second principle is *the development of a weighted score that reflects the core values of an organization and can be applied to each object evaluated in the Impact Assessment so that each of the core values is represented, with the most important value holding the most weight, and the least of these holding the least weight.*

There are three key work products that will need to be created in order to deliver alignment to core values in the impact assessment:

1. A listing of organizational values
2. The assignment of weights to the core values that reflect the most important and least important of the core values as agreed upon by a defined set of stakeholders as they apply to the weighted score
3. A listing of who was and was not consulted when arriving at the weighted score pie chart

To determine the alignment to core values in the impact assessment (which are the most important and which are the least important), key stakeholders should be consulted and agreements should be made as to how the potential impact assessment reflects the core values of the organization. The assignment of a **weighted score** to core values is achieved through building consensus with the organization's leadership and indicating which stakeholders were and were not consulted. A weighted score is the method of taking each of the core values and assigning them a percentage of a 100% total score.

The practitioner can create a **weighted score pie chart** to illustrate core values and the influence these will have on individual objects in the final impact analysis calculation. This is achieved by creating a simple spreadsheet pie chart that reflects a whole score that is broken down by each of the core value considerations. Once this pie chart is created, the percentage values of each core value can be adjusted until the leadership stakeholders agree that the weights of each core value appropriately reflect the value they place on each core value statement. Consider these examples:

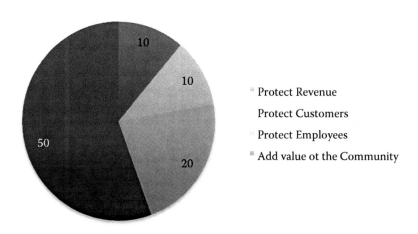

In this first version:

- 50% of the total weighted score will be derived from how a person, process, or technology protects revenue impacts.
- 20% of the total weighted score will be derived from how a person, process, or technology protects the customer.

- 15% of the total weighted score will be derived from how a person, process, or technology protects employees.
- 15% of the total weighted score will be derived from how a person, process, or technology protects value to the community.

In this second version a completely different set of core values is represented:

- 50% of the total weighted score will be derived from how a person, process, or technology protects value to the community.
- 20% of the total weighted score will be derived from how a person, process, or technology protects employee impacts.
- 10% of the total weighted score will be derived from how a person, process, or technology protects customers.
- 10% of the total weighted score will be derived from how a person, process, or technology protects revenue.

From these two samples alone we can see that either we are looking at two very different organizations, or the core values of one organization are widely contested. The first example places an emphasis on the core values of revenue and customers and appears to place the most criticality on protecting those core values. The second example places an emphasis on the community and employees and appears to place the most criticality on those values.

Based on the impact horizon created in the prior chapter, we can now see that the value of objects (people, processes, and systems) inside the impact horizon will be measured based on an alignment to the core values of the organization, by scoring them to create a weighted score.

The work product for the second principle should be delivered as:

- A basic listing of the core value statements of the organization
- Followed by the weighted score pie chart that represents the individual weighted scores for objects
- And a list of who was and was not consulted, which is the key to applying the second principle of aligning impact measures to core values

4.10 WHY THE SECOND PRINCIPLE MATTERS

What viewers, victims, and shareholders (private and public alike) want to understand within the spectacle of disasters and terror attacks is the twofold question: *What caused the impacts and what was impacted?* This is the stuff of headlines, commentary, and conversations across America and around the world whenever disaster or terror strikes. *What happened and what was harmed?* The emergency management or counterterrorism analyst offers the backdrop against which these questions are framed and answered. So many of us in the field fall into the category of emergency management analysts that it is worth highlighting a basic and important truth about our roles.

As discussed in Chapter 1, we should strive for higher learning. Critical thinking and working to build meaningful impact assessments that are aligned to the five guiding principles of postmodern impact assessments best illustrate that what we seek to protect is a means of *living a life devoted to a higher level of professional practice.* Not for honor or glory, or to be imminently contrarian in our practice, but for a much greater and more meaningful cause: to support the truest heroes in our fields—the first responders, counterterrorism field agents, and all the others who put their lives at risk to save others when disasters strike.

* * *

As emergency management professionals, we should support and enhance the vision and the understanding our leaders have in the art of messaging and creating *meaning* in a culture that is consumed with hope and fear.

* * *

Our personal and professional commitment to the impact analysis is our opportunity to rise above the fray of budget and political constraints in order to align messaging and leadership so that we all meet the challenges of a fearful and often critical public, all the while without undermining the good work of first responders or our personal standing in our practice.

We currently live in a culture in which the general public is torn between opposing desires. One set of hopes consists of democratic freedoms, free markets, and aspirations for a better life—a life that is enhanced by open borders and the free exchange of ideas and goods. Yet these noble and basic ideals are threatened by the (also basic) desire to be free from the fear of terrorism and disasters. The Arab Spring of 2011, the desperate and ugly uprising of youths in England in the summer of 2011, and the Libyan rebellion of 2011 are sharp examples of a world reaching for more of what is good and meaningful in life, regardless of how misguided, disruptive, or accidental those acts might seem.

* * *

These are the defining cultural themes of our time: the hope for a better life and the fear of our lives undone at the hands of a terrorist or a disaster.

* * *

In any one news media cycle, we witness these two dominant dialogues play themselves out: on the one hand, great hopes for a better future, and on the other, atrocious acts of terror and mother nature that defy public understanding. In fairness, the profane and novel take up the bits of time left between these paired cultural themes as items related to popular culture and the glamour of fame contend for precious airtime.

This is the broad cultural context in which we practice. These are the roots from which cultural messaging and leadership in disasters and terror attacks must spring forth. This is not a new picture of America or the world; it is one that has been developing since the events of 9/11, and in America, and can most readily be likened to the optimism of a 1950s' America faced with the Cold War. Again, on the one hand, hope, and on the other, fear.

Perhaps the change that should be noted is that this dual cultural condition has "gone global" to some greater extent, and the sharp fluctuations of hope and fear can now be found around the world due to our shared economies, shared corporations and supply chains, and our increasingly shared values. They are coming under threat from disasters and terror attacks that resonate with a global community that seeks a greater good for their local communities. These are the tacit outputs and the natural duality of our postmodern world today.

* * *

The shared cultural condition of our generation is to simply hope and fear.

* * *

It is in this context that the importance of postmodern culture exerts itself on the practice of conducting an impact assessment. In a globally united culture of hope and fear, we are charged with clearly defining how fearful acts will be responded to in the media and positioned in the public discourse during the impact assessment. We referred to the impacts on first responders and our profession earlier in this text as negative perception impacts—impacts that directly affect how the public views our profession and the performance of leaders to whom we might report, but who are not necessarily emergency management or counterterrorism professionals, yet nonetheless rely on us as professionals in this field to inform them.

* * *

This is where professional emergency management practitioners find themselves: between the first responders on the ground fighting for a swift and sure response, and the leadership above who must cope with the media that is driven to feed a starving market of viewers who wish to better understand their fear.

* * *

When we understand that our job is to prepare for negative perception impacts, we can really change the picture of how our profession is perceived, how the message about impacts is delivered, and most importantly, how we can create meaningful leadership messaging around impacts and the response to them.

4.11 SUMMARY

One of the outcomes of the fundamental flaw is that impact assessments are often misaligned with the core values of the organizations they serve. Core values are principles that guide an organization's internal conduct as well as its external relationships with the community and other partners. These are usually found in a mission or vision statement for the organization.

Hurricane Katrina, the Joplin tornado, and the Oslo terror attacks are examples of how an alignment with core values disrupts or assists messaging and can create or avoid negative public perception impacts. The tactics and messaging deployed during these events either aligned to the core values of the public organizations responding to them or did not.

Some emergency managers and their leadership have well aligned their tactics and messaging to core values during a crisis, and others have not fared as well. Tragically, the true cost of misalignment can be more than political—it can be very practical with the ministration of budgets and the narrowing of a program's scope being the rough reaction to poor management and messaging. The purpose of this chapter is to best understand the importance of culture and messaging on impact in the context of establishing an alignment to core values.

Using the five guiding principles of postmodern impact assessments drives toward an executive understanding of the impact assessment process *concisely* by establishing an impact horizon, aligning the impact assessment to core values, then aligning the impact assessment to national or state policy and law to arrive at a weighted score, and finally, ensuring that executives buy in or opt out. This proposed sequence to developing impact assessments deeply informs the potential response tactics and messages that will be communicated before, during, and after an event.

When messaging on impact is done right, we see communications that are hopeful in the face of fear, triumphant in the presence of failure, and controlled in the context of chaos. We believe these are not accidental occurrences, but the results of careful practice and engaged partnership with leadership by emergency managers who are applying the notion of a perception impact to their practice, by extension of their experience.

Often, there is more than one core value at play in the private sector, and an effort to align impacts to each core value from the highest-order impact to lower-order impacts is an important exercise that informs the impact assessment and the resulting tactics and messaging approaches that will come out of this effort. Organizations that align their core values to the impact assessment find that the resulting ranking of criticality for people, processes, and systems is much more affable to the organization at large, normally achieves earlier executive buy-in, and lays the foundation for much more effective messaging and response tactics in the planning phase.

The impact analysis area is our opportunity to rise above the fray of budget and political constraints in order to align messaging and leadership so that we all meet the challenges of a fearful and often critical public, all the while without undermining the good work of first responders or our personal standing in our practice.

4.12 QUESTIONS

1. How can aligning core values of an organization to the impact assessment reduce negative public perception impacts?
2. What does it mean to be on mission and on message?
3. Provide an example of a weighted score based on core values for a public or a private sector organization.
4. What is the meaning and importance of aligning core values to the impact assessment in the private and the public sector?
5. Generate a weighted score pie chart to illustrate an alignment to core values for a sample organization.

ENDNOTES

1. Wikipedia. 2011. Kathleen Blanco. http://en.wikipedia.org/wiki/Kathleen_ Blanco (accessed September 6, 2011).
2. Ibid.
3. Nossiter, Adam, and Dewan, Shaila. 2008. Mayor Orders the Evacuation of New Orleans. http://www.nytimes.com/2008/08/31/us/31orleans. html?pagewanted=all (accessed September 6, 2011).
4. ABC News AU. 2005. Troops Told "Shoot to Kill" in New Orleans. http:// www.abc.net.au/news/2005-09-02/troops-told-shoot-to-kill-in-new-orleans/2094678 (accessed September 6, 2011).
5. CNN.com. 2005. Mayor to Feds: "Get Off Your Asses." Transcript of radio interview with New Orleans' Nagin. http://www.cnn.com/2005/ US/09/02/nagin.transcript/ (accessed September 7, 2011).
6. Meet the Press. 2005. Transcript for September 4. http://www.msnbc. msn.com/id/9179790/ns/meet_the_press/t/transcript-september/#. TwHeuCOkA5s (accessed September 7, 2011).
7. Think Progress. 2005. Katrina Timeline. http://thinkprogress.org/report/ katrina-timeline/ (accessed September 6, 2011).
8. CNN, The Situation Room. 2011. Growing Anger in Search of Missing. http://transcripts.cnn.com/TRANSCRIPTS/1105/26/sitroom.01.html (accessed September 7, 2011).
9. Ibid.
10. Disaster Mortuary Operational Response Teams. http://www.dmort.org/.
11. The City of St. Louis Missouri. ND. Department of Public Safety. http:// stlouis-mo.gov/government/departments/public-safety/ (accessed August 19, 2011).
12. MSNBC Europe. 2011. At Least 85 Dead in Norway Youth Camp Attack. http:// www.msnbc.msn.com/id/43854355/ns/world_news-europe/t/least-dead-norway-youth-camp-attack/#.TmzzTusmHrV (accessed September 6, 2011).
13. Ibid.
14. Ibid.
15. Summers, Chris, Barford, Vanessa, and Spiller, Penny. 2011. As It Happened: Norway Attacks Aftermath. http://www.bbc.co.uk/news/world-europe -14260205 (accessed September 6, 2011).
16. Milligan, Susan. 2011. Norway Reacts to Terror Attack with Commendable Peace. http://www.usnews.com/opinion/blogs/susan-milligan/2011/07/25/norway-reacts-to-terror-attack-with-commendable-peace (accessed September 6, 2011).
17. Ibid.
18. Summers et al. As It Happened.
19. Spinu, Alexandra. 2011. Utøya Survivor: "You Failed," Anders Behring Breivik. http://theforeigner.no/pages/news/utya-survivor-you-failed-anders-behring-breivik/ (accessed September 6, 2011).

141

20. Haaretz. 2011. Glenn Beck Compares Victims of Norway Attack to Hitler Youth. http://www.haaretz.com/jewish-world/glenn-beck-compares-victims-of-norway-attack-to-hitler-youth-1.375388 (accessed September 1, 2011).
21. Ibid.

5

The Third Principle
Consider and Align National and State Laws and Industry Regulations

5.1 KEY TERMS

5.2 OBJECTIVES

After reading this chapter you will be able to:

1. Discuss the meaning and importance of considering state and federal laws as well as industry regulations.
2. Name two industry-specific regulations that require business continuity or disaster recovery planning.
3. Describe the difference between business continuity and disaster recovery.
4. Discuss the requirements of the Dodd-Frank Act in terms of systems safeguards.
5. Discuss the influence of the Posse Comitatus Act on public sector impact analyses.

5.3 OVERVIEW: ADDRESSING UNDERLYING PROBLEMS WITH FEDERAL AND STATE LAWS AND INDUSTRY REGULATIONS

In Chapter 1, the fundamental flaw of impact assessments was described, with the main flaw being described as one of thinking too small. We

Figure 5.1 Key concepts in this chapter are problems created by not aligning impact assessments with federal and state laws or industry regulations, and how we can use the third principle to confront potential rogue outcomes.

looked at the misgivings and problems that underscored this concept, as well as the challenge of *negative public perception impacts*. In Chapter 2, we introduced the five guiding principles of postmodern impact assessments as a method to address these problems and misgivings.

* * *

A failure to align with federal and state laws or industry regulations causes the impact assessment to *undermine* the public perception of first responders, emergency managers, and the organizations they serve, potentially leading us *beyond* negative public perception impacts toward the *rogue outcome* of a community or organization that refuses aid—which then creates civil unrest (Figure 5.1).

* * *

145

In this chapter, we discuss problems that occur when we do not create impact assessments that align with federal and state laws or industry regulations and how we can use the third principle of the five guiding principles to confront (and prepare for) **rogue outcomes** (unexpected consequences) that may become problematic for responders if this challenge is not met. It is important at this point to reflect on the ideas discussed in Chapter 3 regarding the impact horizon and in Chapter 4 regarding the alignment to organizational core values.

Specifically, a well-prepared impact horizon generates two work products:

1. A set of clearly stated disclosures about the impact assessment
2. A RACI matrix that indicates who is responsible, accountable, consulted, and informed regarding the total scope of the impact assessment

Also, alignment to organizational core values generates three work products:

1. A listing of organizational values
2. The assignment of weights to the core values that reflect the most important and least important of the core values as agreed upon by a defined set of stakeholders as they apply to the weighted score
3. A listing of who was and was not consulted when arriving at the weighted score pie chart in Chapter 4

Establishing an impact horizon helps frame the scope of the impact assessment, but it *does not* address the underlying problem of misalignment to core values. We have established that the conditions of postmodernism, market state economies, and globalization are exerting an influence on organizations of all types. One of the challenges that this influence creates is a great diversity of views regarding how laws, at both the state and the federal level, as well as industry regulation, do or do not infringe on public rights and free trade and enterprise at the state or private organizational level. You will recall that in a market state condition, even states will compete for goods and services within a republic of states, or within an organization such as NAFTA, the United Nations, or regional alliances.

While establishing an impact horizon and aligning to organizational core values will assist in generating the scope of a disaster or terror attack, as well as assist in making the response appropriate to the core values of the organization, they do not address the fundamental concepts of

Figure 5.2 Misalignment to state and federal laws and industry regulations holds a greater threat to an organization than misalignment with core values.

freedom and safety in a democratic nation or the challenging legal and regulatory landscape upon which impacts must be considered, so that appropriate response tactics are created and key messaging is delivered to lessen the likelihood of negative public perception impacts, rogue outcomes, and unlawful behavior during a response (Figure 5.2).

While establishing the impact horizon addresses the boundaries of the scope of impacts to be assessed, and aligning the impact measures to organizational core values addresses the need for an alignment of impacts (and the response tactics informed by them) to core values, the third principle (considering federal and state laws as well as industry regulations) *does something neither of the first two principles can*: It considers how we measure impacts and respond in accordance within a legal and regulatory context. The third principle drives the weighted score toward legal and regulatory boundaries *before* conducting a potential impact assessment so that prepared and subsequent response tactics are lawful and appropriate to the organization and the constituents they serve.

* * *

Specifically, the third principle of considering federal and state laws as well as industry regulations will generate results that will avoid negative public perception impacts and identify those legal and regulatory concerns that should be used in the further development of a weighted score.

* * *

To review, the third principle creates an output that is *reflective of due consideration and appropriate alignment as an organization, community, or state to national or state laws and industry-specific regulations.* The principle here refers to the wider policies of the nation or state in which the organization does business. These laws and regulations can take the form of guidance or general policy statements and come from a variety of sources.

* * *

Consideration and analysis of national and state laws as well as industry-specific regulations generates a view that says: "The potential impact assessment should reflect due consideration and appropriate alignment as an organization, community, or state to national or state laws and industry-specific regulations."

* * *

In this chapter, we explore a few industry-specific regulations and illustrate how to deliver the consultative output of "the further development of a weighted score with the enumeration, recital, and clarification of national and state laws and industry regulations that have been considered and are either addressed or not addressed by the potential impact assessment," as called for in the five guiding principles of impact assessments. In Chapter 6, a strong case study is presented regarding national and state laws as they apply to both private and public sector emergency managers.

5.4 THE THIRD PRINCIPLE AND THE PRIVATE SECTOR

Even if business continuity and disaster recovery (**BC/DR**) is not specified in a law or regulation, issues of data integrity, availability, privacy, and internal controls impact our BC/DR initiatives.

5.4.1 Standards and Regulations

There are essentially two different types of regulatory compliance. First, there are standards and requirements that need to be met in order to become a member of an organization. Some examples of such organizations are the International Organization for Standardization (ISO) and the Federal Department of Insurance Corporation (FDIC).

The second type of compliance is government regulations that are imposed upon specific industries, which mandate that in order to do business in that industry, our organization must comply. These regulations are created for the good of the people and create national standards of

Figure 5.3 There are two types of regulatory compliance: standards and requirements to be a part of an organization, and government regulations required in
order to conduct business.

uniformity and quality. Most regulations are mandated for the purposes
of protecting the public, the ability to respond effectively to disaster, information security, and ensured continuity of business practices. There are
several of these that require board members be accountable for their implementation and control. A good example of this is the **Sarbanes-Oxley Act**
of 2002, which pertains to all publicly held companies (Figure 5.3).

5.4.2 In the Business Arena

According to the American Management Association, "About 50% of businesses that suffer from a major disaster without a disaster recovery plan
in place never reopen for business." *The Sarbanes-Oxley Act (SOX) increased
a corporate officer's liability for business continuity.* Section 404 of the act is
about internal controls and is material to financial reporting. In order to
determine whether something is subject to these controls, companies must
perform a business/application impact assessment, commonly referred to
as a business impact analysis. SOX, Section 406 (c)(2) requires "full, fair,
accurate, timely, and understandable disclosure in the periodic reports

required to be filed by the issuer." Essentially, a BC/DR plan determines how a company will comply with this section.

5.4.3 In Healthcare

Mandated by the Health Insurance Portability and Accountability Act (HIPAA), healthcare providers must have a disaster recovery plan, data backup plan, emergency mode operation plan, and risk assessment. Many facilities performed the risk assessment requirement after the first big push in 2005 and then filed it away some place where it now collects dust. Security experts agree that could prove to be a big mistake. Healthcare CIOs and their IT steering committees have a lot on their plate these days, with emerging technologies demanding attention and the average budget being 1–3% of net operating revenue. Attention is greatly focused around barcode medication administration, physician documentation, and inter-active patient portals.

Demands on the healthcare CIO are tight. The world of emergency response, business continuity, disaster recovery, and general "end of the world as we know it" products and services is full of facts, fictions, and flux. The noise on this channel is louder than ever as vendors jockey for position and highlight surveys and analyst quotes to justify their position and gain market share.

Some may still think that a risk assessment is a one-time thing that we do for regulatory requirements and then file away, but we need to think again. Risk assessments are supposed to be *ongoing*. A risk assessment is the first step in an ongoing business continuity and disaster recovery life cycle, as described in *Managing Emerging Risk*.

5.4.4 New Orleans, August 23, 2005—Katrina

After dealing with the surge of sick and elderly seeking shelter from a killer hurricane and a total loss of operational control, Charity and University Hospitals might have thought they had survived a catastrophic event that even the best contingency plans could barely handle. However, the worst was yet to come.

Days after the storm subsided, on September 8, 2005, Richard Angelico of WDSU Channel 6 in New Orleans reported: "The healthcare system is dealing with another major ordeal—its computers. The hospital's IT system was in New Orleans and they lost it. For some reason, their backup system also failed. Now, they have Internet access only on five laptops in their 'war room.'"

We and many others may be tasked with planning for an event like Katrina or another type of disaster for a private organization. Board members are using terms like *disaster recovery plans, business continuity,* and even *continuity of operations,* and they are looking to us for answers. Where do we start? What are the leading practices? How do we alleviate concerns and maintain "business as usual" so our customers can focus on their core competencies?

5.4.5 Know the Terrain

Disaster recovery, business continuity, and continuity of operations are not the same things. These terms are often confused as a result of years of buzzword status and few standards. To clear up this confusion, here is what we should know. Disaster recovery is the practice of designing a repeatable, living process in a data center operations environment that allows a customer to rebuild critical systems at a secondary site after a catastrophe. It is *not* operational resilience (servers that fail over to one another in the same building). It is not business continuity.

Business continuity can best be described as the manual work-arounds and other ad hoc solutions that nurses, doctors, and other healthcare staff would use during an interruption to critical data center systems that support their job functions. Business continuity is about doing what a hospital does without support systems and computer applications running.

The World Health Organization (WHO) and National Center for Health Statistics (NCHS) have initiated changes in the healthcare industry, which impact healthcare providers, insurance and billing agencies, and healthcare facilities. These changes will reshape the way electronic health records are created, updated, and stored for the industry. The National Council for Prescription Drug Programs has also issued changes in order to maintain compliance with the new HIPAA standards. Below is an overview of the expectations and changes in each of these regulatory standards.

5.4.6 HIPAA 5010

The Health Information Portability and Accountability Act of 1996 (HIPAA) implemented revision 4010 as an identifier of the current addendum release. HIPAA 5010 is a new addendum to this act that allows for

ICD-10 and states' other requirements that have been amended, including new standards for the electronic transmission of electronic health records.

5.4.7 NCPDP

The National Council for Prescription Drug Programs (NCPDP) has issued additional regulatory compliance requirements involving the ICD-10 coding and health record transmission in accordance with the HIPAA 5010.

Each of these standards has an impact on data entry, data transfer, data storage, and data recovery. What does this mean to the average healthcare emergency manager? These changes affect every level of healthcare, insurance, and health management organization in the country. All levels of employees in the healthcare community will feel these impacts, although the impact will vary based on the office environment. Even the few physicians that do not interact with insurance billing will have to implement the ICD-10 code in order to manage public health recording and exchange of information with other practices.

There are several items that need to be addressed in order to comply with the new regulations. Very little help is available from the organizations that have implemented them. A complete review of these new regulations is required *just to complete an accurate, regulatory-minded business impact assessment* in the healthcare industry today.

5.4.8 The Dodd-Frank Act

In the financial sector, the **Dodd-Frank Act** of 2010 has changed the regulatory landscape for financial firms. The act is also known as the **Financial Stability Act** of 2010. In all, the act is actually comprised of 16 individual titles. Written in response to the 2008 financial crisis, the act has the primary purpose of protecting America's financial system "by improving accountability and transparency in the financial system, to end 'too big to fail,' to protect the American taxpayer by ending bailouts, to protect consumers from abusive financial services practices, and for other purposes."[1] The act applies to American financial institutions as well as those who have operations abroad, in keeping with new market state realities.

Below is an excerpt from the Dodd-Frank Act on the system safeguards and record-keeping requirements for organizations, including derivatives clearing, swap execution, and board of trade. What you'll see is that best practice guidance suggests that registered hedge funds and private equity firms *will need disaster recovery, data protection, security, and archiving systems in place.*

> **System safeguards:** Establish and maintain a program of risk analysis and oversight to identify and minimize sources of operational risk, through the development of appropriate controls and procedures, and automated systems, that—
>
> (i) are reliable and secure; and
> (ii) have adequate scalable capacity.
>
> Establish and maintain emergency procedures, backup facilities, and a plan for disaster recovery that allow for—
>
> (i) the timely recovery and resumption of operations; and
> (ii) the fulfillment of the responsibilities and obligations of the facility.
>
> Periodically conduct tests to verify that the backup resources of the facility are sufficient to ensure continued—
>
> (i) order processing and trade matching;
> (ii) price reporting;
> (iii) market surveillance; and
> (iv) maintenance of a comprehensive and accurate audit trail.
>
> **Record keeping:** Each organization shall maintain records of all activities related to the business of the facility, including a complete audit trail—
>
> (i) in a form and manner that is acceptable to the Commission; and
> (ii) for a period of not less than 5 years.[2]

In the private financial sector, the Dodd-Frank Act is already law, despite discussions regarding its repeal and the fact that the FDIC and other agencies enforcing the act appear to be generally slow in enforcing the law.

* * *

Financial services organizations would be foolish not to start planning for an implementation based on an impact analysis that considers this law now—especially due to the massive complexity of high-volume transactional systems!

* * *

153

These are just a few industry-specific laws and regulations. An individual case-by-case study is required as recommended in this chapter to generate an impact assessment that is considerate of such laws and regulations and complies with them.

5.5 DELIVERABLES IN COMPLIANCE WITH THE THIRD PRINCIPLE

If the organization we are working for is identified as critical infrastructure or key resources under the National Infrastructure Protection Plan (NIPP), then chances are law or policy regulates it. A discussion with key stakeholders is required to identify which laws and regulations will influence those outcomes of the impact assessment. This is the function of an emergency manager working in, at the very least, an advisory role regarding legal and regulatory issues.

* * *

The emergency manager must place a central fact before the stakeholders during the impact assessment: If impacts inform recovery and response strategies, then the laws and regulations under which we measure impact must be considered.

* * *

You will recall that a weighted score was created to ensure that the second principle assigned numerical weights to core values. The total score of all core values cannot exceed 100% for any single object, but must reflect the whole capacity of the organization from a profit, capacity, or output perspective. To further align the impact assessment we will further develop the weighted score with the third principle in mind—a consideration of national laws and industry regulations.

The principle of considering national and state laws and industry regulations says: "The potential impact assessment should reflect due consideration and appropriate alignment as an organization, community, or state to national or state laws and industry-specific regulations."

The key deliverable of applying the third principle is the further development of a weighted score with the enumeration, recital, and clarification of national and state laws and industry regulations that have been considered and are either addressed or not addressed by the potential impact assessment.

There are four key work products that will need to be created in order to deliver this portion of the potential impact assessment:

1. A listing of national and state laws and industry regulations relative to emergency management, business continuity, and disaster recovery that are organization specific, and which include the exact language of the written law or regulation
2. A legal opinion from the organization's general council or legal department regarding the interpretation of those laws and regulations in writing and how they will or will not impact the overall emergency management program and impact assessment
3. The assignment of weights to laws and regulations that reflect the most important and least important and are added into the weighted score as agreed upon by a defined set of stakeholders in the previous chapter, *or* the decision to override all weighted scores in the face of any regulated or legally mandated process or system
4. A listing of who was and was not consulted when arriving at the weighted score or overrides

Key stakeholders should be consulted and agreements should be made as to how the potential impact assessment weighs the laws and regulations in addition to the core values of the organization. Adding additional weights for laws and regulations through building consensus with the organization's leadership and indicating those stakeholders who were consulted and those who were not are as important in this step as they were in the approach to core values.

The practitioner can now further develop the weighted score deliverable to include legal and regulatory influences and the impact these will have on generating the final impact analysis.

Consider this example:

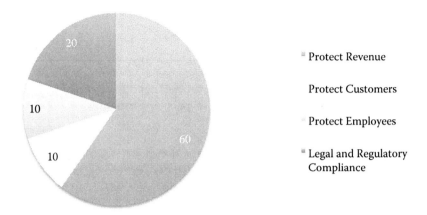

- Protect Revenue

- Protect Customers

- Protect Employees

- Legal and Regulatory Compliance

We can see that the addition of legal and regulatory compliance has caused other core values to shift just by adding a 20% value in the weighted score. In our new weighted score pie chart, we understand that each object (person, process, technology) will be scored based on legal and regulatory compliance, adding value to the community, protecting employees, protecting customers, and protecting revenue, with each total score reflecting individual observations and weighed appropriately within the total 100% measure.

Based on the impact horizon created in Chapter 1, we can see that the objects (people, processes, and systems) inside the impact horizon will be measured based on an alignment to the core values of the organization *and* consideration for national and state laws and industry-specific regulations by scoring them based on the percentage of impact to each core value that is agreed to by key stakeholders.

The principle to consider and align national and state laws and industry regulations says: "The potential impact assessment should align to national and state laws and industry regulations."

The key deliverable of applying the third principle is the further development of a weighted score (an updated weighted score pie chart) with the enumeration, recital, and clarification of national and state laws and industry regulations that have been considered and are either addressed or not addressed by the potential impact assessment.

There are three key work products that will need to be created in order to deliver alignment to national and state laws and industry regulations in the impact assessment:

The work product for the third principle should be delivered as:

- A basic listing of the national and state laws and industry regulations relevant to the organization
- A legal opinion regarding the interpretation of the laws and regulations by the organization
- A list of who was consulted and who was not, which is key to applying the third principle of national and state laws and industry regulations

Important: It should be noted that several organizations may choose not to weigh regulatory or legal issues and may choose instead to override the weighted score completely whenever such an object is encountered.

In this case, the practitioner does not update the weighted score pie chart, but instead places an if/then statement into the impact assessment documentation that reads: "If no regulatory or legal issues are identified, then default to the weighted score. If a regulatory or legal issue is identified, then the score is 100%, and rates at the highest level in the range of criticality values."

Considering everything we have just reviewed that applies to the creation and application of the weighted score, it is very important to note that this is not the end all, be all. First, to stop analyzing data at the weighted score within the confines of the big picture is putting a cap on the vast work done to create the weighted score pie chart. The second point is that by further segregating objects based on the weighted score into an array within the range of criticality values, the analysis of weighted objects by individual weights gives us a very thorough and kaleidoscopic picture of the objects in harm's way within the context of the multiple ways they impact an organization. This will be completely explained in Chapter 7.

* * *

The emergency manager must place a central fact before the stakeholders during the impact assessment: If impacts inform recovery and response priorities and options, then the laws and regulations under which we measure impact must be considered.

* * *

Key stakeholders should be consulted and agreements should be made as to how the core values of the organization, in conjunction with laws and regulations, affect the weighted score. Adding additional weights for laws and regulations through building consensus with the organization's leadership and indicating those stakeholders who were consulted and those who were not are as important in this step as they were in the approach to core values.

5.6 POSTMODERN CULTURE: LEGAL CHALLENGES AND THE REGULATORY CLIMATE

In Chapter 4, by using examples such as the Joplin tornado of 2011, we demonstrated how a lack of clear messaging on impact has hurt our profession. In this chapter we want to take a moment to reflect on what a unified messaging plan can look like and point to some fantastic examples of informed leadership response to the public with clarity. We believe that this type of clear, concise, and positive messaging coming from our profession is the product of extremely skilled professional emergency managers who understand the importance of perception impacts and who have considered how to manage those impacts through communication based on a knowledge of federal and state laws and industry-specific regulations.

Well before Irene made landfall in August 2011, the debate in American culture surrounding the balance between freedoms and safety had ripped its own path of destruction across the American sociopolitical landscape. Left in the wake of this path of destructive debate was a nation divided on the issue of freedoms and safety. There were those who painted counterterrorism, specifically the DHS and FEMA, with a broad brush where each action taken by DHS and FEMA was considered in the context of humanitarian issues, civil rights, and the unlawful use of force. Then there were those who viewed new laws, new tools, and the new policies and practices of DHS and FEMA as a necessity in preparing for, and combating, terror attacks.

While counterterrorism and the war on terror created many new laws (including the Patriot Act), much of the focus regarding DHS and FEMA's activities was on their use, or *potential misuse*, of one very specific law: Federal sector agencies are regulated by a key piece of legislation, the **Posse Comitatus Act** (*Posse Comitatus* is Latin for "power of the county"). This act presents a unique challenge in enabling the alignment of national policy and law discussed in Chapter 4 with counterterrorism impacts. This is important when considering that Americans of a certain stripe love to dispute the legality of the use of the U.S. Army or other military assets within our own borders.

The Posse Comitatus Act is also possibly one of our most important American legal treasures and is commonly viewed as being part of the original to the Constitution drafted by the founding fathers of our country. It clearly outlines the role of American troops and intelligence agencies, and regulates the federal reach within the bounds of state sovereignty. Additionally, during an event, DHS specialists at the federal levels determine state and local-level boundaries and liaise appropriate relationships when responding to a national-level disaster or terror attack (Figure 5.4).

This dispute has become so heated that the public opinion trajectory of DHS and FEMA can nearly be tied directly to perceived abuses of the law through the deployment of U.S. military forces on U.S. soil based on Posse Comitatus. Radio talk show hosts, chat rooms, and public forums buzz

Figure 5.4 Posse Comitatus clearly outlines the role of American troops, intelligence agencies, and the overall federal role in disaster response within the bounds of state sovereignty.

with activity any time U.S. troops are deployed on U.S. soil. For many, this is an act of a "police state" whereby the federal government exerts its power. For some, it hints at a sinister plot to overthrow our democracy with military force. The debate is broad, with the cries of groups that have extreme views, from limiting the power of the federal government to supporting the expansion of the fed's power of influence in the realms of national and state sovereignty. These, and many other views, can spin a reasonable debate into frenzy.

While some may argue that recent Army operations and scope of control statements bypass the need for Posse Comitatus, it should be clearly noted that *any statement by the U.S. Army does not constitute law*, nor does it effectively augment or change Posse Comitatus. Specifically, we refer to the announcement in 2006 that the 3rd Infantry Division's 1st **Brigade Combat Team** (BCT) will be under the command of U.S. Army North (**U.S. NORTHCOM**) and may be "called upon to help with civil unrest and crowd control or to deal with potentially horrific scenarios such as massive poisoning and chaos in response to a chemical, biological, radiological, nuclear or high-yield explosive (**CBRNE**) attack."[3] *This is not a change to the law*—it is a statement of intent regarding the rearranging of military command.

The act of deploying national armed resources in intelligence gathering, disaster response, or for other reasons on U.S. soil is widely regarded as a "no-no" by some Americans. According to the ACLU, "We're setting up essentially a domestic intelligence agency, and we're doing it without having a full debate about the risks to privacy and civil liberties."[4]

To exasperate the challenge, federal and state funding is unclear and hard to navigate:

> If overall federal funding levels for homeland security decrease, it is possible that there will be some level of decrease in Homeland Security Grant Program [which] is comprised of five interconnected grant programs:
>
> 1) State Homeland Security Program,
> 2) Urban Area Security Initiative (UASI),
> 3) the Law Enforcement Terrorism Prevention Program (LETPP),
> 4) the Metropolitan Medical Response System (MMRS), and
> 5) the Citizens Corps Program (CCP).[5]

The Posse Comitatus Act has hindered FEMA and DHS's ability to respond tactically to an event based on potential impacts. Concern around the federal role of fusion centers is a key challenge for DHS as presented under Posse Comitatus. The statement that "the concern is to what extent, if at all, First Amendment protected activities may be jeopardized by fusion center activities"[6] highlights this key issue. Fortunately, the need to be respectful to civil liberties and privacy as a result of 28 CFR Part 23 guidelines, and recommendations by other "think tanks" take further action to ensure that public fusion centers are not put at risk as a result of abuse or infringement on civil liberties.

In the past, these outstanding policy issues for public sector fusion centers, command centers, incident commanders, and first responders have caused agencies at the state and federal levels to muddle through incident management, as we did during Hurricane Katrina. However, more recently, as demonstrated during Hurricane Irene, the Posse Comitatus Act, as well as other policies, have been better integrated into the command and control structure, with intelligence agencies and the Army being able to deliver better assessment and tactical capabilities. Yet, even in the wake of the successes of Hurricane Irene's response, Dr. Mosser's statement still rings true. We must "share criminal information and intelligence analysis to create a Broader Emergency Management Mitigation."[7]

5.6.1 About Posse Comitatus

The genesis of Posse Comitatus is found in England, and was written in the common law to describe and limit the authority of a county sheriff or other law officer to conscript an able-bodied male to assist in keeping the peace or to pursue and arrest a felon. The powers of sheriffs for Posse Comitatus were codified in Section 8 of the Sheriff's Act of 1887. The first subsection of the law stated: "Every person in a county shall be ready and appareled at the command of the sheriff and at the cry of the country to arrest a felon whether within a franchise or without, and in default shall on conviction be liable to a fine, and if default be found in the lord of the franchise he shall forfeit the franchise to the Queen, and if in the bailiff he shall be liable besides the fine to imprisonment for not more than one year, or if he have not whereof to pay the fine, than two years."[8] In England, the common law is now generally obsolete.

However, the law was reborn as a means for limiting the ability of law enforcement or the equivalent to summon a militia or the military for issues at the state level during a difficult time in American history. In the period right before the American Revolution, British military units were sent to the colonies to enforce British control. In the Declaration of Independence, Thomas Jefferson cited the use of the British military in America as one of the colonists' main grievances, saying, "He has kept among us, in times of peace, standing militaries without the consent of our legislatures. He has affected to render the military independent of and superior to the civil power." Once the Union was formed, Americans wanted to protect themselves from an overarching military. The Articles of Confederation limited the role of the military. The Constitution mandated civilian control over the military, with the elected president to serve as the commander in chief.

Prior to the Posse Comitatus Act, soldiers who took on a policing role were usually average citizens, not professional soldiers, and civilian rights were protected under the **Mansfield Doctrine**, which gave citizens the right to sue or criminally prosecute those who abused their powers as part of a posse. One hundred years after the creation and use of these founding concepts in American law, the Civil War required a rethinking of the Posse Comitatus concept.

President Lincoln sent the military to police the Southern states after the Civil War. During this period, Lincoln also suspended the **writ of habeas corpus** (the need for the court to produce the "body of a prisoner") in order to protect the newly stabilized Union and to keep Confederate rebels from using the Constitution against the Union. Congress barred the Supreme Court from challenging Lincoln's decisions.

In the election that followed the Civil War between Democrat Samuel Tilden and Republican Rutherford B. Hayes, U.S. soldiers were ordered to protect the rights of black freedmen during the elections. Once the Democrats agreed to concede victory to Hayes after a contentious election process, the military withdrew from the Southern states.

The Posse Comitatus Act was first formed into law in the wake of the Civil War and a controversial election. As originally drafted, the act states, "Whoever, except in cases and under such circumstances expressly authorized by the Constitution or by an Act of Congress, willfully uses any part of the Army as a Posse Comitatus or otherwise to execute laws shall be fined no more than $10,000 or be imprisoned for not more than two years, or both." The act was passed into law for the first time in 1878. In amendments and retractions over the years, it has become clear that the Coast Guard and, to some degree, the National Guard are *not included* as U.S. military assets as interpreted under Posse Comitatus.

* * *

Claims by would-be constitutionalists that the Posse Comitatus Act is a core constitutional law based on the writings of our founders would be off by roughly 100 years.

* * *

In an article by *Time Magazine* in December 2008, Soihgan Morrisy considered the training of 20,000 U.S. troops from Fort Stewart, as well as others, as part of a $556 million, 5-year training program supported by FEMA and the DOD. In the article Morrisey says:

> Historically, Presidents have suspended the Posse Comitatus Act by invoking the **Insurrection Act**. President Dwight D. Eisenhower did just that in 1957 when segregationists tried to prevent black students from enrolling and attending public school in Little Rock, Ark. John F. Kennedy also used the Act in 1962 and 1963 to send troops to enforce desegregation in Mississippi and Alabama. Similarly, George H.W. Bush sent troops to quell the Los Angeles riots in 1992. Assistant Secretary of Defense McHale notes that the troops being trained for disaster response under the new program would not even be the ones called upon to help quell domestic disturbance in the event of a President invoking the Insurrection Act.[9]

* * *

"Part of the genius of the Insurrection Act is before it can be invoked the President has to make a public declaration that he is doing it," Dycus says. "There is no way the President can use that exception to the Posse Comitatus Act secretly."[10]

* * *

To be clear, if we count the number of times the Posse Comitatus Act has been suspended by U.S. presidents through the use of the Insurrection Act, we will find interesting examples of conflict and have a better understanding of why the president can override the law:

1. In 1957, Posse Comitatus was suspended to protect the rights of black students to attend public school.
2. In 1962, Posse Comitatus was suspended to enforce desegregation.
3. In 1963, Posse Comitatus was suspended again to enforce desegregation.
4. In 1992, Posse Comitatus was suspended to quell the Watts Riots.

The Insurrection Act, Section 333 reads:

> The President, by using the militia or the armed forces, or both, or by any other means, shall take such measures as he considers necessary to suppress, in a State, any insurrection, domestic violence, unlawful combination, or conspiracy, if it—

163

(1) so hinders the execution of the laws of that State, and of the United States within the State, that any part or class of its people is deprived of a right, privilege, immunity, or protection named in the Constitution and secured by law, and the constituted authorities of that State are unable, fail, or refuse to protect that right, privilege, or immunity, or to give that protection; or

(2) opposes or obstructs the execution of the laws of the United States or impedes the course of justice under those laws.

In any situation covered by clause (1), the State shall be considered to have denied the equal protection of the laws secured by the Constitution.[11]

* * *

Despite the grumblings of naysayers and conspiracy theorists, current actions by the DHS and FEMA to strengthen the law and update Posse Comitatus, as it was written over 100 years ago, are moving forward with due legal consideration and a transparent conversation in both Congress and in the commons of U.S. media.

* * *

This then leads us back to the unique circumstances of Hurricane Irene and her potential impacts. In preparing for Irene, four key potential impacts had to be considered:

- The recent "flash mob" riots of England and the looting there created an environment of civil unrest in a modern democratic country, only a month prior to Irene. (For more on flash mobs see *Managing Emerging Risks.*)
- The length of Hurricane Katrina's slow-moving impact lasted well over 2 weeks, from August 26 until mid-September—a much longer disaster timeframe than originally considered in FEMA scenarios.
- There was a credible threat to East Coast targets of a truck bombing that was to coincide with the 10-year anniversary of September 11, possibly at a time when first responders would still be dealing with the first event and the disaster halo effect of Hurricane Irene.
- Finally, the target density in Hurricane Irene's path was simply too important to national security.

During Hurricane Irene, four unique first cause events had manifested themselves within the potential disaster halo effect of Irene, among these, a terrorist threat to our national security. Meanwhile, other critical infrastructures and key resources were also under threat.

Figure 5.5 Understanding the laws and regulations surrounding the public sector will help the emergency manager in the private sector.

Understanding the laws and regulations that impact business continuity and disaster recovery planning in the public sector is helpful in understanding the role of the emergency manager in the private sector. While regulatory compliance may be a driving factor within many organizations, we can also leverage our business continuity and disaster recovery initiatives in the area of regulatory compliance to generate immediate favorable return on our efforts (Figure 5.5).

There are numerous laws and regulations to consider:

- Regulations that apply to all industries
- Financial regulations
- Healthcare regulations
- Government agency regulations
- Utilities regulations
- International Organization for Standardization (ISO) regulations

The good news is that when done correctly, even the Posse Comitatus Act and the thorny issues facing FEMA and DHS can be *managed*.

The key lessons of this and the next chapter together are that some excellent emergency managers and their leadership have provided us with the material for a landmark case study in the legal delivery of response during a multistate event (to be discussed in Chapter 6). There are important lessons to be learned from this success. The value of these chapters is that to best understand the importance of national and state laws and regulations in an impact analysis, we can study the *successes* of our national response to Irene in both the public and the private sector and apply them to our organizations in the form of the third principle: a consideration of federal and state laws as well as industry regulations.

5.7 WHY THE THIRD PRINCIPLE MATTERS

What viewers, victims, and shareholders (private and public alike) will want to know after disaster strikes is whether or not the actions taken and the operations restored are *still operating within the law and regulatory framework that were originally mandated*. If not, there will be negative public perception impacts and, as noted, the possibility for rogue outcomes. Simply put, if a food processing plant can recover its operations but does not adhere to FDA regulations after an event, it is probably heading for bankruptcy. The same is true of medical facilities, banks, and justice systems.

5.8 SUMMARY

One of the challenges created by the postmodern influence on culture is a great diversity of views regarding how laws, both at the state and the federal level, as well as industry regulation, do or do not infringe on public rights and free trade and enterprise at the state or private organizational level.

In previous chapters, we have described how a lack of clear messaging on impact has hurt our profession by using examples such as the Joplin tornado of 2011, among others. In this chapter we took a moment to reflect on what a unified messaging plan can look like and point to some fantastic examples of informed leadership taking their message of responding to fearful events to the public with clarity. We believe that this type of clear, concise, and positive messaging around our profession is the product of extremely skilled professional emergency managers who understand the importance of perception impacts, and who have considered how to manage those impacts through communication based on federal and state laws and industry regulations.

In this chapter we explored key national and state laws that impact emergency management as well as a few industry-specific regulations to illustrate how to deliver the output of the further development of a weighted score with the enumeration, recital, and clarification of national and state laws and industry regulations that have been considered and are either addressed or not addressed by the potential impact assessment, as called for in the five guiding principles of impact assessments.

A discussion regarding the Frank Dodd Act was included to illustrate the postmodern effects of regulation as a reaction to risk and the ever-changing landscape of legalities in private industry specific to our practice.

Based on the impact horizon created in the first chapter, we can see that the loss value of objects (people, processes, and systems) inside the impact horizon will be measured based on an alignment to the core values of the organization presented in Chapter 2 *and* consideration for national and state laws and industry-specific regulations, by scoring them based on the percentage of impact by the organization's core value that is agreed to by key stakeholders in this chapter.

There are three key work products that will need to be created in order to deliver alignment to national and state laws and industry regulations in the impact assessment:

The work product for the third principle should be delivered as:

- A basic listing of the national and state laws and industry regulations relevant to the organization
- A legal opinion regarding the interpretation of the laws and regulations by the organization
- A list of who was consulted and who was not, which is key to applying the third principle of national and state laws and industry regulations

It was noted that several organizations may choose not to weigh regulatory or legal issues and may choose instead to override the weighted score completely whenever such an object is encountered.

The key deliverable of applying the third principle is the further development of a weighted score (an updated weighted score pie chart) with the enumeration, recital, and clarification of national and state laws and industry regulations that have been considered and either are addressed or not addressed by the potential impact assessment.

In this case, the practitioner does not update the weighted score pie chart, but instead places an if/then statement into the impact assessment documentation that reads: If no regulatory or legal issues are identified, then default to the weighted score. If a regulatory or legal issue is identified, then the score is 100%, and rates at the highest level in the range of criticality values.

In Chapter 6, we will take a second look at the third principle of the five guiding principles of impact assessments. We will look at a case study of the third principle in action through the efforts of the U.S. federal government and cooperating state agencies to protect public and private assets, as well as communities facing possible impacts from Hurricane Irene. Concurrent with Irene was the emerging threat of terrorist activity at the 10th anniversary of the September 11 attacks.

5.9 QUESTIONS

1. Describe the meaning and importance of considering state and federal laws as well as industry regulations.
2. What are two industry-specific regulations that require business continuity or disaster recovery planning?
3. What is the difference between business continuity and disaster recovery?
4. What are the requirements of the Dodd-Frank Act in terms of systems safeguards?
5. Describe the influence of the Posse Comitatus Act on public sector impact analyses.

ENDNOTES

1. Pub. L. 111-203, §§ 101-176. (Hereinafter, all statutory citations are to the Wall Street Reform and Consumer Protection Act, Pub. L. 111-203, Subsection 15, Preamble.)
2. Ibid., Section 49.24, System Safe Guards.
3. Cavarallo, Gina. 2008. Brigade Homeland Tours Start Oct. 1. http://www. armytimes.com/news/2008/09/army_homeland_090708w/ (accessed September 4, 2011).
4. Massee, T., and Rollins, J. 2007. *A Summary of Fusion Centers: Core Issues and Options for Congress.* RL34177. Washington, DC: Congressional Research Service.
5. Ibid.
6. Ibid.
7. Mosser, Miriam. 2009. Intelligence Has No Value. Speech Given to George Washington University. Retrieved on September 14, 2009.
8. Sheriff's Act, 1887 [50 and 51 Vict. Cg. 55.]. http://www.legislation.gov.uk/ ukpga/1887/55/pdfs/ukpga_18870055_en.pdf (accessed September 12, 2011).
9. Morrisey, Siobhan. 2008. Should the Military Be Called in for Natural Disasters? *Time Magazine.* http://www.time.com/time/nation/arti-cle/0,8599,1869089,00.html#ixzz1XoU0BW79 (accessed September 12, 2011).
10. Ibid.
11. Cornell University Law School. Legal Information Institute. U.S. Code, Title 10, Subtitle A, Part 1, Chapter 15, Section 333.

6

Taking a Second Look at the Third Principle

6.1 KEY TERMS

6.2 OBJECTIVES

After reading this chapter you will be able to:

1. Describe recent changes to the command structure of DHS to address legal issues presented by the Posse Comitatus Act.
2. Describe the role of a "dual-hatted commander" in public sector emergency management.
3. Provide an example of a negative public perception impact that can exacerbate the response effort based on a contemporary legal emergency management understanding.
4. Describe the Federal Family and what it means in the context of the National Response Framework, and how it was effectively messaged during Hurricane Irene.
5. Compare the approach and scope of resources used during the response to Hurricane Katrina with the scope and resources used during the response to Hurricane Irene.

6.3 OVERVIEW

We are spending a second chapter on the third principle to take a deeper look at how the third principle applies to the public sector (Figure 6.1). Recall that the third principle calls for the professional to *consider and align national and state laws and industry regulations.* There is a significant difference between the laws that a corporation follows, and the laws that municipalities, states, and federal agencies follow, in much the

Figure 6.1 A key concept in this chapter is that negative public perception impacts can be avoided. The response to Hurricane Irene has emphasized our understanding of the importance of messaging and the appropriate response level based on potential impacts.

same way the laws for a civilian driver on the freeway differ from those of a police officer driving on the same road. A corporation found in violation suffers fines and penalties. A police officer in violation of his laws affects himself, his station, and his sheriff, but most importantly, it affects the public—the very thing he is trusted with protecting. The consequences for an officer's violations are vastly different from those of a civilian.

We have discussed in previous chapters the idea of negative public perception impacts and how multinational corporations and public sector emergency managers must be aware of messaging during an event on a world stage. As you'll recall, one of the most damaging aspects of negative public perception impacts is the notion that FEMA and DHS are "evil" organizations in the view of some fringe groups within America. This dialogue is so vitriolic that there is an embedded rogue outcome for public sector emergency managers who are perceived to act unlawfully by this citizenry. Chapter 6 is devoted to dive deeper into federal and state laws as they relate to the public sector.

* * *

It becomes increasingly difficult to render aid if we respond in a manner that is unlawful or is *perceived* to be unlawful. Forced aid is the stuff of dictatorships and totalitarian regimes, *not* democratic governments. However, there are some risk scenarios in which mandatory aid or evacuations are needed—such as pandemics and large-scale natural disasters. These events introduce a slippery slope of ethics and legalities for public sector responders and emergency managers.

* * *

The public sector's adherence to the third principle has a critical impact on the public's perception of municipal, state, and federal actions in their day-to-day operations, especially during times of response to disasters and tragedies. A public agency that creates negative public perception impacts through improper planning and response tactics has the potential to cause civil unrest and insurrection.

For an example of legal issues in the public sector, we are going to examine a contemporary event: Hurricane Irene. This event provides examples of how federal and state laws can be successfully adhered to, and messaging can be used to avoid negative public perception impacts. An interesting component of this example is that Irene also put industry-specific private sector organizations that were supporting public sector missions in harm's way. We will critically examine how the tactics and messaging deployed during this event established how public and private sector emergency managers were able to work together to achieve success in the area of legal and regulatory compliance. This will also serve to show what can be learned from this event and applied to other organizations in preparation for future events.

* * *

Hurricane Irene is a case study in public/private sector emergency management partnership and the mindful delivery of lawful response with exacting messaging and precision—and the reader may be surprised to learn that more than a hurricane threatened America in those August days of 2011.

* * *

6.4 HURRICANE IRENE, 2011: A CASE STUDY IN LEGAL ACTION AND REGULATORY RESPONSE

In contrast to Katrina (discussed in Chapter 4), the tactics and mission objectives used in the response to Hurricane Irene shine because of the fantastic and deft use of the National Response Framework to bring all federal assets to bear on the potential impacts of the hurricane. In addition, a message was quickly formulated and communicated to the governors of the states that were in harm's way as well as other stakeholders. A new message to the field of emergency management in America appeared and resonated (Figure 6.2).

The DHS and FEMA were not publicly positioned in the press as *individual* contributors to the response; rather, the **National Response Framework** (NRF) was used to create a completely new response model, the support model of the **Federal Family**. The Federal Family is a very accurate description of the resources and partnerships that fall under the control of DHS and FEMA based on the Disaster Mitigation Act, the Stafford Act, and the National Response Framework.

Given the political climate of America in August 2011, it would be hard to imagine that a federal family even existed. Budget talks had crumbled, bipartisanship was on the rise, and the commander in chief was on the ropes. Nonetheless, as prescribed and outlined in both the NRF and the Disaster Mitigation Act (DMA), multiple federal resources provided support and aid to state, local, municipal, and tribal communities, resulting in a stunning tactical response.

The response to Irene was the manifestation of a well-honed federal response under the guidance of the DMA and NRF. It worked exactly as it was intended, and a message from the federal government invited governors to participate in the Federal Family's response to the event. With the framework of the federal government's disaster management understood, we will take a look at how the events with Hurricane Irene unfolded.

Figure 6.2 Hurricane Irene is a case study in the Federal Family's state of readiness and preparation, especially when considering it was not the only threat being managed.

* * *

For every example of what does not work in America's current laws and response capabilities, Irene stands up as an example of what does work.

* * *

On August 19, 2011, FEMA began monitoring a tropical storm in the Atlantic.[1] The National Hurricane Center started tracking the tropical storm and began to initiate public advisories. On August 20, the now named storm, Irene, was upgraded to a tropical cyclone.[2] Irene quickly intensified and soon became a hurricane. Irene cut a swath through the Leeward Islands and made its first hurricane strength landfall near Puerto Rico.

FEMA quickly deployed **Incident Management Assistance Teams** (IMATs) to the U.S. Virgin Islands and Puerto Rico to coordinate with local officials regarding their needs and offset any shortfalls of supplies for potential disaster response and recovery.[3] Throughout the day of August 21, FEMA's regional office in New York worked with the Caribbean area office in Puerto Rico and the U.S. Virgin Islands Territory Emergency Management

Agency through its embedded staff in those locations (known as liaison officers) to ensure that the necessary commodities, including potable water, meals, medical aid teams, and cots and blankets, were available to the areas potentially impacted by the storm in the Atlantic and Caribbean. FEMA encouraged local residents of both the Virgin Islands and Puerto Rico to closely monitor the storm and keep an eye on weather conditions.

By August 22, in addition to supporting recovery efforts in the wake of the hurricane in Puerto Rico and the U.S. Virgin Islands, FEMA began contacting U.S. governors on the East Coast from its regional office in Atlanta, Georgia. Included in these discussions were the early identification of needs that might arise should Irene strike the East Coast, and the early identification of potential pitfalls. FEMA deployed a national Incident Management Assistance Team to North Carolina in anticipation of any problems of severe weather. FEMA activated its Regional Response Coordination Center in New York to ensure federal coordination and resources were available that same day. President Obama signed an emergency declaration for Puerto Rico, making federal assistance available to protect lives and property as well as remove debris for all 78 municipalities in the Commonwealth of Puerto Rico.[4]

On August 23, President Obama was briefed on the development of Irene during a call with the Department of Homeland Security Secretary Janet Napolitano and FEMA Administrator Craig Fugate. The call was to discuss a surprising *earthquake* in Virginia that same day; however, the team recognized that the threat of Irene continued. National Incident Management Assistance Teams were deployed to staging areas in Georgia and Pennsylvania. A video teleconference was held with the governors that had been or could be impacted by the severe weather. Craig Fugate, FEMA administrator, and National Hurricane Center Director Bill Read held a teleconference with congressional stakeholders to discuss response operations.

As Irene moved through the Bahamas and skirted past Florida, it became clear that Irene, now a category 3 hurricane, was headed for the East Coast of America. On August 24, Fort Bragg, North Carolina, was designated as the incident support base for Hurricane Irene, and placed staged commodities for response closer to the expected impact area. The U.S. Army Corps of Engineers deployed members of the 249th Engineering Battalion, known as Prime Power, to Puerto Rico to assist with restoring power on the island. The National Oceanic and Atmospheric Administration monitored Irene and flew surveillance missions into the hurricane to provide updated forecasts. U.S. NORTHCOM deployed staff to Puerto Rico to help provide support and coordinate response efforts.

The U.S. Coast Guard (USCG) worked diligently to provide logistical support and to reopen ports in Puerto Rico and the U.S. Virgin Islands. The American Red Cross sent volunteers to North and South Carolina and began moving feeding trucks and communications equipment to the East Coast. Local chapters of the Red Cross set up shelters.

By August 25, the track of Irene was clearly heading up the East Coast of America, and a flurry of activity took place. DHS and FEMA briefed the president on ongoing response and preparation activities, not only in Puerto Rico and the U.S. Virgin Islands, but also up and down the East Coast. President Obama signed a predisaster emergency declaration for North Carolina, as requested by the governor of that state. In advance of the storm, Incident Management Assistance Teams were added to North Carolina and Virginia. In addition, regional IMATs were set up in Connecticut, Maryland, Maine, Massachusetts, New Hampshire, New Jersey, New York, Rhode Island, and Vermont to coordinate with local officials, state resources, and tribal leaders.

On the same day, three additional incident support bases were set up: one at Fort Gordon in Augusta, Georgia, another at Westover Air Reserve Base in Massachusetts, and the third at joint base McGuire–Dix Lakehurst in New Jersey. There were then a total of four incident support bases set up in anticipation of Hurricane Irene, which created the ability to quickly move supplies in and victims out of affected areas. FEMA deployed liaisons to state emergency operations centers in North Carolina, South Carolina, Massachusetts, Connecticut, Rhode Island, and New York and moved liaisons to New Jersey, Virginia, and Maryland. FEMA Deputy Administrator Serino and National Hurricane Center Director Bill Read held a conference with congressional stakeholders to discuss response operations. Later that same day, Secretary Napolitano and Administrator Fugate convened a call with state, local, and tribal leaders as the storm traveled up the East Coast.

Two **mobile emergency response systems** (MERS), one in Raleigh, North Carolina, and one at Fort Jackson, South Carolina, were slated to support emergency response communications needs. The U.S. Army Corps of Engineers 249th Engineering Battalion, "Prime Power," returned from Puerto Rico and was staged at Fort Bragg. The U.S. Coast Guard Water Science Center deployed crews to North Carolina, South Carolina, Virginia, and Maryland in order to deploy storm surge sensors into the coastal waters. Additional sensors were shipped to Florida, Connecticut, and New York. The U.S. Department of Veteran Affairs began preparatory actions in the event that the storm presented the need to evacuate its medical facilities in the storm's path. As local evacuation orders began to go into effect in North Carolina, the Red Cross opened its shelters. The National Oceanic and Atmospheric Association (NOAA) continued to monitor the storm closely. The U.S. Department of Health and Human Services began coordination with states along the projected hurricane path to support public health needs.

The Federal Communications Center (FCC) deployed two **Roll Call Spectrum Scanning** teams to the FEMA regional offices in Atlanta and Boston. These teams conducted post-hurricane scans after it made landfall to determine which critical communications systems might be impacted. NORTHCOM activated the defense coordinating officer to the FEMA Regional Response Coordination Center in Atlanta to support civil authorities as Irene approached. The U.S. Department of Transportation and Amtrak cancelled passenger train service for the period August 26–28 for services operating south of Washington, D.C.

On August 26, President Obama signed an emergency declaration for the state of New York as well as a predisaster emergency declaration for the commonwealths of Massachusetts and Virginia. DHS Secretary Napolitano and FEMA Administrator Fugate briefed the president on activities in response to the hurricane. While the media had been tracking the approaching hurricane and its projected path, President Obama released a statement on the preparations for Hurricane Irene for the first time on August 26. During his statement, the president said, "All indications point to this being a historic hurricane."[5] The statement was issued from Martha's Vineyard, where the president and his family had been on vacation. He continued: "I cannot stress this highly enough. If you are in the projected path of this hurricane, you have to take precautions now. Don't wait. Don't delay."[6]

The same day, President Obama, Napolitano, and Fugate held a teleconference with the mayors of the East Coast's largest cities to determine if additional aid was needed in preparation for the storm. An estimated 55 million people were in Irene's path, according to Reuters. State and local Red Cross shelters began opening from North Carolina to New England as local officials announced evacuations along coastal low-lying areas— many of these were mandatory. The Department of Health and Human Services deployed three **Disaster Medical Assistance Teams** (DMATs) to staging areas.

* * *

A DMAT is comprised of medical professionals such as doctors, nurses, paramedics, and pharmacists who are trained to support medical facilities and health centers.

* * *

Incident Management Assistance Teams were staged in South Carolina, North Carolina, Virginia, New York, Massachusetts, and Vermont, and were deployed to Washington, D.C., Connecticut, Delaware, and Rhode Island to assume the responsibility of federal, state, local, and tribal response activities. The FDA warned consumers to take precautions for storing water and to ensure the safety of their food and medical supplies. The Small Business Administration urged business owners to prepare to evacuate. The Nuclear Regulatory Commission (NRC) assessed power plant preparations, and NRC officials began closing communications with state emergency operations centers.

* * *

All of the activities of the Federal Family were undertaken during Irene *without* encroaching on Posse Comitatus

* * *

On August 27, Hurricane Irene made landfall over North Carolina's Outer Banks and moved along Virginia's coast.[7] Secretary Napolitano and Administrator Fugate, as well as other members of his emergency management team, briefed the president again. During this briefing the president asked to be updated as necessary, day or night. The president visited the FEMA National Response Coordination Center for a complete briefing from his emergency management team and from states already affected, or anticipating to be affected by the storm. He signed pre-disaster emergency declarations for Maryland, New Hampshire, Rhode Island, New Jersey, and Connecticut, with further specificity regarding the types of damage and impacts anticipated in those states. From the previous night, the Red Cross was already sheltering more than 13,000 displaced people and was prepared to open more shelters as needed. More than 150 shelters across eight states were opened, as additional evacuation orders were set into effect. FEMA disability integrations specialists, who help ensure that the needs of individuals with disabilities are addressed during disaster planning, response, and recovery efforts, were positioned in North Carolina, Washington, D.C., Philadelphia, New York, and Boston to help disabled persons.

Continuing throughout the 27th, the U.S. Department of Defense positioned defense coordinating officers at national response coordination centers in Washington, D.C., as well as at Regional Response Coordination Centers in Boston, New York City, Philadelphia, and Atlanta to support and coordinate any request for defense assets and personnel by the states. Governors activated 1,200 National Guard personnel in seven states (or territories), including Florida, Connecticut, North Carolina, New Hampshire, Puerto Rico, Rhode Island, and Virginia, to assist with state response efforts. The Centers for Disease Control (CDC) activated the National Public Health Radio Network, a non-infrastructure-dependent communication method, as a redundant means of communicating with state, territorial, and local health departments in the event that traditional means of emergency communications failed. FEMA then had 18 Incident Management Assistance Teams along the coast to assist with coordination at the state and local levels, with six national urban search and rescue teams comprised of more than 500 personnel placed on alert. The total of DMATs deployed rose to five. The president signed a major disaster declaration for Puerto Rico.

On August 28, the president convened a video teleconference in the White House Situation Room with Vice President Biden, Chief of Staff Daley, DHS Secretary Napolitano, Treasury Secretary Geithner, Transportation Secretary LaHood, Energy Secretary Chu, FEMA Administrator Fugate, Homeland Security Advisor Brennan, and other senior White House officials. Napolitano and Fugate were asked during this call to continue to maintain contact with governors and local leaders along the East Coast. President Obama signed predisaster declarations for Delaware and the District of Columbia. The Red Cross had more than 500 operating shelters in eight states. The shelter population had risen to more than 29,000 people. The U.S. Army Corp of Engineers temporary emergency power mission continued with power teams deployed to incident support bases in Massachusetts, New Jersey, North Carolina, and Maryland. The 249th Prime Power Battalion provided support and logistics to the teams.

Thousands of Red Cross workers were in place and moved in to assist and rescue victims across all affected states as soon as conditions permitted. Partner organizations such as AmeriCorps National Civilian Community Corps and the Southern Baptist Convention were positioned alongside Red Cross workers to offer assistance to those in need. Relief efforts were underway in over 12 states. Real-time monitoring of power outages and other energy-related issues was taken on by the Department of Energy's Response Center. Verizon and other private sector liaisons supported the mission from the National Response Coordination Center. The private energy sector brought in additional crews and utility contractors to deal with pole and pole top equipment and restoration work. Flooding evacuations continued as Irene weakened to a tropical storm and exited the country.

As of August 29, 2011, Hurricane Irene, which was ultimately downgraded to a tropical storm, killed at least 18 people from Puerto Rico to Connecticut and caused $3 billion in damage. More than 4 million homes lost power for extended periods of time across the eastern United States.[8]

In the aftermath of the storm, floods impacted many states. On August 31, FEMA Administrator Craig Fugate said, "You may have heard media reports that the lead up to Irene was over-hyped and that we 'dodged a bullet'—well I can tell you that while the impacts of Irene could have been much worse, there are many areas, especially in the Northeast that are still experiencing dangerous inland flooding and our state and local partners are still very much responding to this storm."[9]

On September 4, President Obama told a crowd in New Jersey, "As President of the United States, I want to make it very clear that we are going to meet our federal obligations—because we're one country, and when one part of the country gets affected, whether it's a tornado in Joplin, Missouri, or a hurricane that affects the Eastern Seaboard, then we come together as one country and we make sure that everybody gets the help that they need."

6.4.1 Hurricane Irene—On Message

Message follows mission, and in the case of Hurricane Irene, the perception impact of FEMA and other responding agencies was very positive. The mission was a nearly perfect example of federal, state, and local coordination as outlined in the National Response Framework. According to a CNN editorial, governors from both sides of the aisle were praising FEMA in the wake of Irene. "FEMA has been very responsive," said New Jersey's Republican governor, Chris Christie. Maryland's governor, Martin O'Malley, a Democrat, also praised FEMA and drew contrasts to a few years ago when, under President George W. Bush, FEMA was "undermined and ineffective."[10] Budget cuts to FEMA and DHS will most likely fall on deaf ears on both sides of the political spectrum in the wake of Irene. A well-managed mission with constant messaging regarding the Federal Family that made that mission possible seems to have mitigated the negative public perception impact of Irene, and perhaps bolstered the confidence in America's system for dealing with disasters.

On September 1, 2011, Vermont's governor Peter Shumlin told a reporter, "I think that the response has been extraordinary, to be honest with you. I mean we got hit with the worst flooding in Vermont's history and any state that hits a historic devastation is going to, obviously, have extraordinary impacts. But this notion that somehow it could have been avoided or that there are other things we could have done, I think is a bit of a Monday morning quarterbacking that isn't justified. Listen, President Obama has been extraordinary. He has his team in here. They're checking with us every few hours. They're flying in supplies. We're rebuilding. We're reconnecting our power grid."[11]

6.4.2 The Tale of Two Hurricanes—A Critical Comparison

Miscommunication, or a lack of understanding of how the states evoke the Stafford Act and how the National Response Framework is set up to fully leverage federal resources during a disaster, has been highlighted in the comparison between Hurricanes Katrina and Irene. The issues of Posse Comitatus are framed by both hurricanes: In one, our military is used as a threat of force, while in the other (with little mention in the press, but full disclosure by FEMA and DHS), it is used in a support capacity (Figure 6.3).

Figure 6.3 During Hurricane Katrina, the U.S. military was perceived as a threat of force, while during Hurricane Irene, the military played a supportive role. The difference between the two was communication from FEMA and DHS.

There is no doubt that one hurricane did more damage, killed more people, and did more harm to our profession and image than the other. However, what the comparison above also illustrates is the full functionality and girth of capability the DHS and FEMA have when under sound leadership.

6.5 THE BACKDROP—A NATION IN CONFLICT OVER FREEDOM AND SAFETY

6.5.1 Applying Resources to Irene Based on Potential Impacts While Following the Third Principle

The third principle of potential impacts, as you will recall, is to consider and align national and state laws and industry regulations. Given the potential impacts of civil unrest, an overlap between the hurricane's impact and the 10th anniversary of 9/11, and a credible threat to targets on the East Coast, the first question had to be: What was in the path of Hurricane Irene? Certainly there were civilians, private property, and other critical infrastructures and key resources (CI/KR) in harm's way. But there were also CI/KR that had a direct tie to our national security, such as the nation's capital, the Pentagon, and several administrative buildings of the federal government, including the DHS, DOD, and FEMA.

In addition, because of an explosive growth of fusion centers,[12] joint operations centers, and other data gathering and DHS locations along the Eastern Seaboard and the rest of America, the target density of both federal and federally contracted private companies and employees from Washington to New York working in counterterrorism had vastly expanded since 9/11. In a 2011 investigative series for the *Washington Post*, Dana Priest and William M. Arkin reported, "At the Department of Homeland Security (DHS), the number of contractors equals the number of federal employees. The department depends on 318 companies for essential services and personnel, including 19 staffing firms that help DHS find and hire even more contractors. At the office that handles intelligence, six out of 10 employees are from private industry."[13]

The corporate property used by these private company contractors and the federal and state facilities they support has also expanded considerably along the Eastern Seaboard, and one should question to what degree these private facilities are hardened for disasters. We can draw a sense of the federal, state, and local counterterrorism assets (buildings, complexes, people, technologies, and tactical controls) that were in harm's way from a state-by-state review of organizations working in the path of Hurricane Irene based on reportage from the *Washington Post*.[14]

South Carolina is divided into four Counter Terrorism Coordinating Council Regions and six emergency management regions within FEMA Region IV. The Defense Coordinating Office in Atlanta is responsible for brokering and arranging federal military support for South Carolina. In South Carolina there are the following private and public sector assets:

- 36 state and federal law enforcement agency offices
- 2 emergency management offices
- 6 counterterrorism offices
- 2 Joint Terrorism Task Force (JTTF) offices
- 4 intelligence public and private organizations
- 1 fusion center

North Carolina is divided into nine domestic preparedness regions within FEMA Region IV. Like South Carolina, the Defense Coordinating Office in Atlanta is responsible for federal military support to the state. In North Carolina there are the following private and public sector assets:

- 47 local, state, and federal law enforcement agency offices
- 2 emergency management offices
- 5 Homeland Security private and public assets
- 3 Joint Terrorism Task Force offices
- 7 intelligence public and private organizations
- 3 fusion centers

Virginia is divided into seven emergency regions, and the Virginia Department of Emergency Management's regional coordinators maintain offices for each region. As defined in the Homeland Security Act of 2002, the state is part of the Metropolitan Washington Council of Governments and the FEMA National Capital Region. In Virginia there are the following private and public sector assets:

- 94 local, state, and federal law enforcement agency offices
- 13 emergency management offices
- 14 Homeland Security private and public assets
- 6 counterterrorism offices
- 3 Joint Terrorism Task Force offices
- 19 intelligence public and private organizations
- 4 fusion centers

Maryland is part of the Metropolitan Washington Council of Governments and the FEMA National Capital Region as defined in the Homeland Security Act of 2002. It is located in FEMA Region III. The Defense Coordinating Office in Philadelphia is responsible for federal military support to the state. In Maryland there are the following private and public sector assets:

- 38 local, state, and federal law enforcement agency offices
- 9 emergency management offices
- 14 Homeland Security private and public assets
- 5 counterterrorism offices
- 1 Joint Terrorism Task Force office
- 21 intelligence public and private organizations
- 4 fusion centers

Delaware is located in FEMA Region III. The Defense Coordinating Office in Philadelphia is responsible for federal military support to the state. In Delaware there are the following private and public sector assets:

- 10 local, state, and federal law enforcement agency offices
- 2 emergency management offices
- 6 Homeland Security private and public assets
- 3 counterterrorism offices
- 1 Joint Terrorism Task Force office

The District of Columbia is part of the Metropolitan Washington Council of Governments as defined in the Homeland Security Act of 2002. It is located in FEMA Region III. The Defense Coordinating Office in Philadelphia is responsible for federal military support to the state. In the District of Columbia there are the following private and public sector assets:

- 20 local, state, and federal law enforcement agency offices
- 2 emergency management offices
- 8 Homeland Security private and public assets
- 3 counterterrorism offices
- 1 Joint Terrorism Task Force office
- 6 intelligence public and private organizations
- 2 fusion centers

Pennsylvania is divided into nine emergency response/counterterrorism regions. It is located in FEMA Region III. The Defense Coordinating Office in Philadelphia is responsible for federal military support to the state. In Pennsylvania there are the following private and public sector assets:

- 62 local, state, and federal law enforcement agency offices
- 3 emergency management offices
- 10 Homeland Security private and public assets
- 6 counterterrorism offices
- 3 Joint Terrorism Task Force offices
- 9 intelligence public and private organizations
- 4 fusion centers

New Jersey is located in FEMA Region III. The Defense Coordinating Office in New York City is responsible for federal military support to the state. In New Jersey there are the following private and public sector assets:

- 44 local, state, and federal law enforcement agency offices
- 2 emergency management offices
- 13 Homeland Security private and public assets
- 2 counterterrorism offices
- 1 Joint Terrorism Task Force office
- 7 intelligence public and private organizations
- 1 fusion center

New York is divided into five emergency management regions. The state is located in FEMA Region II. The Defense Coordinating Office in New York City is responsible for federal military support to the state. In New York there are the following private and public sector assets:

- 95 local, state, and federal law enforcement agency offices
- 4 emergency management offices
- 35 Homeland Security private and public assets
- 12 counterterrorism offices
- 4 Joint Terrorism Task Force offices
- 15 intelligence public and private organizations
- 6 fusion centers

Connecticut is divided into five emergency management regions. The state is located in FEMA Region I. The Defense Coordinating Office in Boston is responsible for federal military support to the state. In Connecticut there are the following private and public sector assets:

- 23 local, state, and federal law enforcement agency offices
- 2 emergency management offices
- 9 Homeland Security private and public assets
- 2 counterterrorism offices
- 1 Joint Terrorism Task Force office

- 2 intelligence public and private organizations
- 1 fusion center

Rhode Island is located in FEMA Region I. The Defense Coordinating Office in Boston is responsible for federal military support to the state. In Rhode Island there are the following private and public sector assets:

- 10 local, state, and federal law enforcement agency offices
- 2 emergency management offices
- 6 Homeland Security private and public assets
- 2 counterterrorism offices
- 1 Joint Terrorism Task Force office
- 1 intelligence public and private organization
- 1 fusion center

Massachusetts is divided into five Homeland Security planning regions. The state is located in FEMA Region I. The Defense Coordinating Office in Boston is responsible for federal military support to the state. In Massachusetts there are the following private and public sector assets:

- 37 local, state, and federal law enforcement agency offices
- 4 emergency management offices
- 10 Homeland Security private and public assets
- 5 counterterrorism offices
- 2 Joint Terrorism Task Force offices
- 9 intelligence public and private organizations
- 4 fusion centers

Vermont is located in FEMA Region I. The Defense Coordinating Office in Boston is responsible for federal military support to the state. In Vermont there are the following private and public sector assets:

- 11 local, state, and federal law enforcement agency offices
- 2 emergency management offices
- 12 Homeland Security private and public assets
- 0 counterterrorism offices
- 0 Joint Terrorism Task Force offices
- 1 intelligence public and private organization
- 1 fusion center

New Hampshire is located in FEMA Region I. The Defense Coordinating Office in Boston is responsible for federal military support to the state. In New Hampshire there are the following private and public sector assets:

- 29 local, state, and federal law enforcement agency offices
- 3 emergency management offices
- 6 Homeland Security private and public assets
- 2 counterterrorism offices
- 1 Joint Terrorism Task Force office
- 1 intelligence public and private organization
- 1 fusion center

Maine is located in FEMA Region I. The Defense Coordinating Office in Boston is responsible for federal military support to the state. In Maine there are the following private and public sector assets:

- 13 local, state, and federal law enforcement agency offices
- 2 emergency management offices
- 1 Homeland Security private and public assets
- 3 counterterrorism offices
- 1 Joint Terrorism Task Force office
- 1 intelligence public and private organization
- 1 fusion center

* * *

Across these 15 states combined, in the direct path of Hurricane Irene, was the lion's share of DHS and FEMA private sector assets: *a total of 98 buildings and complexes* housing technologies and personnel dedicated to the protection of our homeland and deterring national security threats in the form of terror attacks.

* * *

These joint teams, operating under NIPP and other Homeland Security and FEMA directives, were faced with a tough challenge. A natural disaster was bearing down on the critical infrastructure and key resources used to fight the war on terror—just days before the 10th anniversary of the September 11 attack.

While Irene was being downgraded to a lesser hurricane than Katrina, it was moving slowly, and the effects on citizens and property *would be felt*. It was possible that the immediate impacts of Hurricane Irene itself would be felt for as many as 20 days (as was the case with Katrina), taking the response effort from the storm well into the 9/11 anniversary.

Coinciding with preparation for Hurricane Irene's landfall, hundreds, if not thousands, of joint operations were already underway in the counterterrorism arena as DHS and the complete set of infrastructure and assets outlined above worked on tracking down all manner of investigative leads. Finally, there was an emerging credible threat of a chemical, biological, radiological, nuclear, or explosive (CBRNE) attack on the East Coast. It is apparent from this activity that civil unrest and the possibility of revolution were a top priority as Hurricane Irene approached the United States. It is important to note that the Occupy Wall Street movement was gaining momentum across the United States, and there had been several uprisings across the globe that had been occurring throughout the year.

Across the Atlantic, just before the events of Hurricane Irene from August 6–10, 2011, in England there was revealed a risk of rioting and looting never before seen in a modern democracy. Rioting, looting, and arson occurred in at least a dozen towns for a period of 4 days, resulting in 3,100 arrests, 5 deaths, and over 3,000 crimes committed by disenfranchised youths, some as young as 11 years old. Tony Blair, in an op-ed for the *Guardian*, stated, "The big cause is the group of young, alienated, disaffected youth who are outside the social mainstream and who live in a culture at odds with any canons of proper behaviour."[15] However, if you'll reflect on the impacts of postmodernism on society as discussed in Chapter 2, Mark Easton's quote in the BBC News UK brings us much closer to the *root cause* of the riots. England's civil unrest bears a striking causal resemblance to the Occupy Wall Street movement—calling themselves the 99%.

> Within weeks of coming to power in 1997, Tony Blair set up a Social Exclusion Unit inside the Cabinet Office specifically to deal with what his party painted as Margaret Thatcher's underclass—hundreds of thousands of people, workless, skill-less, often homeless and hopeless, a group cut off from mainstream society—dubbed the entrenched 5%.[16]

* * *

The global, large-scale undertone of civil unrest and revolution as caused by the postmodern condition had to be a "top of mind" concern as Hurricane Irene approached.

* * *

6.5.2 A Thorny Problem

The question of impact must have come into sharp focus on the days leading up to Hurricane Irene's landfall. There were the obvious potential impacts to people and property as a result of storm surges, flooding, and high winds. There would be power outages. Private sector support organizations actively working a credible terror threat would be impacted. There would be a loss of communications. Certainly, some of the assets listed above would be impacted. Assets that were supporting pre-September 11, 2011, investigations, tracking a credible bombing threat, and also supporting international counterterrorism efforts were all in harm's way.

There could be no margin for delay as a result of the approaching hurricane. There could be little to no interruption of counterterrorism activities in the face of the now credible threat of a bombing on the East Coast. There could be no civil unrest in the wake of the hurricane, no matter how severe the damage to cities, municipalities, and tribal areas might be.

* * *

In the face of Hurricane Irene, the storm damage would pale in comparison to a CBRNE attack on any one of the major cities in the storm track, and the death toll could be in the millions. A natural disaster combined with the potential weakening of our counterterrorism capabilities and an active, credible bomb threat was and still is a nightmare scenario.

* * *

The bomb threat in late August and early September of 2011 was significant. Out of all the chatter, threats, investigative leads, and international and domestic actions occurring simultaneously in the run-up to the 10-year anniversary of 9/11, for a threat to become public and to be reported as credible was significant. According to Matt Chandler, the spokesperson for DHS, the threat of an attack in Washington or New York using a car or truck bomb and tied to 9/11 was "specific, credible, but unconfirmed."[17] An unnamed official told the *New York Times* that intelligence agencies were urgently pursuing leads overseas in an effort to gauge the seriousness of the threat. The assets used to provide intelligence, surveillance, and command and control of those operations were all in Irene's path.

Chandler brought to attention that a notebook seized after Osama bin Laden was killed had speculated about mounting an attack 10 years after September 11. Commissioner Kelly of the New York Police Department said, "Officers will work 12-hour shifts, instead of 8-hour shifts. Vehicle checkpoints will be installed. The police will conduct bomb sweeps in parking garages and elsewhere. More police cars will be equipped with cameras that scan passing license plates. Convoys of police cars will swoop down at predetermined spots in shows of force. Increased numbers of illegally parked cars will be towed." He continued, "All of these precautions are on top of an already robust counterterrorism overlay in place for the 10th anniversary commemoration at the World Trade Center site."[18]

The thorny problem of Hurricane Irene was not just that the hurricane itself would have multiple public and private sector impacts to lives and property. The problem was that it would hamper our ability to protect against a threat to American lives—a threat that, if nuclear or biological, would be several magnitudes higher in impact than the hurricane itself.

6.5.3 A Low-Profile, Highly Tactical Response

As preparations and responses to Hurricane Irene were executed, a low-profile but highly tactical response was executed. As noted in Chapter 4, this response was extremely mission oriented, involving multiagency response and preparedness. Governors readily called in the Coast Guard and the National Guard for support. However, on August 27, the U.S. Department of Defense positioned defense coordinating officers at national response coordination centers in Washington, D.C., as well as at Regional Response Coordination Centers in Boston, New York City, Philadelphia, and Atlanta, to support and coordinate any request for additional U.S. military assets and personnel by the states.

The U.S. Army Corps of Engineers 249th Engineering Battalion, Prime Power, returned from Puerto Rico and was staged at Fort Bragg. Incident support bases were set up: one at Fort Gordon in Augusta, Georgia, another at Westover Air Reserve Base in Massachusetts, and the third at joint base McGuire–Dix Lakehurst in New Jersey. These prepositioned liaison officers and the engineering battalion were just the tip of a spear ready to react if things "snowballed" during Irene and the additional bomb threat. Clearly, the U.S. Army was on standby and ready to assist. Out of Boston, Philadelphia, New York City, or Atlanta, the liaison officers at incident command centers throughout the region had U.S. NORTHCOM at their disposal.

6.5.4 Negative Public Perception

The *Savannah Morning News* reported that soldiers with the 3rd Infantry Division's Combat Aviation Brigade had been deployed to North Carolina to assist with relief efforts in the wake of Irene. "The brigade sent a total of nine UH-60 Blackhawk helicopters last weekend to help support efforts in case the storm caused major damage,"[19] the report said. "Basically we went up there to support FEMA," Army Cpt. Christopher Cobert told the reporter. "We performed aerial surveillance of the North Carolina coast." This action was deemed as a "support task" and was not in violation of Posse Comitatus.

According to the *Army Times*, "6,500 active-duty troops were on post-Irene standby."[20] Defense Secretary Leon Panetta ordered 6,500 active-duty troops to be ready in case there was an order for them to help with Hurricane Irene relief work. The prepare-to-deploy order was issued to all military branches. A majority of these were from the National Guard, which is legal under Posse Comitatus, even if they are referred to as active-duty troops. The problem in negative public perception was that it was hard to tell the difference between National Guard troops, equipment, and transport from active military branch troops, equipment, and transport (Figure 6.4).

While the Posse Comitatus Act is not one of the freedoms our forefathers wrote into the original Constitution in 1787, *what is* is Article II: "The President shall be Commander in Chief of the Army and Navy of the United States, and of the Militia of the several States, when called into the actual Service of the United States; he may require the Opinion, in writing, of the principal Officer in each of the executive Departments, upon any subject relating to the Duties of their respective Offices, and he shall have Power to Grant Reprieves and Pardons for Offenses against the United States."

While the author supports the public's right to the statements below, as they are protected through the freedom of speech, and agrees that such comments are necessary in the course of political debate, the opinions below *do not* reflect the author's opinion, but only serve to illustrate the great debate facing emergency managers and counterterrorism professionals in 2011.

* * *

The freedoms of religion, press, and expression are part of the Bill of Rights, a series of laws written in 1789, a mere 2 years after the original Constitution. They appear as Amendment 1. Anyone who is laying claim

Figure 6.4 Even though Posse Comitatus was adhered to during the Hurricane Irene response, it was difficult for the public to discern the legal use of the National Guard from the illegal use of active-duty military forces.

to the "intent of our forefathers" should be doing so on the basis of the original Constitution and the Bill of Rights.

* * *

Conspiracy theories around the 3 weeks during Irene abounded. To begin with, the earthquake in Virginia, the hurricane itself, and other natural disasters just seemed to be coming on too rapidly. An unnamed blogger posted the notion that all of the events were linked to HAARP (High Frequency Active Auroral Research Program), saying, "Is it connected to the Earthquake that rocked the East Coast, Hurricane Irene, or other natural disasters? Seems odd that a Hurricane is heading to the East Coast the week of an Earthquake. Could the powers that be try to use HAARP to cause an Earthquake to redirect Hurricane Irene? Something to think about." In conspiracy circles, HAARP is the source of all "evils," from brainwashing to militarized global climate control.

Many people took videos of military hardware and troops and posted them to YouTube and Internet video sites, with dire wording and warnings. "Military Convoy in New York City!" said one poster. "What the fuck are military convoys doing on civilian streets, a violation of Posse Comitatus!" decried another.

Infowars.com reported that the Pentagon was exploiting Hurricane Irene in effort to further "militarize" disaster response, citing that Fox News never used the word *militarize*. "Under the cover of fixing supposed delays, duplications and gaps after Katrina hit the Gulf Coast in August of 2005, the Pentagon has further crippled Posse Comitatus—restricting military involvement in domestic law enforcement—and limited the participation of the state in disaster and emergency response," wrote Kurt Nimmo at Infowars.com on August 29, 2011. He went on, "Obama's fancy command center is part of the effort to sell further militarization of law enforcement."[21]

Of course, the ranting of conspiracy theories moved on to the fringes of the political scene. On September 1, 2011, presidential hopeful Congressman Ron Paul told Alex Jones: "You can have a breakdown of law and order so the people will unfortunately be begging for stabilization, and they'll be inviting the federal government to come in and destabilize things, so I think they are making plans along those lines." When asked by Jones who "they" were, his response was FEMA, "who have come in for harsh criticism from the congressman in the aftermath of Hurricane Irene."[22]

This strange line of dialogue continues in the article, with the statement: "U.S. troops returning from Iraq were being re-allocated to occupy America, running checkpoints and training to deal with 'civil unrest and crowd control' under the auspices of a NORTHCOM program that revolved around deploying 20,000 active duty troops inside America to 'help' state and local officials during times of emergency."[23]

On August 8, 2011, in a blog post to VisiontoAmerica.com, a poster wrote: "Amidst riots in central Europe that have now spread to London and a debt downgrade that threatens to plunge the United States into a double-dip recession, Americans' lack of confidence in their leadership is so crippled that they are now 'pre-revolutionary,'" according to pollster Pat Caddell.[24] This blog post in particular spurred many comments from online readers. Among them:

- "The government sees the American people as nothing more than servants to it, treats its people with disdain, injustice and contempt. Is it any wonder America is in a pre-revolutionary mode?" R

- "I do believe there is a clause in the Constitution saying that our military can go against any enemies in our country. I realize the National Guard is supposed to take care of America internally but frankly I don't think they are going to be prepared enough. It's going to take more than just them to take care of Washington plus all the outlying states with Nazis running them." Judy Y
- "The only wonder is that we have not had more people in the streets and breaking store windows, but we really must avoid that at all costs as it would allow Mr. Obama to declare martial law, cancel the election and name himself 'President for the duration.'" Adrian Vance[25]

With this sentiment growing, presidential candidate Ron Paul took his FEMA and Irene comments to NBC, saying that there was nothing magic about FEMA and that "we should be like 1900, we should be like 1940, 1950, 1960 ..." (Figure 6.5).

The sentiments toward FEMA and the federal government, up to and during Irene, could be said to be malicious. Certainly, in some circles, they were taken as just downright nasty. The discourse and negative public perception around Posse Comitatus and the federal response was sure to be tested during Irene, even without the other potential threats moving in concert with the event. How to quell the negative public perception impacts regarding actions that were necessary and required by governors and the White House would be key. Fortunately, lessons learned from Katrina had laid a legal framework out that would allow for troop deployment without breaking the law of Posse Comitatus, and if further action was required, the Insurrection Act could be evoked.

* * *

For those professionals working for FEMA and DHS, as public servants or as private sector consultants, one thing should be entirely clear, they are results-oriented organizations.

* * *

6.5.5 Changes in the Military Structure

The span of influence and relationships as outlined under NIPP alone involves deep relationships with the U.S. military and the FBI, CIA, NSA, and others. In the wake of 9/11 and Katrina, it was clear that something had to be done within the boundaries (both implicit and implied) of the

Figure 6.5 Ron Paul put forward the idea of shutting down FEMA under the auspices that there was nothing magic about it and we should return to a political system similar to that of the early 20th century. (Used with permission, copyright Rich Koele/Shutterstock.com.)

Posse Comitatus Act that would allow for U.S. military involvement and support during a national disaster or terror attack without forcing the commander in chief to evoke the Insurrection Act. Jeffery W. Burkett of the Center for Army Lessons Learned observed:

> Louisiana Governor Kathleen Blanco's opposition to federalizing the state National Guard and her rejection of President Bush's offer to appoint an Active-duty officer instead of using a state National Guard officer as a dual-status commander highlight the clash between top-down (Federal) and bottom-up (state) philosophies. Some experts have argued that Hurricane Katrina is a political anomaly and should not be used for comparison. Nevertheless, Hurricane Katrina and the flooding of New Orleans constituted the first missed opportunity for USNORTHCOM and the National Guard to demonstrate the utility of a National Guard dual-status command for a no-notice event.[26]

Notable changes occurred quickly after 9/11. "First, Presidential authority established U.S. Northern Command (USNORTHCOM) in 2002. Second, the National Guard reorganized itself at the state level and launched a series of homeland defense and security programs. Likewise, the National Guard Bureau (NGB) also transformed itself by improving its national coordinating ability and refining its supporting role for state governments and the national defense community. Finally, Congress changed the Federal law (Title 32) that governs the National Guard to create the legal framework for the executive branch to employ the Guard in homeland defense and civil support actions."[27] These changes also required additional training and changes to the internal structure of the U.S. military and the National Guard.

Since Posse Comitatus allowed for the involvement of the National Guard, and the U.S. Coast Guard reported directly to the DHS framework and was not a U.S. military asset, a solution began to emerge after 9/11 that certain U.S. military officers could have dual status, as both guardsmen and military officers within their unique branches. Dual-status commander training began at the U.S. Northern Command headquarters (NORTHCOM) after the 2001 terrorist attacks to help DHS defend the homeland and to assist civilian authorities with domestic crises and emergencies. This did not change the law; it changed the structure of the military ranks so that a National Guard commander could lead both U.S. military forces and guardsmen during a crisis.

Dual-status command has been described thus:

> The dual-status command structure addresses the unity of command dilemma directly. Under this construct, National Guard commanders on Title 32 status are ordered to Federal Active duty (Title 10 status), retaining their state commission when activated. This dual-status provides the statutory authority for one person to command both state and Federal military forces simultaneously. This permits the dual-hatted commander to control a unified military response at the operational level in support of the state ... the chain of command beginning with the President and Governor. National Guard forces in state Active-duty or Title 32 status perform state missions under the authority of the Governor, and assigned Title 10 Federal forces perform defense support of civil authority for U.S.NORTHCOM.[28]

As training commenced, special emphasis was put on the legalities of authority and legal restrictions in "support and report" activities as a dual-status commander of both guardsmen and U.S. troops. When Hurricane Katrina struck, no single commander had authority. In practice, and in almost every case of deployment on U.S. soil, the program seeks to place a Guard officer in command of a mission because of the Guard's familiarity with his or her home state and because the National Guard is specifically trained in disaster response, and thereby can command both U.S. troops in support roles and guardsmen in tactical roles.

Today, there are four commanders in the Guard who have completed this rigorous training and are committed to working to merge command over U.S. military and National Guard assets during a crisis. They are Brigadier General Michael Swezy of the New York Army National Guard, Brigadier General Carolyn Protzmann of the New Hampshire Air National Guard, Brigadier General James Trogden III of the North Carolina National Guard, and Colonel Donald Lagor of the Rhode Island Air National Guard.[29] We should all be proud of these fine men and women for learning to walk a delicate line between our liberties and our safety.

NORTHCOM is commanded by Army General Charles H. Jacoby Jr., who comes from the **North American Aerospace Defense Command** (NORAD), the U.S. and Canadian command that defends the two countries from airborne threats and monitors maritime traffic off their shores.

The ability to command both active-duty troops and guardsmen that report directly to a dual-status commander effectively makes that unit a National Guard unit, with the commander reporting to DHS and U.S. NORTHCOM during a crisis. In this way, the dual-status commander has access to both National Guard and U.S. military assets as needed for support. Irene was the first time dual-status commanders were used to respond to a national crisis. In fact, the appointment of the aforementioned dual-status commanders occurred on the weekend of August 27–28, 2011—just after Irene made landfall. The reason for this is that the implementation of dual-status commanders on U.S. soil could be best achieved with the joint support of governors willing to consign their states' National Guard units to the federal mission.

The Department of Defense announced the appointments, and four governors and the Defense Department made the selections of these officers jointly for Irene. Involving the governors is illustrative of the sensitivity to having U.S. active-duty soldiers on the ground during a disaster. The states to which these units were deployed included New Hampshire, New York, North Carolina, and Rhode Island. According to the Associated Press, Bill Illing of the National Guard Bureau said a review of how the appointment process went, as well as any logistical or coordination issues that arose once Irene was over and the military's role there was done, would occur.[30]

With the benefit of dual-status command finally being put to the test during Irene, it seems clear that more than just the disaster of the hurricane was averted. Perhaps the impasse between governors who were not willing to give up state sovereignty during a crisis and the need for active-duty military aid during a crisis were resolved as well. This may not have quelled the dissenting voices of the radical extremes in the negative public perception debate, but it did seem to work. The stated benefit of the dual-status command approach is that dual-status command includes a governor retaining authority over the response, clear lines of command, and the ability to integrate federal military forces operationally to achieve unity of effort. Conversely, presidential C2 is preserved. (**C2** is military shorthand for command and control.)

6.5.6 In Summary: Irene and Other Impacts

What few realize is that the dual-status commander involvement in the Irene response, along with that of National Guard and active-duty U.S. military, may have well been a response to more than just the potential impacts to life and property. The impact horizon of this event overlapped with a disaster halo effect of two, if not three, first event scenarios: the hurricane, a bomb threat, and the potential for civil unrest.

Many of the commentaries regarding Irene did not consider the threefold threats and multiple impact potentials that were manifesting along the Eastern Seaboard in late August and early September of 2011. Even fewer can grasp the density of critical infrastructure and personnel supporting our mission in the war on terror, both at home and abroad, which were in harm's way during Irene.

The bomb plot seems to be unsolved, and no attack occurred on the 10-year anniversary of 9/11. Perhaps the enemy was evacuated from the storm area, diverted from the target, or even drowned. We may never know. We do know that Janet Napolitano announced on September 13, 2011, that "we consider it an ongoing threat and we continue to lean forward into confirming that threat,"[31] in testimony before the Senate Homeland Security and Governmental Affairs Committee. FBI Director Robert Muller said, "Since we first had word of that threat we have conducted hundreds of interviews, we have been pursuing a number of leads and consequently as a result of that we have now been able to eliminate some aspects where we thought we ought to be looking in order to determine whether it was indeed a valid threat, but there's still work to be done."[32]

In an earlier statement, Muller discussed his biggest concern surrounding the anniversary of 9/11: "A radiological attack is not so remote, because it's relatively easy to get radiological materials and have some sort of radiological improvised explosive device. Although the damage would be far less than from a nuclear detonation, the threat is still there today."[33]

* * *

While talk of liberties and freedoms based on the Constitution is neces-sary in a democracy, we should understand that any one of the pedes-trian threats outlined in *Managing Emerging Risk* or the detonation of a nuclear device could lead us into a country without freedoms and liber-ties worth protecting. In this case, the boundaries and limits of working within our current legal context, by necessity, must be, and are, explored by professionals.

* * *

Irene and the bomb threat of 2011 combined to create a potential impact horizon that included lives, property, critical infrastructure, key resources, our national security, and perhaps, perception impacts that could have had a devastating impact on FEMA and the DHS. However, the public and the media seem to be quite pleased with how Irene was handled, with the exception of the outlying conspiracy theorists. For them, all we can offer as professionals is, using the new tools and agree-ments available to us, we found success where we once failed, and we did it with the third principle of potential impacts, *by considering national and state laws and industry regulations.*

6.6 SUMMARY

This chapter covered the differentiation of the third principle in a fed-eral environment as opposed to a public organization. We saw in the case study of Hurricane Irene a response that went through great efforts to maintain compliance with federal, state, and municipal laws.

We also saw the negative public perception impact of the use of military resources in preparation for the response to Hurricane Irene's landfall. As illustrated, while Posse Comitatus was not violated, the mere presence of military activity spurred conspiracy theorists and instigators into action. They spread messages that promoted only distrust and suspi-cion of *any* action the federal government made in its efforts to protect its resources and citizens.

These serve as examples of how federal and state laws can be suc-cessfully adhered to and the delivery of precise messaging can avoid negative public perception impacts. An interesting component of this example is that Irene also put industry-specific regulated private sector organizations in harm's way. Further, we explored some key private sector industry-specific regulations, including:

- Regulations that apply to all industries
- Financial regulations
- Healthcare regulations
- Government agency regulations
- Utilities regulations
- International Organization for Standardization (ISO) standards

Moving forward, we will discuss the application of rigorous data analysis and (1) the creation of a range of criticality values, the scoring of objects based on the weighted score, creating a weighted object; (2) the placement of a weighted object into this range of criticality values; and (3) the establishment of a logical order and a common taxonomy that are required in completing an impact assessment.

6.7 QUESTIONS

1. What recent changes have been made to the command structure of DHS to address legal issues presented by the Posse Comitatus?
2. What two government branches are incorporated in the dual-hatted commander role in public sector emergency management?
3. Provide an example of a negative public perception impact that can exacerbate the response effort based on a contemporary legal emergency management legal *perception.*
4. Describe the Federal Family. What does it mean in the context of the National Response Framework and how can it be effectively messaged in future events?
5. What are the differences in the approach and scope of resources used during the response to Hurricane Katrina compared with those used during the response to Hurricane Irene?

ENDNOTES

1. FEMA. 2011. Tropical Storm Irene: Overview of Federal Family's Preparations and Response. http://www.fema.gov/news/newsrelease.fema?id=57478 (accessed September 6, 2011).
2. Ibid.

3. Ibid.
4. Ibid.
5. MacInnis, Laura, and Bull, Alister. 2011. Obama Says Hurricane Irene "Extremely Dangerous." http://www.reuters.com/article/2011/08/26/us-storm-irene-obama-idUSTRE77P4IM20110826 (accessed September 8, 2011).
6. Ibid.
7. Biesecker, Michael, and Peltz, Jennifer. 2011. 2 Million Ordered to Leave as Irene Takes Aim. http://www.boston.com/news/nation/articles/2011/08/26/waves_swells_from_irene_begin_hitting_nc_coast/ (accessed September 6, 2011).
8. Armstrong, Drew. 2011. Irene: Deaths, Flooding, Power Losses State-By-State. http://www.bloomberg.com/news/2011-08-28/irene-s-damage-a-state-by-state-look-at-deaths-flooding-power-outages.html (accessed September 6, 2011).
9. Fugate, Craig, FEMA administrator. 2011. Irene Update 36: Seeing the Team in Action in Vermont. http://blog.fema.gov/2011/08/irene-updated-36-seeing-team-in-action.html (accessed September 6, 2011).
10. Kohn, Sally. 2011. Another Disaster: Conservatives' Attack on FEMA. http://edition.cnn.com/2011/OPINION/08/29/kohn.conservatives.fema.index.html (accessed September 6, 2011).
11. Shumlin, Peter, Vermont governor. 2011. Vermont Governor Peter Shumlin on Rebuilding after Irene: Transcript from the Take Away (radio show). http://www.thetakeaway.org/2011/sep/01/governor-shumlin-rebuilding-vermont/transcript/ (accessed September 6, 2011).
12. Burton, Kevin. 2012. *Managing Emerging Risk*. New York: CRC Press, p. 149.
13. Arkin, William M., and Priest, Dana. Top Secret America: A Washington Post Investigation. http://projects.washingtonpost.com/top-secret-america/ (accessed September 12, 2011).
14. Ibid.
15. Blair, Tony. Blaming a Moral Decline for the Riots Makes Good Headlines but Bad Policy. *Guardian*, August 20, 2011. http://www.guardian.co.uk/commentisfree/2011/aug/20/tony-blair-riots-crime-family (accessed on February 19, 2012).
16. Easton, Mark. 2011, August 11. England Riots: The Return of the Underclass. BBC News UK. http://www.bbc.co.uk/news/uk-14488486 (accessed February 19, 2012).
17. Shane, Scott. 2011. Investigators Assess Threat of Bombing Tied to 9/11. http://www.nytimes.com/2011/09/09/us/09threat.html?_r=1&scp=1&sq=bomb%20threat%202011&st=cse (accessed September 12, 2011).
18. Ibid.
19. Dickstein, Cory. 2011. 3rd ID Helicopter Crews Return from Hurricane Irene Deployment. http://savannahnow.com/latest-news/2011-08-31/3rd-id-helicopter-crews-return-hurriance-irene-deployment#.TnJbkHMYSIQ (accessed September 12, 2011).

20. Army Times. 2011. 6,500 Active-Duty Troops on Post-Irene Standby. http://www.armytimes.com/news/2011/08/ap-military-active-duty-troops-on-post-irene-standby-082711/ (accessed September 15, 2011).
21. Nimmo, Kurt. 2011. Pentagon Beta Tests Tighter Military Control of Disaster Response. http://www.infowars.com/pentagon-beta-tests-tighter-military-control-of-disaster-response/ (accessed September 12, 2011).
22. Watson, Joseph P. 2011. Ron Paul: Feds Preparing for "Breakdown of Law and Order." http://www.infowars.com/ron-paul-feds-preparing-for-breakdown-of-law-and-order/ (accessed September 12, 2011).
23. Ibid.
24. Watson, Joseph P. 2011. Pollster: Americans Are "Pre-Revolutionary." http://www.infowars.com/pollster-americans-are-pre-revolutionary/ (accessed September 13, 2011).
25. All posted comments taken from Pollster: Americans Are "Pre-Revolutionary."
26. Burkett, Jeffrey W. 2009. Command and Control: Command and Control of Military Forces in the Homeland. http://usacac.army.mil/cac2/call/docs/10-16/ch_3.asp (accessed September 9, 2011).
27. Ibid.
28. Ibid.
29. Department of Defense. 2011. Dual-Status Commanders to Support Irene Relief Efforts. http://www.af.mil/news/story.asp?id=123269826 (accessed September 15, 2011).
30. Elliott, Dan. 2011. Irene Tests Military's Revamped Disaster Response. http://www.military.com/news/article/irene-tests-militarys-revamped-disaster-response.html (accessed September 14, 2011).
31. Yager, Jordy. 2011. FBI, DHS Warn That 9/11 Anniversary Terror Threat Still Unresolved, "Ongoing." http://thehill.com/news-by-subject/defense-homeland-security/181171-fbi-dhs-warn-that-911-anniversary-terror-threat-unresolved-still-ongoing (accessed September 14, 2011).
32. Ibid.
33. Kessler, Ronald. 2011. FBI on Heightened Alert for 9/11 Anniversary. http://conservativewatchnews.org/?p=21311 (accessed September 15, 2011).

7

The Fourth Principle
Apply Rigorous Data

7.1 KEY TERMS

7.2 OBJECTIVES

After reading this chapter you will be able to:

1. Establish an applicable range of criticality values that can apply to people, processes, and technologies.
2. Discuss the meaning and importance of using the constraints and liberties created in the second and third principles to allow for

flexibility when applying weights and creating a weighted score that is applicable to multiple objects.

3. Specify the benefits of interview-based data collection combined with the use of big data in scoring objects using the weighted score.

4. Describe a logical order and the hierarchical relationships of objects scored using the weighted score and placing them within the range of criticality values.

5. Provide an example of an applied taxonomy and the creation of a common naming standard for a set of technological components.

7.3 OVERVIEW: APPLYING THE SECOND AND THIRD PRINCIPLES AND CREATING A RANGE OF CRITICALITY VALUES BASED ON A LOGICAL ORDER AND A COMMON TAXONOMY

The fundamental flaw of impact assessments has been described as a tendency to think too small, which leads to other problems and misgivings (Figure 7.1). Some of these include a lack of appropriate scope as a result of not having a clearly stated impact horizon. There are also negative public perception impacts based on the misalignment of core values, and there is the potential for civil unrest or negative brand impacts based on the misalignment of core values with national and state laws and industry-specific regulations. The five guiding principles of postmodern impact assessments have been introduced in Chapters 2–6 as a method to address these problems and misgivings.

* * *

The five guiding principles of the postmodern impact assessments encourage practitioners of emergency management to indulge in a deeper level of critical thinking *prior to measuring any impact at all*. Taking the time to lay the foundation and framework of the analysis is the hallmark of a well-crafted impact analysis—an analysis based on *the core values* and *the fundamental context* of the organization.

* * *

The application of the first three principles will have established a well-stated impact horizon, the core values of the organization will have been analyzed, and any legal or regulatory conditions that would

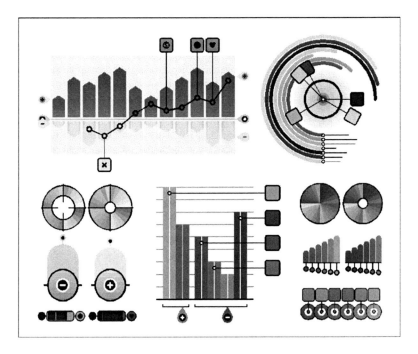

Figure 7.1 Key concepts in this chapter are creating a range of criticality values based on a logical order and common taxonomy.

influence the analysis will have been addressed. Complying with these principles results in the following deliverables:

1. The first principle delivers an impact horizon statement.
2. The second principle delivers the development of a weighted score that reflects the core values of an organization and can be applied to each object evaluated in the impact assessment so that each of the core values is represented, with the most important value holding the most weight, and the least of these holding the least weight.
3. The further development of a weighted score with the enumeration, recital, and clarification of national and state laws and industry regulations that have been considered and are either addressed or not addressed by the potential impact assessment.

With these deliverables, we have already completed the lion's share of our work and the keen practitioner now has a clear scope in the form of an impact horizon, an initial weighted score pie chart for each object he or she is about to measure based on organizational values, and an understanding of how specific laws and regulations will influence the weighted score pie chart. What is missing is a range of criticality values that is determined based on the organizational appetite for risk.

The key deliverable of applying the fourth principle will result in (1) the creation of a **range of criticality** values, the scoring of objects based on the weighted score, creating a weighted object; (2) the placement of a weighted object into this range of criticality values; and (3) the establishment of a logical order and a common taxonomy that are required in completing an impact assessment.

The fourth principle allows us to continue pressing forward and enables the application of significant analysis based on the organizational realities discovered using the second and third principles. This analysis yields a range of criticality values to which multiple weighted objects can be applied, and also generates a matrix of logically ordered people, processes, and technologies that make up the enterprise, with the use of a common taxonomy.

* * *

As we have worked through the material presented thus far we have found a truism presented in Chapter 1—that the old method of creating impact analyses is ad hoc. The highly specific method of applying the five guiding principles described in this volume yields a much more *prudent* and *informed* analysis of impacts than simply "jumping right in."

* * *

To be clear, the five guiding principles do more than demand prudence in our approach to starting an impact analysis; they demand rigor in conducting the actual scoring of impacts and assigning them a place in our range of criticality values. The fourth guiding principle of postmodern impact assessments consists of three essential analytical tools that will yield the most accurate of results in the final impact analysis deliverable:

1. A range of criticality values
2. A logical order of all things measured
3. A common taxonomy or language for naming what is measured

Emergency managers are responsible for crafting detailed, concise, and considered analytical work in the form of a superior postmodern impact assessment. Success can only be achieved with the application of solid analytical models, exacting logical, relevant, and clear language and taxonomies. The value of this chapter is that we can deliver a detailed description of the data and analytics used to create a range of criticality values to which multiple weighted objects can be applied, in a logical order, defined by a common taxonomy.

7.4 THE IMPACT ASSESSMENT AS A BUSINESS CASE

In Chapter 1, we briefly described how the traditional business impact assessment is often described as a business case for business continuity and disaster recovery programs. Taking a wider view, an impact assessment is *actually* the baseline for all **remediation** and **mitigation** activities and tactics undertaken by public or private organizations. *Remediation* is the act of improving or "setting right" a weakness found during an impact assessment, which can lessen the impact if that object is lost or damaged *before* a disaster event. *Mitigation* is the act of lessening the severity or intensity of damage to an object through taking action *after* a disaster has occurred. Remediation and mitigation are different things—often to the surprise of our stakeholders!

Remediation requires that resources be used *now*, prior to an event, to lessen the potential impact. Mitigation also requires that resources be used *now*, to address the impacts as they manifest themselves after the event through the use of specific response tactics and plans. To the extent that the use of such resources will require the outlay of money, people, and time, a sound impact assessment *can* be used as a business case for a business continuity, disaster recovery, or emergency management program. However, the author believes that the determination of an organization to move forward with a business continuity, disaster recovery, or emergency management program has much more to do with the strong consultation and analytical work delivered by the practitioner, as delivered using the first three principles, than it does with the perception of possible loss.

* * *

Poor business impact assessments that do not hold up to analytical scrutiny and are not logically sound are nothing more than scare tactics used to sell expensive insurance policies and frankly sit below the level of accuracy needed in the context of today's business and emergency management world.

* * *

While some claims are made that the impact assessment is required to create a business case for emergency management, business continuity, and disaster recovery programs, we suggest that the application of core values, laws, and regulations is the most influential organizational value delivered when an impact assessment is well crafted. Using the approach detailed in this volume, a business case becomes self-evident and is founded in the views, values, and legal and regulatory constraints of the organization we are serving.

In this text, we use the term *program* to refer to policy, strategy, plans, tactics, and operations, as well as the goals, missions, and objectives that are required in tasking teams during response operations in business continuity, disaster recovery, or emergency management situations.

In understanding how we might specifically measure impacts, we can better align our program to the overriding program policy of the organizations we serve by improving our **weighted scores** and refining the range of criticality values we've arrived at, using expert interviews, strong data, and logic as we complete the work in this chapter.

7.5 ESTABLISHING RANGES OF CRITICALITY VALUES USING LOGIC AND THE WEIGHTED SCORES

Using the fourth principle, impact assessments can score many objects based on the weighted score, thereby creating a weighted object. The weighted object can then be placed into a value within the range of criticalities. We have already started assigning weights to the weighted score determining core values and applying legal and regulatory weights in Chapters 4 and 5.

7.5.1 Getting Started with Data Normalization in the Weighted Criticality Score Values

As you will recall from Chapter 5, for illustration purposes, we created a weighted score pie chart for a fictional organization that functions with core values of health and safety in mind, including legal and regulatory compliance. To review, that weighted score pie chart looked like this:

The Weighted Score V3

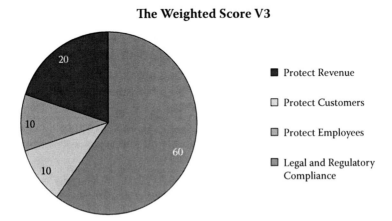

In Chapters 4 and 5, we initially developed the weighted score above by aligning impact measures to the core values of an imaginary organization (the second principle) and further developed the weighted score with the consideration and alignment of national and state laws and industry regulations. For calculation purposes, the weighted score above consists of weighted components. The weighted components for this example's weighted score are composed of:

- Protect revenue: 20%
- Protect customers: 10%
- Protect employees: 10%
- Legal and regulatory compliance: 60%

Therefore, we will not be using executive overrides or deviations to address the value of legal and regulatory compliance.

In order to arrive at a final impact analysis we need to take the weighted score and apply it on an object-by-object basis yielding multiple weighted objects. These multiple weighted objects are then placed within the appropriate range of criticality values. Since we already have our weighted score, we must create a range of criticality values before we apply the weighted score to individual objects (creating weighted objects). The range of criticality score values *is not the weighted score.*

7.6 THE RANGE OF CRITICALITY SCORE VALUES AND THE PLACEMENT OF OBJECTS IN THE RANGE

7.6.1 Create a Range of Criticality

Once we have the weighted score (shown above), we want to be able to rate the loss value of objects (people, processes, and technologies) based on the weighted score by creating weighted score objects, and then arranging them across a range of criticality values that is ordered by **quartile** (in this example).

For this example, the quartile is one of four values in a statistical analysis. The quartiles may be called "mission critical," "critical," "business essential," and "desirable." They may also be numbered or assigned an alphabetical designation such as tiers A, B, C, and D, or tiers 4, 3, 2, and 1.This ranking of objects into one of the four quartiles is called *assigning a criticality to an object.* Each quartile is made up of a portion of a 100% score arrived at through the distribution of impacts across the complete range of values, i.e., 100–75%, 74–50%, 49–25%, and 24–1%. It's important to note that the quartiles can vary highly depending on the organization's appetite for risk. For example, an organization that provides security may decide that the first quartile is made of any object falling into the 100–50% range, while a retail organization may choose only to have its top scored objects fall in the 100–90% range. Nonetheless, how each quartile score is arrived at is based on the organization's appetite for putting value at risk (Figure 7.2).

A weighted object score, considered in a range of criticality values, will vary and is used to frame each weighted object within a **common loss grouping**—the quartile value within the range of criticality value. Clearly, the larger the number of scored objects that exist in the analysis, the more statistically significant the criticality quartile-ranking scheme becomes.

Generally, it is important to note that irreplaceability always trumps performance in concordance with the five guiding principles and should result in a weighted score that captures potential performance loss as well as **single points of failure**, or those objects that may be irreplaceable. A single point of failure is one person, one process, or one computing system

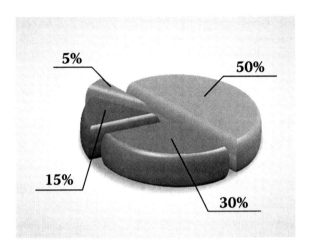

Figure 7.2 The weighted score is a critical component to understanding the values of an organization.

for which there is no interrelationship, manual workaround, or backup. In short, a single point of failure or irreplaceable object should, by nature of the five guiding principles, score in the top quartile.

7.6.2 Apply the Weighted Score to Individual Objects

An impact score rates the overall value of people, processes, and technologies within the context of the weighted score. When we look at objects from a weighted score point of view we need to apply individual impact scores to each of the weighted components (revenue, customers, employees, etc.):

Critical Loss	High Loss	Some Loss	Minimal Loss	No Loss
5	4	3	2	1

When reviewing the weighted score pie chart above, the weighted score version 3 is being used to capture all of the weighted components going into a weighted score for one object that can then be placed in one of the common loss groupings (quartiles of the range of criticality values). The weighted score is based on the components found in the organization's core values, laws, regulations and policies, impact values, and other factors described in the five guiding principles of postmodern impacts. They are *drawn out* by the professional consultation of the real-world experience of the practitioner doing the analysis. The organizational values that make up the components will vary from organization to organization, but will most always fall within one of the consultative narratives presented in the five guiding principles of postmodern impact analysis.

As an example, we are going to apply impact scores to individual weighted components based on the weighted score to five objects (see Table 7.1). For this example we will be using the weighted score version 3 above.

The objects:
- **Mr. A** is the visionary CEO of the organization and the genius behind the organization's multiple patents and discoveries (think Steve Jobs).
- **Dr. B** is the engineering and science director, and a darn good one at that!
- **The China plant** is a newly built facility that produces 40% of the organization's goods for market in the United States that were sold in the past fiscal year.
- **The new data center** is a $15 million computer center in the basement of the San Jose, California, headquarters of the organization.
- **Mrs. C** is the incredibly talented industrial designer who designs and packages Mr. A's products for marketability and has an innate sense of trends based on years in the electronics industry.

7.7 APPLYING COMMON LOGIC

We need to take our criticality scoring under consideration and apply it to the specific objects we are measuring based on the second and third principles and the resulting weighted object scores. If we measure a fire extinguisher with a weighted object score ranking of 80%, that would place it in the critical loss range. Does the same logic work for processes? Sure, if extinguishing a fire is very important it should score in the range of 76–100. What about other infrastructure like power? Absolutely!

There are not separate scales for humans and machines. There are not separate scales for water and gas. Whatever objects we are measuring, if informed by the second and third principles and this notion of interoperability logic, the result will be a uniformed scoring methodology that can

215

Table 7.1 Example—Calculating Individual Object Scores

Mr. A

Weighted Component	Impact Score	Weight	Component's Weighted Score	Weighted Object Score
Protect revenue	5	(×20%)	1.0	4.7
Protect customers	3	(×10%)	0.3	
Protect employees	4	(×10%)	0.4	
Legal and regulatory compliance	5	(×60%)	3.0	

Dr. B

Protect revenue	1	(×20%)	0.2	1.4
Protect customers	2	(×10%)	0.2	
Protect employees	4	(×10%)	0.4	
Legal and regulatory compliance	1	(×60%)	0.6	

The China Plant

Protect revenue	5	(×20%)	1.0	2.0
Protect customers	3	(×10%)	0.3	
Protect employees	1	(×10%)	0.1	
Legal and regulatory compliance	1	(×60%)	0.6	

The New Data Center

Protect revenue	4	(×20%)	0.8	3.2
Protect customers	5	(×10%)	0.5	
Protect employees	1	(×10%)	0.1	
Legal and regulatory compliance	3	(×60%)	1.8	

Mrs. C

Protect revenue	2	(×20%)	0.4	1.2
Protect customers	1	(×10%)	0.1	
Protect employees	1	(×10%)	0.1	
Legal and regulatory compliance	1	(×60%)	0.6	

(continued)

Table 7.1 Example—Calculating Individual Object Scores (continued)

Note: All scores are based on an impact scale of 1–5 across the four weighted score components. The highest impact score possible is 5. The highest weighted object score is also 5. Keep in mind that in this scoring method, a 5 would be critical loss and a 1 would be no loss. These scores are based on expert interviews and are created at the discretion of the practitioner when working with the client. It is possible in our model to use as many or as few weighted components to create a weighted object score for any given object as long as the data are normalized accordingly (see below). In Section 7.9 we will discuss the positive attributes of a model that generates these weighted object scores based on the combination of big data and expert interviews.

apply to *any object.* Inspection of what we are measuring to see if there are logical hierarchies that will help us determine how to group what we measure can also be helpful in asserting a logical order.

The inspection, or definition of a critical hierarchy based on *relationships*, is the practitioner's largest challenge. It takes into consideration the many names applied to the same objects, as well as the interrelationships between those objects, and sets out to codify them. For many organizations, working with a professional from our field is the first time the organization has had to move away from cultural naming conventions and assumptions about the relationships between objects and actually pin down a convention and thesaurus.

At the highest level, one of our measures might be to protect revenue, but revenue is generated by various means and we want to limit the number of variables we measure in order to keep this process manageable. Here is the logic of the corporate world of revenues: Processes generate revenue, people do processes, and people need computers to aid with processes. Therefore if we rank a process as "critical" based on a high revenue score, then the people and technologies that support that process *inherit the criticality.* This is called **inherited criticality**, which means *criticality is given because of the highest-order measured variable*, which in this case was the process.

The term *inheritance* suggests parents, children, and grandchildren, in which a trait (in this case the importance and impact) is inherited, much like the gene for eye color. This is a sound and well-used methodology for conducting potential impact analyses. The method proves out **dependencies** and **interdependencies** between systems, people, and processes. A dependency is the requirement for one object to have a dependency on another object for it to operate. Interdependency is when more than one object will require other objects or even sets of objects to operate. Thinking of it this way, we can see that a **naming convention** and a logical order must be in place for us to align and map the relationships between many objects to arrive at weighted criticality scores for grouped objects that infer not only their dependencies and interdependencies, but also their inherited criticality.

* * *

This is the best part of our role as emergency managers, counterterrorism, disaster recovery, and business continuity professionals—if we understand all of the working parts of the organization and their importance, we have a clear view, unlike many others, of what makes an organization run. Leveraging this knowledge is a key to boosting career visibility and performance.

* * *

7.7.1 Core Objects and Metadata

Here is another example—the "ensure public safety score" logic might work like this: First responders ensure public safety. First responders need to be safe to ensure public safety. To be safe, first responders need working equipment, including vehicles, active communications, and running water. Therefore if we think public safety is critical, all of the things that make up a solid first response capability are also critical based on the inherited public safety score. Finding the **highest-order measure** (the highest logical category or grouping) for each object in the impact assessment will lower the number of objects scored as long as we link the core object score to its metadata. The **core object** is the highest logical order of what we are trying to protect; the **metadata** are the objects that enable the core object to function and deliver value, safety, or other core values or legal and regulatory capabilities as expressed in our weighted score.

* * *

We must identify the weighted components that are applicable across anything, and then arrange them so that the core object can be measured. It must allow for inherited criticality to inform the potential loss and importance of the metadata objects associated with the core object.

* * *

Here is a logic tool the practitioner can use to test his or her reasoning: How can a person who delivers revenue be any less important to protect than the computer he or she uses to do the job? How can a first responder be any less important than the equipment he or she uses to do his or her job? It will be hard for us to apply hierarchal logic, and we will have to work through the logical order of things to ensure that inherited criticality is exact and that the concept is not overused. However, it is important to know that it is acceptable and probable that something will defy this logic.

Identifying the few objects that stand outside the applied logic is an important exercise. It means that there are stand-alone objects (people, processes, or technologies) that have no direct relationship to anything else in the organization or delivery of a valued and critical process considered within the impact assessment. By definition, these objects are single points of failure.

Once we have applied hierarchal logic, we will have identified our core objects, their interdependencies, and inherited criticality. Finally, and most importantly, we now must find a common language and taxonomy for what we are about to go out and measure.

7.8 APPLYING A COMMON TAXONOMY

To truly have a method that is cross-functional in the private sector as well as in the public sector, and one that plays across multiple subdisciplines within emergency management and counterterrorism, we must create a common **taxonomy**, and ultimately a common language that is extensible across these interests.

Here is an example. An emergency manager is told that DHS has currently put the National Terrorism Advisory System at *elevated* by his DHS commander in chief, and by a military DOD liaison that the current threat level has a WATCHCON of 4, and a TEMS commander tells him that there are 700 persons already triaged with injuries rated as *urgent*, and the incident manager for airborne surveillance from the USCG says that there are *potential impacts* to a National Special Security Event (NSSE), and finally, a private sector telecommunication incident commander is reporting *impacts* to 20 essential communications systems. Given all this, it might be hard for the manager to understand what the current impact potential of the first event he or she is working on actually is.

The DHS uses the **National Terrorism Advisory System** (NTAS) to indicate one of only two types of threats: *elevated* watch status, which means that the public is being warned of "a credible terrorist threat against the United States,"[1] or an *imminent* threat alert, which means that "a credible, specific, and impending terrorist threat against the United States" exists. The DOD uses a **WATCHCON** to communicate a hierarchy of stages ranging from 1 to 4. A WATCHCON 4 is usually in effect during normal peacetime. A WATCHON 1 is in effect during war.

A **Tactical Emergency Medicine Unit** (TEMS) will often report non-casualty persons in triage as urgent, or needing care in 2 hours; priority, or needing care in 2–4 hours; or routine, or needing care in 4 hours.[2] A **U.S. Coast Guard** (USCG) airborne commander reporting an **NSSE** in harm's way means he is identifying a target using DHS parlance for a national special security event, which includes anticipated attendance by dignitaries, or a large-sized event, or a significant event. Finally, a private sector report from a communications company of losing 20 "essential" systems could mean *anything*. Is "essential" more important than "mission critical"? How could we possibly know?

Here's the *real* meaning of the potential impacts in our example above. The emergency manager is faced with a credible terrorist threat reported by his command at DHS. The DOD has reported a peacetime condition. A rapidly deployed Tactical Emergency Medical Unit is reporting that 700 persons are in need of urgent care within 2 hours. The Coast Guard has reported active surveillance of a national special security event involving possible dignitaries and large crowds during a significant date or at a significant target, and the private sector telecommunication incident commander is reporting system impacts to essential systems that, in his or her terms, need to be recovered in no less than 4 hours, but are *not* mission critical.

In translation then, there is a credible terrorist threat, during peacetime, with 700 people already needing care within 2 hours, a high-profile special event target, and some high criticality systems damaged. The emergency manager has conflicting data, but it is clear the potential impacts are high, just not clear enough. There is no common measure of impact criticality.

Imagine if the same report *was* given using a commonly architected system that possessed uniform language for potential impact. The emergency manager is told that DHS has currently put the National Terrorism Advisory System at level 1 by his DHS commander in chief, and by a military DOD liaison that the current threat level has a WATCHCON of 1, and a TEMS commander tells him that there are 700 persons already triaged with injuries rated as level 1, and the incident manager for airborne surveillance from the USCG says that there are potential impacts to a level 1 target, and finally, a private sector telecommunication incident commander is reporting impacts to 20 level 2 communications systems. If there was a common potential impact measure and level 1 indicated *critical* and response needed within 30 minutes and level 2 meant *urgent* and response needed within 60 minutes, he would instantly understand his or her challenge.

This is not a "pipe dream" or a "blue sky" vision for the future of emergency management or counterterrorism. DHS and FEMA continue to urge public sector involvement and partnership in countless news conferences and briefs. However, to quote Elsa Lee, from the introduction to her book *Homeland Security and Private Sector Business*, "The problem is not that we all could die tomorrow in an attack. The problem is that we cannot seem to perform the basic functions of diagnosing and treating the problems so that it is manageable. Public and Private partnerships are essential to the success of this management and should already be further along than they are to create partnerships and information-sharing collaboration."[3]

* * *

The emergency management and counterterrorism profession has matured to the point at which a common taxonomy is required that imposes a common impact vernacular that enhances interoperability, provides extensible flexibility, can be used across multiple public and private professions, reduces operational overhead and cycles, and increases response effectiveness.

* * *

A **standard naming convention** is like a decoding ring and tells us that what one person calls accounts receivables is also related to a system called pay me and a group of employees in a group called collections. While each stakeholder may be describing a person, place, thing, or system by a different name, at the end of the day they are all talking about receivable revenue. We might encapsulate that grouping into a logical key potential impact called revenue retrieval.

The challenge is that there is very little common nomenclature within a single organization (let alone across multiple organizations). Information technology workers will call a system one thing, while the office workers who use the same system every day will call it something different. For example, everyone refers to the system that allows them to communicate on their computers as email; however, the IT folks might call it the exchange server, or just exchange. What's more, the email server is just part of a larger communication system made up of several servers, routers, hubs, switches, and other devices that ultimately lead us to two key support items, power (as in electricity) and the Internet (as in connectivity).

These last two items are so basic and so fundamental to the order of things in the naming of potential impact items that we could refer to them as superstructure systems. **Superstructure systems** would be places, systems, infrastructure, or even personnel support teams that must be in place for a key potential impact score to exist. For instance, one of the superstructure systems needed for customer support is customers. Without customers, the potential impact to customer support is negligible.

Naming systems take decades or more to generate in most scientific and professional practices. Medicine has taken decades to arrive at a common naming convention for medications, and is just now wrestling with ICD-10, a common naming system for coding diagnoses. In the world of natural science, we have struggled with the taxonomy of living things, from the times of Aristotle (who introduced the idea of ranking "beings"), to the works of Linnaeus (who gave us terms such as *substance*, *species*, and *genus*), and forward to more contemporary naming and classification schemes, such as the well-known text *On the Origin of Species* by Charles Darwin, in which he discusses biological classification at length (Figure 7.3).

The works of Linnaeus and Darwin have somewhat cemented our ideas on biological classifications to the hierarchy of species, genus, family, order, class, phylum, and kingdom. However, if you ask a young person today to explain biological classification to you, he or she will add that above the highest order of kingdom, there exists a classification of domain. The idea of domains was added to biological taxonomy in the 1990s and is currently under debate among scientists in this field. We are pointing out the challenges of modern classification because it is easy to see that any suggested classification scheme will be contested and debated for some time before it becomes anything near a standard, and most schemes are always changing. That should not prohibit us from moving ahead with them.

To continue with our biological classification scheme example, the latest development in this area is an orientation toward globally unique identifiers in the form of life science identifiers (LSIDs). An **LSID** strives to link identifiers to databases and the World Wide Web and create a naming and ranking convention that can be extended as our knowledge of new

Charles Darwin.

Figure 7.3 Charles Darwin went through painstaking detail to give us a con-temporary naming and classification scheme in his work *On the Origin of Species*. As we apply this same thinking to our field, we are stepping into Darwin's shoes!

species and families increases. The naming convention is interesting, as it suggests a standard use formula such that any thing can be classified as follows:

LSID = <Authority>:<Namespace>:<ObjectID>(:<Version>)

In this scheme, the source or authority is followed by the name or namespace, and then an object ID or a short name, and finally, the version or release of that named object. The reason that the LSID is important is that it surrounds the biologically classified name in the namespace with other data, specifically, the authority, the object ID, and a version number surrounding it. This allows for the realization that over time, one person's namespace use may vary from another's, and that the versioning use of that namespace will change over time.

A company in Austin, Texas, uses taxonomy and semantics to generate comprehensive classifications and identifiers for named objects in a relationship-based system for several fields and applications, among them defense-related taxonomies, terrorism taxonomies (3,000 entries of terrorists, tactics, groups, attacks, venues, weapons, and characteristics), and geospatial taxonomies (terrain, climate, paths, vegetation, and other topics). The applied use of taxonomies and standard naming with applied heuristics and knowledge management systems has created a fantastic source of common valued and named objects that are searchable and standardized.[4]

This system could be easily leveraged to quick-start our industry toward a common taxonomy and set of naming conventions if adopted.

* * *

Applying a taxonomy built on relationship-based information is often a compound of common naming conventions, heuristics, and knowledge that should not be viewed so much as a "tree" or a hierarchy of items, but a thing without shape—the objective is not to create a dictionary, but a thesaurus, and this approach to taxonomies has been applied for hundreds of years across a multitude of disciplines.

* * *

In the *Joint Forces Quarterly*, July 2005, Richard D. Downie wrote about defining integrated operations, exploring a project undertaken by General Richard Myers, USAE, and the then chairman of the Joint Chiefs of Staff. General Myers noted, "We need to transform our military competencies for joint operations to integrated operations." He went on to say, "One of the first—and easiest—things we can standardize is the terminology we use to define important, though perhaps amorphous, operational concepts."[5]

Based on this, Richard Downie set out to define a common set of terms saying, "Toward the Chairman's goal of standardization, this commentary offers a taxonomy of terms to describe various types of interagency and integrated operations. The intent is to generate discussion on how to standardize the way we define and address such operations. The faculty of the Center for Hemispheric Defense Studies at the National Defense University developed the terms. We based our approach on differentiation and categorization of the entities participating rather than on the functional objective of an operation (such as peacekeeping, disaster relief, or counterterrorism)."[6]

In all efforts to create common terms of use and taxonomies, some rules are applied that inform the naming convention and build out the framework. These rules of thumb or approaches to experienced-based problem solving and learning are called **heuristics**. The process of studying terms used to identify things and what the terms mean in any given taxonomy is called **semantics**. Semantics is the study of the meaning of words, phrases, and signs. *Together, semantics and heuristics, or the terms and rules, when applied, can help generate taxonomy.* In order for us to be able to create a common taxonomy in our field and capture potential impact items that can be encapsulated into key potential impacts, we will have to apply some basic semantics and heuristics and gather agreement from our stakeholders as to how these terms and rules apply to our framework.

7.8.1 A Proposed Taxonomy Framework

7.8.1.1 Location

Within the range of potential impacts, practitioners should be using a global view to build out a common naming convention and logical order of things. Within a global scope an organization could have three types of impacts based on location. As an example, the first set of categories will be based on location. Since we want our locations to be measurable in terms of their impact, we will apply some basic rules of thumb around location impacts, specifically that location impacts can be:

1. Global
2. Regional
3. Local

Therefore we can start with the statement that those impacts happen where risk manifests itself, and that those impacts affect that location (and our client's organization) globally, regionally, or locally. A naming standard for this first level of potential impact item will be <Location>:<Impact Scope>. The string we are creating for these named items has its beginnings with a location and an impact scope. For example, if our company has a global headquarters in Los Angeles, the beginning of this name will be L.A. HQ: G, meaning Los Angeles, global. Some companies have location identifiers for properties that work very well in the location identifier field, and an alternative approach is to use that code versus a shorthand version of the location name. Location names and their associated impact rules are like domains, they work very well in defining a place and its range of influence.

7.8.1.2 Superstructure Systems

Within these domains of location and impact influence are large superstructure systems required for the locations to operate and support people, processes, and technologies. Since these superstructure systems can be said to be required for all people, processes, and technologies, we suggest naming them potential impact items. Given this concept, our next level of naming an object will be to identify its superstructure system dependencies. For this example, we could identify four core superstructure systems:

4. Location accessibility (A)
5. Power availability (B)
6. Network connectivity (C)
7. Voice connectivity (D)
8. All of the above (E)

What our four superstructure systems help us identify are impacts to the larger systems on which our lower-order potential impact items rely, specifically, the ability for people to access the location, the availability of power, a connection to the network or the Internet, and a connection to voice communications by landlines or other means. We can shorthand the identifiers for these superstructure systems in the following way:

9. S3A
10. S3B
11. S3C
12. S3D
13. S3E

S3 stands for superstructure system. A, B, C, and D each stand for the type of connectivity or access needed to support activities at that location with E standing for all. Now we can extend our naming string to identify an item at our Los Angeles headquarters to include its required superstructure systems. In our example the string can now lengthen to <Location>:<Impact Scope>:<S3 A>, meaning Los Angeles, headquarters, global scope. All superstructure systems are needed, as the string would read <L.A. HQ: G: S3 A>.

7.8.1.3 Functions

Next, we can identify the functions being carried out by our organization at various locations. Sometimes practitioners refer to these functions as departments or divisions, which may be an applicable third level naming convention; however, we can consider the alignment to departments or divisions of an organization as a product of organization charts and human resources and not a practical naming convention tier in this example, so that we can apply the framework to more than corporate hierarchies. A function, in this example, can be a roll-up of individual processes and systems that deliver a certain capability or an input or output to the organization. Sometimes they will align with department or divisional names, and sometimes they will not. Let's try an example.

The global organization we are looking at has five key functions. In real-life applications of this approach, we will generally encounter between 20 and 75 functions. In even larger organizations, the number of functions can increase into the hundreds. Here are five sample functions: sales, production, advertising, research, and administration. We can shorthand these down to:

14. Sales
15. Prod
16. Advert
17. Research
18. Admin

Now we can lengthen our naming string to <Location>:<Impact Scope>:<S3 A>:<Prod>, meaning Los Angeles, headquarters, global scope, all superstructures needed, production. The string would read <L.A. HQ: G: S3 A: Prod>.

7.8.1.4 Processes

Next, we can break down the specific function of production into several processes and systems that support those processes. For purposes of this example, our global organization produces counterterrorism intelligence in real time for the U.S. government. Among their produced products are intelligence, tracking, mapping, health and safety impact tracking, and incident monitoring tools. All of these are critical to Homeland Security and other agencies that rely on them, such as FEMA, the NSA, the CIA, the FBI, and others. These are online, subscriber-based tools and services that are delivered on secured Internet connections and via satellite communications.

Within the functional group of Prod, we then could have five product processes. In our example, their short names could be:

19. INT
20. TRACK
21. GIS
22. H&S
23. IMT

Also, each functional group may have multiple large systems attached to it that we need to identify. This is often one of the most confusing parts of doing an impact assessment, or in our terms, a potential impact assessment. There is often very little difference between the name of an application and a system. For example, the system that is used in the production of health and safety tracking may simply be called the H&S system, but it is made up of several applications, including a web page, access control, a messaging bus, a database, and a decision engine. Sometimes it is hard for information technology workers to differentiate the system from its applications, but this work is very important because it identifies system objects with loss potential individually, which is where failures often occur.

* * *

A **system** is any group of applications that, when used together, create an organizational input or output. An **application** is any single package of executable code that is written in the same language or resides on a single machine that enables a system.

* * *

To continue with our functional description we must include system-level identifiers that enable the process. In our example, the function of health and safety tracking will need these other systems to deliver an output: the health and safety system, email, an accounting system, a satellite control system, and a geographic information system (GIS).

Within the functional group of Prod, we have five systems that support the function. In our example, their short code names could be:

24. H&S
25. Email
26. Acct. S

27. SCS
28. GIS

Now we can lengthen our naming string by adding multiple identifiers to our string, which will now read as <Location>:<Impact Scope>:<S3 A>:<Prod>:<(H&S):(Dependent Systems)>. So Los Angeles headquarters, global scope, all superstructures needed, production, health and safety impact tracking using the health and safety system, email, an accounting system, a satellite control system, and a GIS would read <L.A. HQ: G: S3 A: Prod: H&S: H&SS/Email/Acct. S/SCS/GIS>.

Within the production process of health and safety tracking (H&S) there are a multitude of subprocesses and applications. We need to identify each of these that are paired to or are unique to the H&S process.

7.8.1.5 Subprocesses, People, and Applications
The final addition to our proposed naming schema or taxonomy must include the ability to name low-level processes, people, and applications that support the function. In the example of health and safety tracking, there could be myriad objects. This level of detail is essential, as it speaks to what we referred to earlier in this chapter as configuration items. Each of these items is configurable in the enterprise because it can move, take on new responsibilities, or be added to another functional group to add capability and redundancy. For example, a person working in the administration of health and safety tracking may change roles and be "reconfigured" to be an administrator of the intelligence product.

Subprocesses, people, and applications are very hard to track and are usually moving within the enterprise. They are very rarely static, but they are the most important level of understanding we can reach when performing a potential impact analysis, because they tell us exactly what type of resources can be impacted.

To continue with our example, health and safety tracking may consist of three subprocesses, three personnel types, and five applications:

Subprocesses:
- H&S operations
- H&S administration
- H&S analysis

Personnel types:
- Operator
- Administrator
- Analyst

Applications:
- Intranet
- H&ST web
- Time tracker
- Customer satisfaction
- Trouble ticketing

Looking at just one personnel type we can show a unique identifier for a person working in the health and safety tracking area, as well as the function he or she belongs to, the process he or she does, his or her job type, and the applications he or she uses. This string would be a complete representation of one employee type for which we may have a number of employees with the same description.

For an analyst in this role, the string might read: <L.A. HQ: G: S3 A: Prod: H&S: H&SS/Email/Acct. S/SCS/GIS>: H&S Ops: Operator: H&ST Web>. The meaning of this long string is: In Los Angeles, at headquarters, using all superstructure systems, in the production of health and safety tracking, using the systems called health and safety system, email, accounting, satellite control system, and geological information system, there is a subprocess called health and safety operations that has an operator who uses the health and safety tracking web application.

Another way of looking at this taxonomy is to ask: What will the loss impact be of an employee at headquarters in the health and safety tracking group? Our taxonomy says that the response is: <L.A. HQ: G: S3 A: Prod: H&S: H&SS/Email/Acct. S/SCS/GIS>: H&S Ops: Operator: H&ST Web>. This is the proposed code sequence for one employee doing one subprocess, using one application, and who utilizes multiple superstructure systems and other systems (email, accounting, etc.) to add value to the function of health and safety tracking operations.

7.8.1.6 Finding the Point of Measure

As we have indicated, there are two points of impact measure that we must locate. One is the key potential impact (KPI), which is a roll-up or executive reporting level measure, and the second is a potential impact item (PII), which is a single object that, when composed into a function, is the measure of loss impact for a single item.

Using our taxonomy, we can now identify these two levels of measure. The first, our key potential impact, can be at the level of Los Angles headquarters, global, all super systems, production H&S. This measure point is bolded in the long string for a health and safety tracking system employee as <L.A. HQ: G: S3 A: **Prod: H&S**: H&SS/Email/Acct. S/SCS/ GIS>: H&S Ops: Operator: H&ST Web>.

The second measurement point is the individual employee working in health and safety as an operator. Everything he or she is dependent on is embedded in the naming convention, with the specific measurement point being placed in bold in the name string as <L.A. HQ: G: S3 A: Prod: H&S: H&SS/Email/Acct. S/SCS/GIS>: **H&S Ops:Operator**: H&ST Web>.

As long as we know we are in the domain of Los Angeles headquarters, these two indicators of impact produce two important views, a functional roll-up of impacts as key potential impacts, such as Prod:H&S, and the lower-level parts of that function, which could be anything from H&S Ops: Operator to Ops: H&S Analyst.

Even though we have now articulated a proposed naming convention, or taxonomy of what we are going to measure and the range within which these measures will fall, we have not assigned any criticality scores to key potential impact or potential impact items. We have, however, created a framework under which potential impact items can be named, along with their key potential impact relationships, and all of their dependencies and interdependencies and places within a range of criticality.

The successful framework outlined in this chapter accomplishes three things: It creates a range of criticality, key potential impacts and potential impact items, and provides a logical order for the creation of a common taxonomy.

7.9 USING BIG DATA TO CREATE RANGES OF CRITICALITY—A BETTER APPROACH

Interviews that create opinions out of qualitative data are biased because they are based on a personal feeling, at a specific place, within a specific time. The interviews are relative and can easily change based on the person being interviewed, the day, location, time, and even the interviewer who is determining the range of criticality. This is a good start because the organization is aware of its need to understand its areas of impact. A better way to conduct an impact assessment is through combining the subjective interviews with objective data. The most effective way to determine the *actual* value and criticality of an object to the organization is by viewing interviews through the lens of real data about the object. This is **big data**.

Big data can be of any size—from 100 gigabytes to 1 petabyte. What's important about big data is that they have metadata around them, they have systems generated, and they are all based on quantitative, real information. To make this tangible, look at the iPod analogy again. Your iPod only has 30 to 60 gigabytes of data on it. However, for every song there is a genre, the date you added the song, the last time it was played, the number of times it has been played, how many beats it has per minute, and more. This is what metadata look like and how they are used.

You might rank the song as "five stars," but by looking at the metadata around the object you are given tools to more completely understand it. Building our example from the iPod song analogy, we can get our weighted score and tiers of criticality from the combination of informed opinions and validate them with real, quantitative data found in the iPod application (called iTunes), such as number of plays, date added, and genre. This same logic applies in almost any setting for which we have measures.

The author believes that mixing qualitative and quantitative scores is balanced logic, and that interview-based data collection combined with quantitative facts *creates a meaningful perspective for determining response tactics.* In other words, to determine the essential 1,000 songs to put on your iPod Nano, you will get the most satisfying collection of music by creating a playlist based on the number of times you listen to a song within a certain timeframe, when combined with the subjectivity of rating songs with three to five stars. The benefit is that you'll not only have a playlist based on your feelings about songs, but one that reflects your actual preferences over a period of time within objective frameworks you choose.

7.9.1 Generating the Weighted Score and Ranges of Criticality with Big Data

Having a weighted score and the proposed ranges of criticality are essential, but using informed, interview-based data collection to get there is only a good approach to creating a quality impact analysis. A better approach would be to include evidenced data to support our interview findings. To make this clear, apply this thinking to the medical field.

The weighted score would be the equivalent of the picture of a healthy human. The combination of breathing, heart rate, nervous system function, and blood pressure would equal a 100% picture of health. Applying this weighted score of health to a range of criticalities, a doctor can then determine with a quick glance how critical a patient would be and apply a simple triage tag, much like a criticality value or tier. If a doctor stopped there (simply reading the triage tag), would any effective work be completed? No! The reason for this is that while the triage, based on the criticality determined by the weighted score, indicates the overall severity of injury or illness, it does not tell the doctor how to proceed with treatment.

A patient could be diagnosed "critical" with *any number* of impacts that would severely limit his ability to survive, such as a blocked airway, a severed limb, or a heart that is not beating. The doctor can determine from any of these causes that a patient is critical, but without further dissecting the weighted score into its components (breathing, heart rate, nervous system, and blood pressure), he would not know how to diagnose and solve the problem. Just like triage does not diagnose and cure, a tier assignment based on a weighted score alone does not always provide the correct solution.

The weighted score and range of criticalities are important, but they do not lead to an ultimate, impact-appropriate treatment and cure. They form a great business case, but a business case left unused does not lead to solving problems caused by impacts. As we will explore, the weighted score must be broken down and applied to a specific object, or sets of objects, in order to be truly effective and worth all of the effort that has been spent on designing it. However, prior to doing this work, we should consider a different approach to creating tiers.

* * *

The simple logic question we are presenting is one of quality and currency. Do we use subjective, informed opinions, or real data to populate our weighted scores in order to place an object on a tier? This is not an either/or question—the best option is the combination of both.

* * *

As we've said, a good option is to start with interviews to get the impact scores; the better option would be to combine the interview information with data to evidence the claims made in the impact scores. However, here is the best option: Now that the weighted score is in place, we apply thorough analysis and glean the most knowledge from big data. Creating a range of criticality validated with real data is a much better approach than using interview-based data collection alone. While the range of criticality can be expressed as desirable, important, essential, or critical, it is better to base those opinions on real numbers and expert views.

Consider this: Tiers and ranges of criticality are very different from one organization to another—and they should be. They are necessary for determining the overall health of the organization, and as such, each organization is going to determine its health by the organizational values, state and federal laws, and regulations that impact their own business. Going back to the medical analogy, humans have different standards of health than animals. While humans and fish both require oxygen for survival, you wouldn't put an oxygen mask on a fish that is out of the water!

Working forward with the knowledge that these tiers are used as a method of triaging the overall health of an organization, it is also important to recall that they do not diagnose and they do not provide solutions. The purpose that they serve is to indicate a status of health and *a general level of criticality that moves the emergency management program forward.*

Using the big data approach, we can gather real data from systems in the organization we serve and see the health of the organization in *real time.* Here's how. For financial impacts we can create a database schema for inspecting that data on a financial system that will provide us real numbers, such as an accounting system. For customer impacts, we can look to our customer satisfaction database and pull in real data from there to inform us about how many real customers we have and how happy or unhappy they will become if we are hit by a disaster. For adding value to the community we may need to bring in the total hours of community service done by our employees or the financial total of donations to charitable causes from another system.

While this may sound daunting, the upside is that meshing big data into a weighted score is now a common practice in many computer sciences and industries because the benefits are orders of magnitude above the old practice of interviews alone. The reason for this is threefold:

1. The numbers are real and validate existing interview opinions of importance.
2. The data can be represented as a visual indicator, but also as true values.
3. The data change and can be reviewed at any time for purposes of updates and revisions.

Anyone can see that creating a range of criticalities using big data is hard, taxing work, but this work is not without its reward. As we continue to move forward with an impact assessment, it will prove to be the

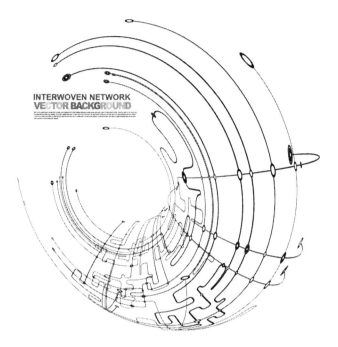

Figure 7.4 Using the fourth principle gives us the pieces we need to build a beautiful puzzle that provides far more value to an organization than any business case ever can.

necessary pieces to a beautiful puzzle that, when completed, provides far more than any business case can. Now we can progress in our impact assessment to the next step of scoring objects (Figure 7.4).

7.9.2 The Set of Objects as Big Data

At this point we have our weighted score based on the values of the organization and its applicable laws, values, and regulations. We have also determined what tiers and ranges of criticalities are appropriate for determining the urgency for response after any impact. Now that these pieces are in place, we need to start applying these data to objects and sets of objects to determine where the people, processes, and systems stand in relation to maintaining the health of the organization.

Determining criticality can be applied to any object within the organization. It can be applied to Robert in accounting (and his associated systems, even the computer he uses, for inherited critical-ity). Criticality can be determined by applying data to the objects that provide employee comfort and safety, such as air conditioning and air filtering. The objects themselves can be anything that carries any level of perceived value.

However, individual objects and their place in the ecosystem are only one piece of the picture, and this is an opportunity to get out of the web of the fundamental flaw—thinking too small!

The idea of applying our weighted score to a set of objects requires a true understanding of what an object *is*. It is, in the author's opinion, not limited to the traditional objects of simple people, processes, and technologies that has been alluded to in previous chapters, but is also a more complex arrangement of objects. Consider the following defini-tions of objects.

Objects are liminal, networked, traced, and vectored to geographies written out as Global Positioning System (GPS) coordinates. They are con-nected by the nature of their workforce, their mobility, their architectures, and the systems of technologies, relationships, and connections that bind them. They are objects when they are stood up alone, the worker who may or may not be with the firm for longer than 3 years, or the system that may or may not be "here" after the next technology refresh. An object exists in time and is relative to its output. In this is the condition; the object only exists in its relationship to other objects. The productivity of the object is not measured in hours at the office or time of use, but by its criticality and its output.

All objects are meaningless in the postmodern context without under-standing their relationship to other objects that constitute production for the organization. The thing to take away from this is the importance of an object's output and production. This serves as an excellent segue into the next segment: determining the criticality of an object.

7.9.3 What Is an Object, and How to Determine Criticality Based on the Conjunction of Expert Interviews and Big Data

As the emergency manager approaches the step of assigning values to objects in order to determine a weighted object score, he or she also reaches the step that is pregnant with the possibility to combine interview-based reasoning with the quantitative value of big data, thereby broadening the horizons and ability of the professional to practice the skill of the rigorous application of data.

If the reader will recall, in Chapter 2 it was said the argument for the fourth principle is simple and elegant. This is where the iPod fits into this step of an impact assessment (Figure 7.5).

The current process for determining object criticality involves deploying surveys or pursuing interviews conducted by the emergency manager, or his team. While this is a good start, the process yields static results that are only valid for the *moment* they are gathered. There is a way to improve and validate this interview process through the application of big data and expert opinion.

Comparing this to an iPod, do you use stars to rate your favorite songs? Chances are, you do. If you were to give someone your iPod and ask her to determine your favorite songs and taste in music by those star ratings, how accurate would she be? Working from your starred songs, she would be able to determine your favorite, neutral, and deplored songs within a limited field of vision. Remember that these stars, outside of the occasional, indispensible 1980s' favorite, are very subjective. You liked or disliked the majority of your songs at a particular moment in time, based

Figure 7.5 The familiarity of an iPod and playlists allow us to easily demonstrate the value of combining interviews with real data.

on a particular location, weather, event, and mood. How would you rate Beach Boy songs as you drove down the Pacific Coast Highway in your convertible, smelling the ocean, and basking in the sun? Probably all of them, with the probable exception of "In My Room," would earn the illustrious five-star rating.

Now put yourself in New York City in the dead of winter. You've got the worst cold you've had in 6 years and you've just stepped out of a cab and into fresh snow that goes over the top of your shoe, into your sock. Even if "Sloop John B" started playing, *especially* if "Sloop John B" started playing, you would fight the urge to vomit on the street corner and swear like a sailor as you pawed at your iPod with your gloved, fat fingers to stop the Beach Boys' mockingly melodious and cheerful voices.

This is how it is with interviews and opinions. Depending on the day, time, interviewer, and lighting, the rating an object receives is biased. We cannot get results that will stand the test of time from the use of this method alone.

Now we change the scenario, just slightly, and yield entirely different results. It's the same iPod and iTunes library. All of the stars are still there, but they are not used as the only source of input for this survey. In addition to the stars, we are going to look at the "Plays" and "Last Played" metadata. These two views of your iTunes library give a very realistic and believable picture of your music preferences and tastes. Yes, it still shows five stars on every single Beach Boy song, but it also shows that you only listened to half of the album once, and that was done on an afternoon at the end of July. Just by adding the simple pieces of data "Plays" and "Last Played," we can now begin to see that this is a combination of qualitative and quantitative data we can work with over a long period of time.

Just by adding the "Plays" and "Last Played" columns to your iTunes library the analyst can see that of your 4,000 songs, you've only listened to Bob Marley's *Legend* once, and that was sometime around 2 years ago—but you swear that you love the album! The analyst can also determine that you have 14 songs that have been listened to more than 25 times, and they're on an album by another artist with many listens, so it's a reasonable deduction that the Bee Gees' *Spirits Having Flown* appears to be your *true* favorite album. The analyst can also determine that 25 listens seems to be a demarcation line for some reason—there's the potential for more work to determine what causes this distinction in music listens.

This is an area where the subjectivity of interviews, in this case star ratings, comes into play and adds value. While the big data of your

Bob Marley *Legend* album is true, what is not accounted for is that Bob's CD is always in your car playing during your city commute—every single day. *Legend* truly *is* your favorite album, even though it is not represented by the big data of your iTunes library. Now to account for the Bee Gees—well, you can't help that this was the album you and your first girlfriend listened to during high school, and being a sentimental fellow, you like to listen to it on Sunday mornings while working in the yard.

While the topic of an iPod and starring versus play count is lighthearted, it is easy to see how powerful analyzing objective, real-world usage is when combined with applying a rating of 1–5. This is especially true when considering it in the context of an impact assessment and the importance that it carries.

How is this principle applied within the setting of a business? Businesses and organizations are not an iTunes playlist. The people, processes, and technologies that make the business function are given the most accurate values when interview-based data are validated by subjective reporting data. These objects are real, tangible, and have a visible, measurable impact on the business every day. Inside or outside of the building, more or less than 3 years, janitor, server, or CEO—each object that affects the business can and most likely will *change*. As an emergency management professional, it is a responsibility that the best work is done to determine an object's value. We must determine that value with the combination of an informed opinion and a measurable and objective appraisal.

* * *

The author realizes that this is a best-case scenario and a goal to be aimed at, but there are ways in which this measurement of value can begin to be implemented today. Until then, here is a simple formula, regardless of which value is being protected: Informed employees knowledgeable in the objects they are scoring can complete a good assessment. A better assessment can be completed by interviews with informed executives and evidenced data. The best assessments are completed by the combination of informed executives and analyzing real-time data. All assessments are valuable, and all can be continuously improved.

* * *

7.9.4 Back to the Weighted Score and the
Rigorous Application of Data

A lot has been accomplished thus far, and yet there's still more ground to cover. The weighted score and a range of criticalities can be determined based on big data. The needs of the organization have enabled the visualization of organizational health. The objects have been rated and valued based on the ranges of criticalities. But this still is not enough. At this point, the practicing emergency manager is a highly trained soldier, carrying himself with professionalism, and is a valuable asset on the battlefield, but he's not a member of the Delta Force … yet.

Now that the professional is in possession of real-time, valuable, meaningful data, it is time to put them to work with the weighted score. The weighted score, the foundation of this entire exercise, is not an end unto itself. For these purposes we will go back to the analogy of a doctor using the weighted score to determine overall health. Recall that the limitation of the weighted score is that it does not provide a solution to the problem—only that the patient is in danger. The weighted score provides a business case for action, but if that is all it is being used for, let's hope you never see this doctor!

The doctor, looking at the patient tagged "critical," needs to know what action to take in order to save the patient's life. The trained professional he is, he quickly takes hold of the weighted score and tears it into the components that comprise a healthy individual. The doctor checks airway, pulse, blood pressure, and nervous system function.

Comparing the patient to these elements of health, the doctor quickly determines that the problem endangering our patient's life is a blocked airway. With the precision of a machine, he quickly performs a tracheotomy, saving the patient's life and moving to the next "critical" patient. This next one is different; he has a severed hand, is losing blood, and his blood pressure is critically low. With the same speed and efficiency, the doctor applies a tourniquet and orders the patient to immediate surgery. The next patient only has a mild burn and is barely affected according to the elements of the weighted score. The doctor orders water, bandaging, and pain management.

In the context of business and government, the weighted score not only provides the foundation for a valuable and effective impact assessment, but it also provides the tool that allows the emergency management professional to slice-and-dice the data in numerous applications. For example, not only can the set of objects be valued by the impact of their loss within the range of criticalities, but they can also be compared to each component of the weighted score for a cross-sectional view of organizational impact.

As opposed to rating objects by the total weighted component score, we can now view the individual weighted components applied to each object or set of objects. It is here that we introduce the concept of viewing objects based on a single component as opposed to the total weighted object score and provide a new example for using big data. This is the true power of big data, and it enables us to view objects, or sets of objects, with a multifaceted view—much like light refracting through a prism, or the view given by a kaleidoscope. We will identify this as **the component-based weighted score** (Figure 7.6).

To be clear, the same mathematical principles used in Section 7.8 apply. However, it is the method for obtaining the data that is being illustrated below.

For this example, the weighted score will be composed of these components:

Protecting revenue	10%
Protecting customers	10%
Protecting employees	20%
Community value add	20%
Legal and regulatory compliance	40%

Looking at the real-time data we see that even though Brenda is in the finance department, she only touches money when helping a customer solve a problem with a fraudulent order. Therefore, according to this measurement, she scores low on revenue.

Applying customers to her, we see that she has customer involvement when intervening in fraudulent orders. Therefore her customer value goes up in an area we did not see by looking at only the weighted score. Going through this method we see that she also plays a big role in compliance, and in revenue, as a poorly handled fraudulent purchase can end up costing more in regulatory fines. It can also cost in the loss of a customer and negative public perception. By applying the components of the weighted score to Brenda, we see that she holds a much higher value to the company than indicated by the weighted score alone. *Consider the possibilities!*

Figure 7.6 A component-based weighted score gives us a multifaceted view of the organization by viewing individual weighted components applied to an object or set of objects.

7.9.5 Creating a Range of Criticality Based on Big Data

To summarize this section, it is important to note that rigorous analysis does not rely on one data source alone, and does not take any data for granted, but applies it in many different ways to create a holistic view of the impacted objects within an organization. Each piece of the puzzle is important alone and together with the other pieces. In *Managing Emerging Risk,* it was discussed that the effective emergency manager has to be able to apply data. He or she has to know how to work the data and apply them to real-world scenarios—to think about them and not just take them at face value.

7.10 SUMMARY

Based on the impact horizon created in Chapter 1, we can see that the objects (people, processes, and systems) inside the impact horizon will be measured based on an alignment to the core values of the organization presented in Chapter 2 *and* consideration for national and state laws and industry-specific regulations by scoring them based on the percentage of impact to each core value that is agreed to by key stakeholders. In this chapter we have discussed a means for measuring potential impacts using an established range of criticality, a logical order, and a common taxonomy.

The work product for the fourth principle should be delivered as scores of objects in value ranges generated from the combination of interviews and big data.

Establishing the range of criticality and logical order of all measured potential impacts based on a common taxonomy generates four deliverables:

1. Three or four criticality scores applied to the weighted score
2. The population of a range of criticalities based on scored objects or a set of objects utilizing a key performance indicator or data-driven approach
3. A logical order of all scored objects or sets of objects in the range of criticalities
4. A common taxonomy for all things scored in the range of criticalities

It should be noted that the application of these concepts is complex; however, it should be given that the impact assessment establishes more than a business case—it sets our policy toward disasters and terror events. Moving forward, we will discuss how to deal with specific executive overrides in depth. Also, Chapter 8 will create increased certainty in the weighted score algorithm we have just discussed that will illuminate what we measure, along with a common taxonomy of what will be measured, and a logical order of how to group and cross-reference what we measure.

7.11 QUESTIONS

1. How would you establish an applicable range of criticality that can apply to people, processes, and technologies?
2. What is the meaning and importance of using the constraints and liberties when using the first three principles to allow for flexibility when applying and analyzing the final weighted scores across multiple objects?
3. How would you specify the limits of interview-based data collection analysis versus the use of big data and expert opinion in scoring objects across the range of criticality?
4. Describe a logical order and the hierarchical relationships of objects measured using a weighted score and placed within the range of criticality.
5. Provide an example of an applied taxonomy and the creation of a common naming standard for a set of technological components.

ENDNOTES

1. U.S. Department of Homeland Security. 2011. NTAS Public Guide. http://www.dhs.gov/files/publications/ntas-public-guide.shtm (accessed September 16, 2011).
2. Schwartz, Richard B., McManus, John B., and Swienton, Raymond E., eds. 2008. *Tactical Emergency Medicine*. Philadelphia: Lippincott Williams & Wilkins.
3. Lee, Elsa. 2008. *Homeland Security and Private Sector Business: Corporations' Role in Critical Infrastructure Protection*. Boca Raton, FL: Auerbach Publications.
4. Cycorp. About Cycorp. http://cyc.com/cyc/company/about (accessed September 27, 2011).
5. Downie, Richard D. 2005. Defining Integrated Operations. http://findarticles.com/p/articles/mi_m0KNN/is_38/ai_n15631260/?tag=content;col1 (accessed September 27, 2011).
6. Ibid.

8

The Fifth Principle
Document Deviations and Overrides

8.1 KEY TERMS

8.2 OBJECTIVES

After reading this chapter you will be able to:

1. Understand and describe the nature of executive overrides and deviations.
2. Apply the appropriate course of action given a specific type of override request.
3. Differentiate between expert opinion and process bias.
4. Apply common sense and spot overrides before the stakeholders do.
5. Demonstrate a deeper appreciation for the cultural biases that shape the quality of our impact assessments.

8.3 OVERVIEW: DOCUMENTED DEVIATIONS AND OVERRIDES

Working our way to the last of the five guiding principles of postmodern impact assessments, we have generated multiple work products and deliverables that have led to a final set of objects that have been scored across a range of criticality and that can be discussed using a common taxonomy.

The application of the first four principles has taken us from an established impact horizon to a final set of value-scored objects across a range of criticalities. We've considered some options (in Chapter 7) about how to achieve the final scoring in the range of criticalities, including the use of interviews, or the use of expert interviews, big data, and real data flows. Remarkably, no matter how one arrives at the final deliverable of scoring objects across a range of criticalities, the practitioner will encounter **deviations** and **overrides** to the logic used to generate the final results by either stakeholders or other practitioners. A deviation is a requested recalculation of the impacts based on missing data or poor logic. An override is an

Figure 8.1 Key concepts in this chapter are addressing overrides and deviations based on expert opinion, cultural needs, and the application of common sense.

executive or key stakeholder simply demanding a change to an object's criticality based on opinion or observation (Figure 8.1).

In this chapter, we can move forward with the fifth and final principle, to better understand, manage, and document these deviations and overrides.

* * *

Even with the sound applications of the first four principles, deviations and overrides are to be expected and can be the result of biases, missed expert input, or cultural conditions. While the first four principles do much to eliminate the "noise on the channel" of our analysis, outliers, deviations, and overrides are part and parcel of any analysis—including a potential impact assessment.

* * *

The fifth guiding principle of postmodern impact assessments consists of a simple method for dealing with deviations and overrides in the final impact analysis deliverable. Specifically, what is called for is the documentation of such deviations and overrides and their source. While the remedy for deviations and overrides is simple, exploring the personal biases, professional and expert perspectives, and cultural issues surrounding our criticality scoring of objects is much more nuanced. It is as necessary to understand what to do with these outliers as it is to understand the why of deviations and overrides. We will be exploring these concepts in this chapter. In doing so, we can deliver our final potential impact assessment.

The fifth principle of documenting deviations and overrides generates a view that says: "All deviations, including non-actuarial findings, opinion-based scores, and executive overrides to the process should be documented." It also creates a result that requires that *key stakeholders accept a detailed exception list that describes the expectation to guidance, the individual responsible, and the date of the deviation or override.*

While this task is simple, as we just mentioned, understanding *why* such deviations and overrides occur can be a very interesting exercise in professional judgment.

* * *

There are all manner of reasons why a sound analysis may find itself challenged with deviations or overrides. There are common reasons behind deviations and overrides. They include personal bias, expert opinion, or cultural challenges.

* * *

The key deliverable of the fifth principle is the documentation of any changes to our final range of criticalities, or the scored objects within them, based on overrides or deviations to our analysis.

While this task is simple, as we just mentioned, understanding *why* such deviations and overrides occur can be a very interesting exercise in professional judgment.

The key lessons of this chapter are that emergency managers are responsible for completing the potential impact assessment with a keen understanding of any deviations or overrides based on personal bias, expert opinion, or cultural challenges. While a sound analytical model will minimize most deviations and overrides, it will not eliminate them. The final impact assessment must consider the who, what, when, and why of any deviation or override to be considered complete. The job of the emergency manager here is to finalize his or her findings with the documentation of any deviations or overrides to scores of objects within the range of criticalities—especially the why!

8.4 WHY DEVIATIONS AND OVERRIDES OCCUR

Our approach to developing a potential impact assessment thus far has been to generate a thoughtful and considerate approach to understanding all of the factors that go into an analysis of impact, understanding that these impacts are only potentials that will occur *if* risk manifests itself. You'll recall from the first chapter of this text that we differentiate between risk and impact. Risk can come from anywhere and be manifest in a number of ways both probable and possible; however, impacts are *knowable*.

Emergency managers often struggle with a process that calls for the first two major deliverables in a program being the risk assessment and the impact assessment, and end up falling into a sort of "analysis paralysis." Stakeholders can, and often do, take issue with what *could* be a risk to their organization compared to what *will be impacted* if a risk manifests itself as an actual event. This paralysis often stalls the program and holds the emergency manager in limbo as stakeholders contemplate the risk and impacts, rather than moving on to the strategies of remediation, mitigation, and planning activities. In turn, this stall leads to overrides, which are caused by two primary reasons. The first reason is due to **personal biases**. A personal bias is an emotional reaction toward a factual issue that impairs judgment.

A simple example will illustrate what so often happens in the course of delivering a complete solution to organizations, both large and small. When a doctor is presented with a healthy, nonsmoking patient who harbors no known bad habits or genetic disposition to disease, the patient and the doctor could agree on one thing—that he would never get cancer from smoking. However, the patient might not agree that he has a "low

Figure 8.2 Just like it is difficult to convince a healthy person about the possibility of disease, it is difficult to convince a healthy organization to minimize the impact of a risk that has not occurred.

risk of cancer diagnosis," believing he has *some* risk of cancer—as many people who get cancer are nonsmokers.

The patient is correct that his risks are lower than normal; this does not change the fact that *the risk simply exists,* and many people develop cancer for myriad reasons besides smoking. Uncertainty may enter the patient's mind regarding the risk, realizing there is a chance, but from here it becomes much more difficult for the doctor. In our example, an emergency manager is like a doctor that is then required to explain the potential impacts of cancer to a patient that has not been diagnosed with the disease (Figure 8.2).

Explaining the impacts of cancer to a recently diagnosed patient can be a grueling process for the doctor and patient. There may be a harsh treatment schedule, constant tests and blood work, radiation exposure, surgery, and perhaps even death. While the facts are necessary for the patient to understand when beginning the treatment process, discussion of the facts themselves may cause an even lower quality of life.

While a patient diagnosed with cancer would listen to the doctor, the healthy patient may have tuned out the doctor's impact assessment, as he simply does not believe the risk is possible, let alone the sordid impacts of a ravaging disease that has never been considered.

In *Managing Emerging Risk*, we discussed at length how to deal with individuals who cannot understand or imagine risk. However, impacts are much more personal, detailed, and to a certain extent, harder to accept because they are very real. Talking with the cyclist Lance Armstrong about the impacts of cancer before he ever had it might have been a difficult, if not impossible task.

Even as a professional athlete, understanding the impact cancer would have on his life would be very challenging. As the master of his destiny with a rigorous diet, workout schedule, and regimen of vitamins, he might simply deny that the risk was even there, and surely would have nothing to do with the impacts of cancer to his career or life—let alone prepare for them!

It is in this case, as is the case with many stakeholders, that the emergency manager is being asked to describe impacts of an event not yet experienced, but impacts that are factual should the event occur. It is the emotional reaction to the facts that causes the personal bias. Like a healthy patient listening to a doctor describe the impacts of cancer, stakeholders may react with denial, abstraction, misunderstanding, and even outrage over the discussion of impacts that have never manifested themselves in a risk.

* * *

Personal bias is often the root cause of executive overrides.

* * *

The second reason for an override or deviation is *expert opinion*. Here, we encounter a third party that has not been consulted during our original evaluation and analysis. Sticking with our example of a professional bicycle racer, we could use the analogy of the team coach. The coach, on hearing that we are discussing the impacts of cancer to his best rider, will simply state that in his expert opinion none of his racers have ever had cancer. While that might be true, it is not the risk of cancer (which is built into our lives as humans) that we are discussing; *it is the impacts*. Nonetheless, because he was not consulted and has never witnessed the impacts of cancer on one of his racers, he disagrees and offers his own opinion about the impacts we have measured. By not including this "expert" in every step we missed an important expert view that can now result in significant deviations in our analysis and even override our findings altogether.

* * *

Expert opinions are often the cause of overrides and deviations.

* * *

251

Finally, an impact assessment conducted in a culture with views that vary from our Western conventions will nearly always create disagreement, deviations, and overrides. Staying with our example, another coach of another team may consider the same impacts of cancer for one of his riders as a minor inconvenience, or a major assault on his or her worldview. For example, in China a diagnosis and description of cancer impacts might be considered a certain type of heresy toward the People's Republic. In France, it could be considered a nonissue because team riders are easy to replace. In either case, these cultural views will result in deviations and overrides. Not understanding the culture in which we are conducting our impact assessment is a recipe for confronting all manner of overrides and deviations in our final delivery.

* * *

Opinions based on cultural perceptions are often the cause of overrides and deviations.

* * *

In the coming sections we will review some key challenges surrounding the personal biases, expert opinions, and cultural perceptions that are the most common whys of overrides and deviations in potential impact assessments. You see, once we measure potential impacts, we obviously *have to do something about them*—either remediate the impact or plan for it through mitigation. Suddenly, our impact analysis has real consequences, and if we have not applied the first four guiding principles, and are not prepared to be challenged with overrides and deviations, there are two possible impacts to our study. One possible impact is that the impact analysis findings are changed. The other is that the program itself is just stopped completely—dead in its tracks.

8.5 PERSONAL BIASES

In Chapter 2, we discuss the influence of personal opinion and executive overrides as a common occurrence in our profession. These personal biases not only shape the nature of the data collected in the course of our analysis, but also often radically challenge our findings as we near the completion of our work. Employees tend to overstate their contribution to the value of the organization, only to retract those statements when

Figure 8.3 Personal opinions can derail an impact analysis if not validated with real data and planned for by involving the right stakeholders.

confronted with need to back up systems, design meaningful delegation and succession plans, or participate in the remaining tasks of mitigation and planning (Figure 8.3).

Further, key executives often rely on the inputs of their managers or line workers to provide expertise in their respective areas of impact only to disagree with the broad picture of impacts of our five guiding principles. Clearly, each of the first four principles requires a listing of who was consulted and what the results were. So, as we have moved through the process of establishing an impact horizon, generating and weighing core values, assessing legal and regulatory issues, and establishing a range of criticality, common logic, and final scoring, we would *hope* that practitioners are involving senior management and executives in those decisions.

Yet often, this is not the case. Private sector impact analyses are often done with little or no consultation with key executives. Public sector

CATASTROPHIC IMPACT AND LOSS

impact analyses often have some leadership oversight. However, they do not generate the four touch points outlined in the first four principles that would negate an executive override. Overstated impacts, poorly rendered data, and a complete misunderstanding of what is in harm's way are often the result. Executive overrides, as you will recall from Chapter 2, are often used to forward agendas other than those that are prudent and based on principle. Even though the consideration of deviations and overrides is the fifth principle, it should be stated that an experienced practitioner would enter the first principle and every other principle thereafter with his or her eyes wide open, *looking for sources of potential executive overrides.*

Executive overrides are the expression of a personal bias by an individual who has the power to change a criticality score or the basis of findings in the impact analysis. The what and who of this business are fairly straightforward. The what is that no matter how much effort has been placed into the analysis, there is new information, or withheld information, that changes the criticality scores or alters the whole analysis. The who is quite simply a key stakeholder with executive power.

While it is understood that business dynamics, operational realities, and even the core values of the organization can change during the analysis, it is important that these executives are met with often in order to keep the approach on track and spot any such changes early. If not, we can be certain that any executive override is the result of poor project management and communication during the impact analysis. In this case, the why of an executive override is a failure of the emergency manager to effectively communicate his or her findings to key stakeholders during each step in the five guiding principles.

That considered, it is often the case that a major change in the organization's approach to business continuity, disaster recovery, or emergency management has been withheld from the analyst during the construction of the potential impact analysis and will only be revealed by key stakeholders or executives at the last moment, during the final draft review of the results. In this situation, the why of executive overrides may be due to many factors. Among them, we might encounter several biases and agendas that simply need to be documented as the who, what, and why of any changes that occur to our findings. Let's consider some of the significant reasons executives will change criticality scores late in the analysis.

Perhaps the first and most common reason for an executive to override a change in the criticality scoring of an object, or set of objects, using our method is an obvious and simple one: The objects were not scored correctly due to the fact that they are **data outliers**. Outliers are people, processes, and systems that defy our scheme of a weighted score, do not have legal or regulatory issues that might compel them to be more critical, but are obviously necessary during the response effort for the organization.

For example, Blackberries and iPhones do not, if lost, result in a loss of financial, customer service, brand, or regulatory impacts. However, an executive, based on his expert view of the enterprise and what will be required first to effectively run the organization, will override the analytical score to correct for this error. Here, the smart emergency manager has an opportunity—to get in front of the obvious!

If we see objects that defy our scoring logic but are clearly required to affect rapid recovery after an event, *recommend them for overrides before an executive does.* Do not wait for a sharp stakeholder to find you so beholden to our approach for sound analysis that we miss the obvious outlying person, process, or system that has a major impact on our objects ranked by criticality.

* * *

The sharp emergency manager can spot outlying people, processes, and systems that should be adjusted manually or by override based on logic that is outside of the systemic analysis before a key stakeholder does. Not beating the stakeholder to the punch and recommending an override is a great method of undermining the impact analysis altogether!

* * *

The identification of outliers is a necessary result of any structured analysis and relies on keen, expert practice and oversight to catch. Using the best judgment available, the emergency manager should capture these early and recommend that they be scored by virtue of override, not the logic created by applying the first four principles. If we fail to do so, the key stakeholders and executives we are working with are likely to find them for us.

The second most common reason for executive overrides is that the initial goals of the impact assessment were never truly understood. In this scenario, key stakeholders have misstated the impact horizon and the analysis is unfounded based on the core values or regulatory conditions under which the analysis has taken place. If the underlying reason for an impact assessment is to simply meet the first step of a regulatory guidance and not to take further remediation and mitigation actions, there will be a multitude of executive overrides at the end of the analysis.

The smart practitioner will watch closely as the core values and regulatory framework for the analysis are crafted. An early emphasis on regulatory requirements with a shortsighted impact horizon and little consideration for core values is an early indicator of an impact assessment being crafted for audit reasons only. Only the prudent and mindful practitioner will spot these early indicators and adjust the assessment approach to reflect these realities early. If the customer or organization withholds this information altogether, there will be a multitude of changes in the criticality scores based on executive overrides.

Here is the why of misunderstood outcomes for an audit-oriented impact assessment: Often, organizations fear that the impact analysis will be tainted by the reality that they have no intent of doing anything other than passing an audit using the resulting data in an impact assessment. Document who made the overrides, what changed, and the reason, in the final report and move on. This client or organization has lied to itself and the professional serving it. *We cannot put pretty on the pig.* There are executive overrides in this case due to regulatory considerations. If we did not see it coming, shame on us; the five guiding principles put many opportunities on the table to spot this organizational position and we missed them!

Finally, executive overrides can be based on a resistance to disclose or take action on the findings. In the case of disclosure, it may be that the organization is about to be sold to a competitor or is undertaking merger and acquisition activities that were not apparent or discussed at the onset of the analysis. Document the reason for the changes to criticality scores as a reorientation of goals and move on. The findings are correct, but their impacts have been adjusted for ease of use during a large-scale organizational change.

In the case of resistance to taking action, this often occurs in both the private and the public sector. A resistance to take action is often directly tied to the imagined cost of backups, redundancies, and planning efforts that must take place in the face of loss of multiple, highly critical objects. An executive override or deviation will be requested to lower the perceived cost of taking action based on the findings. The skilled practitioner should mark these requested overrides as "changed due to cost considerations." If the customer or organization refuses to take responsibility for changing *real* potential impacts due to cost considerations, a professional emergency manager is encouraged to *not change the documented reason for the override.*

The final document should state, in fairly concise terms, that these are the correct scores, and reflect the impact horizon, core values, legal and regulatory issues, and scoring criteria that the organization agreed to in each phase of the project. The practice of the five guiding principles includes who was consulted and who was not for each phase. The only ethical response is to change the scores based on the reason given—cost. Let the customer know that it is welcome to change its internal documentation upon the completion of the professional review using a template provided; however, do not change the final deliverable without documenting the reason for the change based on the factors given.

Whether the overrides and deviations are a result of executive bias, outliers, misunderstood drivers, changes to the underlying dynamics of the organization, or a resistance to forward actions and costs, the role of the emergency manager is to be in front of any changes that might occur, and to truthfully document the changes that do occur. The importance of handling executive overrides and deviations with professionalism and clarity is the basis for professional excellence. Using every tool available in the five principles, a sound analysis and strong practitioner should spot deviations and overrides early, document them honestly, and serve the clients' needs completely with professional integrity.

8.6 EXPERT OPINION

There are many process-oriented methods of arriving at ranges of criticality and scoring of objects. Six Sigma, Kaizen, and other continuous improvement methods that use key performance indicators as part of the define, measure, analyze, design, and verify (DMAIC) approach to continuous process improvement can all generate weighted scores. The author has extensive experience with manufacturing firms such as Caterpillar, Motorola, Toyota, and Honeywell that subscribe to these quality management tools and methods.

Even with extensive experience in using these tools and approaches, it is important to note that even the most practiced emergency manager may not be a content expert in the enterprise in which he or she is working, or even in the geographical or political area in which he or she is serving as a public servant. For example, in Six Sigma there is a certification level of Black Belt that requires years of practical experience in using these analytical tools and multiple qualifying exams. With this in mind, it is easy to see how an "expert opinion" may be introduced late in the development, and even at the time of the delivery of an impact analysis, and can

Figure 8.4 Process-oriented methods of scoring criticality can disrupt the delivery of an impact assessment based on the five guiding principles. Get in front of these disruptions by involving experts at the beginning of the impact analysis.

radically disrupt the findings through requests for deviations and overrides based on the perception of a new process expert (Figure 8.4).

To be clear, the application of the five principles is designed to seek out key stakeholders early and to gather their input regarding the impact horizon, core values, regulatory and legal issues, and scoring methods that resulted in the final criticality range and scores. However, it is not uncommon to be confronted with an expert in process at the end of the analysis and to have multiple deviations and overrides requested as a result.

First, the professional should review the approach and verify that checkpoints have been met, and stakeholders who participated in the analysis with the expert, and verify that all assumptions, data, and logic applied have been considered before any changes were documented. Often, the requested changes are because the expert does not understand the process from which the final scores were derived. A conversation about how the final tiers and scores were created will help to inform the expert. From this position, the practitioner can then take expert opinion under consideration and apply any overrides or deviations with the notation that they were made based on expert judgment by the appropriate (and documented) new stakeholder.

An interesting article appeared in the November–December 2006 issue of *USA Army Logistician* regarding Six Sigma that stated: "The dangers of a single paradigmatic orientation (in this case, that of technical rationality) can blind us to values associated with double-loop learning and the learning organization, organization adaptability, workforce creativity and development, humanizing the workplace, cultural awareness, and strategy making."[1]

Based on an interesting example provided by a friend, the author would like to discuss what can only be referred to as a process blindness that is built into the myriad process management "isms," one that not only inflects itself on expert opinion, but the very crafting of potential impact analysis presented in this text. Below is the story.

My editor is very active at a local gym (which for the purposes of this book will remain unnamed). He was at his gym and in between sets of working out ventured to a drinking fountain for water.

This event in and of itself is nothing out of the ordinary. However, it is important to note that the water fountains were in a state of disrepair as other members of the gym had pounded them and the easy-to-use buttons had been beaten off of the aluminum housing. This left open gaps in the housing of the buttons, and all that was left to be pressed to turn on the water were two very small buttons on the front or the side of the device.

My editor, deciding to go for the button on the left, pressed it in and noticed a sensation of electricity in his fingertip. Having once worked in the property and casualty insurance business, thoughts of liability raced through his mind and he sprang into action!

Approaching the manager he casually said, "Hey, I just got shocked using the fountain." The manager of the gym responded, "Yeah. I know. I put in a ticket for it." (To put in a ticket is to request a repair via an email or other system that tracks repair items and the response to such requests.)

My editor was caught off guard by the honesty, quickness of response, and general lack of concern for his well-being, and stammered as his brain battled the idiocy of the process. While he is quite the wordsmith when it comes to editing my work, in this instance the words painfully escaped his lips, "You need to put a sign on it, or mark it somehow … that, you know, it's broken!"

With the same general lack of concern, the manager replied, "Huh. Yeah. You're right." With that, the editor returned to his workout, with the larger shock coming from the process-oriented lack of judgment exhibited by the manager of the gym—not the electricity flowing freely into the water fountain.

Fortunately, neither the editor nor an elderly patron of the gym with a pacemaker was injured. However, the potential for a larger impact had been present for an unknowable amount of time. This experience illustrates a great point that is difficult to explain without a real-world example.

With all of the processes corporate America embraces, and in a world where we "submit a ticket" when there's a problem because *that's the process*, we oftentimes find that the commonsense thing to do is left stranded outside in the rain, staring at the problem, able to help, but listlessly waiting for the process to somehow take care of the immediate issue.

Sadly, this example too often reflects the reality of how problems are dealt with in the day-to-day resolution of issues. Management and executives often lose sight of the commonsense response of putting out a sign that says "Do not use" because *they possess an idolatrous confidence in a "process."* They literally cannot see the end of the trail through the forest of process-isms they have created, inherited, revised, and trusted in so much. Just like submitting a ticket for repair for an electrified water fountain does not remove the nearly certain negative impact to a gym member, neither does submitting to a process ensure protection.

The extra step of thought, foresight, and a simple, genuine interest in your job and the welfare of your constituents demands that the goal be seen through the obstacles—that of protecting what is valuable to the organization. Whether it is customers, processes, employees, or servers, the processes should still be followed, but not at a loss for the application of common sense. *Common sense* is an amazingly powerful tool because the first thing it does is slows down, or prevents, further impacts through the impact horizon.

In this specific case, the submission of a ticket alone showed more concern for the water dispenser than for the customers of the gym. The water fountain was treated with more respect than the people who used it. The facilities were given a higher priority than the members who pay to keep it open. It would have been better for the company to designate the fountain unsafe and to *never repair it*, than for one member to go through harm (as trivial as it may have been) because of a lack of common sense.

This leaves us with a simple observation. Expert opinion, when executed based on process, knows the limits and boundaries of the process, and knows when exception, deviations, and overrides to the process are necessary.

Consideration of expert opinion should be done with the practitioner who took up the role of conducting a process-based impact assessment, giving solid consideration to the expert opinion of the new stakeholder, making overrides necessary based on expert opinion, and challenging new process assumptions when they defy common sense.

In conclusion, expert opinion overrides and deviations should be captured early by identifying the right key stakeholders and consulting them often. When this is not possible, the boundaries and limits of process must be considered in conjunction with the careful application of the five principles and a deviation-by-deviation discussion must be had, with each resulting change documented and a clear reason for the change captured.

8.7 CULTURAL ISSUES

In Chapter 1 we discuss how we are living in the information age, which includes a much broader impact horizon based on globalized supply chains, labor arbitrage (moving knowledge and other workers offshore or onshore to leverage lower labor costs), and the cultural challenges that are embedded in the postmodern business context. We've briefly discussed negative public perception impacts in Chapters 2 and 3; however, we have *not* discussed how or why cultural issues in a multinational context can result in deviations or overrides in an impact assessment.

It is important to understand that lacking a view of impacts that does not include globalized operations, cultural boundaries, and varied local and national worldviews is setting up an impact assessment that is doomed to fail from the start.

You might also recall that we referenced these challenges in Chapter 3, while discussing legal and regulatory issues, saying:

> The American approach to criticality is culturally biased, and to believe that these same criticalities based on American impacts inform the same mission objectives in China, India, Mexico, or Europe is just poor judgment. In China, for example, any effort to privately recover your business after a catastrophic failure that includes the release of information to the public, which downplays the People's Republic of China's role in keeping your company safe, could be construed as spreading "rumors during a disaster" and will land you in jail.

Here is a closer look at what we want to explore in the context of deviations and overrides regarding cultural issues. Cultural issues can manifest themselves in three unique ways during an impact assessment that will lead to an unraveling of the data and logic used to create a range of impacts and criticalities, as well as radical deviations in the final analysis. The three issues are international law, cultural perspectives, and international finance. As U.S.-based emergency managers, we may think these issues will not play a role in our impact analysis; however, if we reconsider the underlying thesis of this book, which is that impacts are evolving based on postmodernism, we must come to terms with the need to consider impacts to the organization we serve that may well manifest themselves from overseas.

8.7.1 International Law

For the global, and highly mobile, emergency manager who sees himself or herself traveling to China to conduct an impact analysis for a key supplier in the organization's supply chain, or even an internationally owned subsidiary of the U.S. organization that we are working for, here are some interesting things about China's laws we may want to consider. As reported from the U.S. State Department:

> Participating in unauthorized political activities or protests against Chinese policy in China, may result in lengthy detentions and may impact your eligibility for future visas to visit China. Foreigners engaging in pro-Falun Gong or pro-Tibetan activities have been detained or immediately deported from China, usually at their own expense, after being questioned. Several reported they were subject to interrogations and were physically abused during detention. In addition, some alleged that personal property, including clothing, cameras, and computers, was not returned.[2]

We can assume that we will not be participating in political activities or protests while we are in China doing our work, that is, until we better understand what China considers to be a protest.

Consider the case of Xue Feng, a geologist, who has been held for 8 years and counting after a 2½-year-long trial for "spying." Mr. Feng is a U.S. citizen of Chinese ancestry who provided data to a U.S. company (his employer) regarding an oil industry database he had created. The PRC saw this act as one of "selling state secrets." He is still in a Chinese jail,

Figure 8.5 Chinese law serves as a great example of the need to consider the cultural issues that will arise when working in the international community. Something considered standard procedure in the United States could earn you a long prison stay in China! (Used with permission, copyright Hung Chung Chih/ Shutterstock.com.)

and "the geologist has claimed that interrogators burned his arms with cigarettes and hit him on the head with an ashtray" (Figure 8.5).[3]

Back to the U.S. State Department, which says:

> If you are arrested in China, the U.S.-China Consular Convention requires Chinese authorities to notify the U.S. Embassy or nearest Consulate General of your arrest within four days. If you hold the citizenship of another country, including China, and entered China using a passport of that country, Chinese authorities are not required to notify the U.S. Embassy or a U.S. consulate of your arrest. Typically, the police will not allow anyone other than a consular officer to visit you during your initial detention period, including your family or even an attorney. Bail is rarely granted in China, and you can be subject to detention for many months before being granted a trial.[4]

However, how could conducting a U.S. company's impact assessment land an emergency manager from the United States in jail? Consider international law, in this case the Chinese law for counterterrorism, that according to a report by China's English news media, "China View," has 70 clauses; here are 2 of them:

1. Units and individuals are prohibited from fabricating or spreading false information regarding emergencies and government efforts to cope with emergencies.
2. Behavior that contravenes public security management rules or criminal statutes will be prosecuted.

So here's a nonlegal, but serious question about how to approach an impact assessment in China. If the organization we work for wants us to start asking questions about response times and intergovernmental response to disasters and terror attacks in China, the behavior can be construed as "fabrication," spreading of "false rumors," and "contravening public security management rules." This is behavior that will land a foreigner in jail.

Even if you are a *U.S. employee* of a *U.S. company* that is doing business in China, you should understand that "foreign managers or company owners have in some cases been physically 'held hostage' as leverage during dispute negotiations. The Embassy and Consulates General have no legal or law enforcement authority in China and cannot get involved in private disputes nor give legal advice."[5]

Chinese employees of a U.S. company may not be forthcoming with data, and worse, may consider the questions regarding terrorism and natural disaster impacts as illegal, and report the offending emergency manager to authorities. China is a communist country with no extradition agreements with the United States. There is little that can be done by a host company or by U.S. authorities for a U.S. citizen charged with espionage, spying, or simply creating a "commercial dispute."

Here, the deviations and overrides we are most likely to encounter will be those of a part of the organization that we are considering unable or unwilling to contribute to the effort, and an international legal system that is constraining (to say the least!) in conducting the affairs of an impact assessment!

To deal with these deviations, the author recommends remote interviews and data collection, *with an emphasis on data, not speculation*, and erring on the side of caution in terms of international travel. The international stakeholders should not override the scores, and the organization may want to consider not publishing the data found in the impact assessment of its overseas operations in China at all. Publishing the data puts all U.S. executives of the company at risk of prosecution when they are in China.

We have discussed China at length in this section; however, Mexico, India, and even the EU have some very interesting international laws that must be considered and understood to affect an accurate impact assessment. Not the least of which is that in several of these countries, it is a *criminal offense* to not protect the well-being of employees—not a civil liability, as it is widely considered in the United States.

On a lighter note, China does not seem to have many terrorists, and therefore people that live and work there often do not understand the U.S. concept of terrorism-generated impacts. There are only two terrorist groups in China: the East Turkestan Islamic Movement (ETIM) and Tibetan monks. The ETIM is suspected of planning attacks during the 2008 Olympics, and the Tibetan monks keep immolating themselves in protest over the Chinese occupation of Tibet. In China these are not terrorists, they are *separatists*.

8.7.2 Cultural Perspectives: India

India and Japan prove to have interesting cultural perspectives regarding terrorism and natural disasters. For starters, the data regarding natural disasters in India are very poor and natural disasters are rarely reported. There is an effort at the nation-state level to gather data; however, these data are biased by the want for U.S. businesses to do more offshoring of manufacturing and information technology work in India.

This cultural bias of downplaying natural disasters comes through loud and clear if one is an emergency manager trying to interview a facilities manager in Bangalore. One will not be given readily available information on earthquakes or floods in the region, and terrorism is rarely discussed openly. In India, discussing such things is incredibly counterproductive to the aspirational goals of the nation.

Further, while India continues to portray a vision of low seismic activity, Bangalore, the nation's seismic equivalent of our Silicon Valley, has recently been discovered to be sitting on an active fault capable of producing quakes in the 4.0- to 5.0-magnitude range. This is low by U.S. standards; however, many of the buildings in Bangalore are made of mud, the city has a substandard water distribution system, and emergency response is very immature. Therefore, a 5.0-magnitude earthquake would result in much higher potential impacts in Bangalore than it would in San Francisco.

It should also be noted that India ranks third on Nationmaster.com's terrorism activity list, with the United States and Iraq holding the top two spots. Driving around Bangalore, it is hard to miss the IBM/Dell facility with its armed guards, 12-foot fence with razor wire topping, a building set far back from the perimeter, and well-hidden office complexes. This is the face of American business in India. Many other companies settle for much less in terms of security, let alone building integrity. The cultural perception in India is one that says, "There is not much to worry about" in terms of impacts, but the stance of the largest U.S. companies there tells a different story.

8.7.3 Cultural Perspectives: Japan

Meanwhile, the cultural perceptions surrounding natural disasters and terror attacks in Japan, another major supply chain player in the postmodern world, are ones of humility and a nearly frantic need to be "normal" in the face of disasters and terror. This has a great influence on the impact data one might gather there. Consider the 1995 sarin gas attacks on the Tokyo subway system.

The reader may recall that these attacks were perpetrated by the Aum Shinrikyo cult and were one of the earliest modern uses of chemical or biological weapons by a terrorist group in modern history. Sarin is 26 times more deadly than cyanide. Haruki Murakami, an internationally acclaimed author, studied the attack through direct interviews with every witness, victim, or responder he could locate. A telling condition of the Japanese feelings toward impacts is only "40% of the 140 individuals he could locate would consent to interviews"[6] about the attacks. In contrast, in America, at least 300 victims of 9/11 gave their testimony to Congress.

While the 9/11 attacks undoubtedly produced more victims, those victims do not feel a need to "put the event behind them," as Murakami reports that his Japanese countrymen do. This culture of quiet suffering is part of the sociological makeup of Japan. A culture that seems to say "I am not a victim" is one in which understanding impacts can be very difficult.

Understanding that cultural perspectives skew potential data collection and can result in deviations and overrides is an important role in the process of conducting an impact assessment for multinational organizations. To assume that impacts will be reported, or even viewed in the same manner as a U.S. organization would view them, is to be naïve. They must be tracked and understood on their own national and sociological terms, and they must be annotated as appropriate.

8.7.4 Cultural Perspectives: Israel

If there is one word to describe Israel's attitude toward impacts, it is *prepared*. The nation of Israel, in its brief national existence since 1948, has endured seven wars, two intifadas, and countless surges of terrorist attacks against military and civilian targets. This doesn't even consider the Holocaust and numerous persecutions and murders the Jewish people have suffered through their millennia of existence.

The Israeli government, and the general population, has placed a supreme emphasis on the value of human life. In a line of ancient Jewish thought too complex to explain here, the Talmud asks, "Why was Adam created alone? So that every person should say, 'the entire world was created just for me.'" This, combined with a sense of responsibility to repair the world (known as *tikkun olam*), means that the loss of a single person, regardless of cause, is considered as the loss of an entire world, or an entire creation.

Therefore Israel's sense of duty toward mankind as a whole is great. When it comes to impacts, Israel's experience with and preparation for catastrophes enables her to be a country at the forefront of global response to disasters. It goes without saying that prevention is foremost on the agenda, but when prevention fails, Israelis act to minimize the impact by neutralizing the threat and treating casualties. During an impact, there is only time to act. Action is enabled only by preparation. Preparation is enabled by the knowledge of impacts.

With as much suffering as she has endured, and the supreme value of life she holds, she is in a unique position with a unique worldview, to care exceedingly well not only for her own, but for the world around her. Israel invests value to the world around her and does not hesitate to help nations from all over the world recover from disasters—even the countries that are antagonistic toward her!

When a disastrous event does occur, Israel's response teams are highly organized, well equipped, and ready to spring into action at a moment's notice. From professionally trained soldiers and medical units to common civilians, responses are so well practiced that they are carried out in minimal time through muscle memory. In addition to this high state of professional preparedness, there is also a strong sense of community in Israel that ties people together and assists with response. While there are the common bonds of humanity, family, and geography that compel all of us to assist our neighbors, it is not unfair to say that living in a small country surrounded by danger compels its citizens to spend a little extra effort focusing on one another's safety. Combined with the high value of a single life, Israel has a truly unique worldview in its reaction to impacts.

Another important note on Israel's culture is its socialized model of government. There is a high level of governmental control in all aspects of daily life, from education, to medical care, to military service requirements. This centralized government model does provide an advantage in disaster response. Because the government regulates nearly every aspect of response tactics, communication is tight between intergovernmental organizations, preparation, and even the response plan. Combined with training, this results in a standardized, rapid response that is well ordered and efficient.

Moving on from an Israeli worldview to actual examples of Israel's response tactics, we will look at three Israeli organizations: the Western Galilee Hospital, ZAKA, and MASHAV.

The Western Galilee Hospital is a shining star of preparedness for and response to mass casualty events (MCEs) in Israel. Originally founded in 1956 as a maternity hospital, the Western Galilee Hospital (WGH) is now the second largest in Israel, serving a community of 500,000 people. The WGH is a 627-bed facility that employs over 2,000 people, 300 physicians, receives 400 emergency room patients a day, and hospitalizes 60,000 people a year.[7] This hospital has played a central role in response to Israeli disasters and is no stranger to disaster itself. Since the 1970s, the hospital has been frequently attacked with shells and rockets. The current building has a unique floor plan that protects patients and staff and even allows business to carry on during an attack. In addition to decontamination facilities, the hospital features underground facilities that protect staff and patients. The Jewish Federation of Greater Indianapolis notes an especially significant accomplishment of the WGH: "During the Second Lebanon War in 2006, the hospital remained fully functional even while under fire for 34 days straight."[8]

With such significant capabilities, the hospital has served the greater global community by holding Emergency Response Group (ERG) courses. Dr. Paul Boumbulian states, "The ERG program trains American physicians in Israeli mass casualty procedure to both prepare for situations where Israeli physicians would need to assume their military roles and provide American physicians with knowledge of Israeli cutting edge mass casualty procedures so that they can integrate them into their institutions and communities."[9]

Dr. Boumbulian goes on to say that Israel's response to mass casualty events (MCEs) is treated as a national priority as opposed to America's view that they are "exception events."[10] This has a lot to do with the very real, very daily threat of an attack in Israel, whereas we are fortunate to consider it an exception here in the United States. That said, recalling that a fundamental flaw is thinking too small, there is a lot to learn from Israel's level of preparation and ability to respond in order to increase response capabilities in the unfortunate event of another MCE on American soil.

ZAKA stands for *Zihuy Korbanot Ason*, which translates to disaster victim identification. ZAKA serves in a very special capacity within the duties of impact response. Recall the moral obligations and sense of duty the community—the other side of this coin—relates to death. Within the tenets of Judaism, a timely burial is as important as preserving life. Judaism is especially particular in this aspect because it is important that all recoverable remains of a person be buried, not only as a matter of Jewish law, but as a matter of respect for the person, who can no longer care for himself or herself. Pertaining to accidents and terrorism, this can be a particularly grueling and demanding task.

ZAKA is a volunteer-only organization, composed mostly of Orthodox Jews, and is officially recognized by the Israeli government. The mission of ZAKA is to "assist ambulance crews, aid in the identification of the victims of terrorism, road accidents and other disasters, and where necessary gather body parts and spilled blood for proper burial. They also provide first aid and rescue services, and help with the search for missing persons and participate in international rescue and recovery operations."[11]

ZAKA's response to impacts is fearless, meeting the task with a greater sense of responsibility to the deceased, their family, and the greater community as a whole. ZAKA's volunteers are not biased in their collection of remains. They observe the identical level of attention to detail for all those killed. Whether the victims are Jewish, non-Jewish, Christian, or Muslim, all receive the same level of respect. In the cases of terrorism, ZAKA does not deny its services to the bomber and assists in the recovery and identification of even his or her remains.

Israel is also quick to respond to disasters on a global scale and has taken a particular interest in developing countries where their expertise and experience can be used for recovery and educational purposes. In 1958, Israel's international efforts formally began with the creation of MASHAV—Israel's Agency for International Development Cooperation. One of the many areas of focus for MASHAV is emergency and disaster medicine.

> In the last few years, MASHAV has sent numerous teams to partner countries to instruct in Emergency and Disaster Medicine. These teams

train cadres of doctors, nurses, medical technicians and administrators to deal with mass casualty events and to treat multiple trauma patients, sharing clinical expertise and procedures for organizing response to mass casualty events. Theoretical training is accompanied by practical simulation exercises, sometimes with the participation of Civil Defense, Firefighters, Police and Hospitals, in accordance with scenarios relevant to the specific region.[12]

We can see that Israel's attitude toward impacts focuses on having a well-organized, prepared, and fearless response to its unfortunate reality. Impacts cannot always be prevented, but through preparation and organized response, they can be minimized. Israel's history, though sadly rife with disasters and impact, has enabled her to be one of the leading countries when it comes to response. Her knowledge and organization have benefited not only her, but also the countries she has helped and educated.

8.7.5 International Finance

In terms of finance and financial impacts, one cannot enter the realm of postmodern business constructs without some appreciation for the highly nuanced and regulated world of international finance. As an example, consider this: Are potential financial impacts being calculated in U.S. dollars? If so, do those dollars exist in the United States or is there another currency in play? For instance, if the U.S. dollar loss potential is actually a trade on the Japanese yen, the financial impact of a factory loss in Japan has a potential loss of real dollars that fluctuates every *second* as currency exchange rates change.

The multinational organization, in all of its private and public permutations, is subject to these changes in currency. If you want to see a currency trend in an upward swing, watch what happens to it after a national disaster. Consider this example: After the Tōhoku earthquake, the Japanese yen surged after a brief 0.04% drop against the dollar as domestic investors scrambled to repatriate their yen for investments into rebuilding their country. By 7:29 a.m. New York time, the yen had jumped up to 1.2% of its pre-earthquake value against the dollar. This cutting back of overseas risk and bringing a currency home for rebuilding and security reasons is called **repatriation**, and it is the means to buy or move a currency back into its domestic, or national, market.

By comparison, the stock markets of the United States were closed for 6 days after the 9/11 attacks and reopened in a free fall, with the Dow Jones Industrial (DJI) losing 684.81 points. The dollar was saved from a precipitous dip only by the Federal Reserve, European, and Japanese investment. In short, a nation in debt, recession, or decline will suffer as a result of a disaster, while a nation moving in a positive direction will repatriate its monies to rebuild or reduce overseas risks.

This is how a broad understanding directly impacts deviations and causes executive overrides based on international finance. If the plan is to measure potential financial losses to overseas operations in U.S. dollars, it must be understood that two key international finance issues factor in the current cost of repatriating those dollars into America either for use within America or to reduce the international risk. First, the currency being traded back into U.S. dollars will have changed (either positively or negatively based on the currency exchange rate), and second, as of this writing, there will be 35% taxation on those funds coming into the United States from U.S. operations abroad.

This second issue is huge. In effect, it says that the financial impacts to overseas operations (if calculated in repatriated dollars into America) will actually be 35% *more* than originally calculated! Simply put, for every $1 at risk overseas, there is $1.35 at risk if the multinational company ever wants to see that money in a U.S. bank account again. The deviation that occurs when international risk is not accompanied by international financial intelligence is simply too costly.

The recommendation here is to be mindful as emergency managers regarding international finance and to consult experts to truly grasp the potential cost of lost dollars that are at risk in overseas markets.

8.8 SUMMARY

The final goal of a sound impact assessment is to consider any overrides, deviations, and outliers that may come from scoring objects or sets of objects incorrectly or requested deviations or overrides that come from the personal, professional, cultural, or expert opinions of stakeholders. First, we must realize that the application of the first four principles should keep the emergency manager well "in the loop" with regard to the identity of his or her final audience. Second, we must seek to understand each override, deviation, and outlier based on its own merit and seek to understand the why as a means of improving the impact analysis process. Finally, the deliverable of the fifth principle is to document the person that made the request for an override, why, and when.

The work product for the fifth principle should be delivered as:

1. A basic listing of the who, what, why, and when of each override
2. A separate work paper that describes any core issues with the analysis based on new information given or overrides and deviations observed
3. The final updated and scored objects and sets of objects

By applying the principles in Chapter 7, we have a much higher likelihood of generating scores that do not contain arguable or disputable data. To be specific, a solely interview-based approach will yield a set of overrides and deviations by an order of magnitude greater than it will when combined with an objective data-driven approach. Data can certainly be manipulated, but by their nature, well-sourced data are just data and do not have an opinion. Simply stated, systems cannot lie, and objective facts validate or refute interview-based conclusions.

Perhaps the most significant test of the validity of an impact assessment is to consider how much it changes during this final process. Absent the five guiding principles, the delta between the original analysis and the final delivery result will be very high, and the criticality of the scored objects will have changed vastly.

The biggest gains in closing the gap between the analytical findings and those findings that are rescored by override, deviation, or as outliers is found in the notion of applying big data to our approach. Given the three options, which are to not use a structured analytical framework, use a structured framework with biased interview-based data, or use a structured framework informed by data mining and big data analysis, it is clear that the lowest level of deviation would occur using the third, and recommended, method.

Using the five principles, we can narrow the amount of deviation and overrides, but not eliminate them altogether. However, there are so many key stakeholder touch points in the five principles that there would be a significant close in the gap of overridden or deviated scores at the end of the analysis than just "jumping right in" and scoring based on interviews without an impact horizon, core values, and regulatory and legal concerns being completely established.

The author understands that he is tasking the community of emergency managers, business continuity community, and disaster recovery community with a method for approaching this work using prudence and a new set of tools. However, we believe that the stakes are too high to simply keep moving ahead with ad hoc approaches and lose logic in the face of today's emerging impacts, as we discussed in Chapter 1.

Finally, the reader will find in Chapter 9 an interesting discussion regarding the depths of knowledge and working skills deployed by the revolutionary mindset we discussed in Chapter 1. We are, in our field, confronted with chaos and an intelligent enemy. Any reader that is skeptical about the need to rethink our approach to impact assessments should not render his or her final judgment about our need to do so until he or she has read Chapter 9.

If we are not utilizing the five principles presented in this text, it will become very clear in Chapter 9 that we *must do something to improve our understanding of impacts.*

8.9 QUESTIONS

1. What are the three common types of executive overrides and deviations?
2. What is the appropriate course to respond to an expert opinion-based override request?
3. How do we differentiate between expert opinion and process bias?
4. What do the five guiding principles do to avoid multiple overrides?
5. Demonstrate a deeper appreciation for the cultural biases that shape the quality of our impact assessments by applying a cultural understanding to a country of your choice.

ENDNOTES

1. Paparone, Christopher R. 2008. A Values-Based Critique of Lean and Six Sigma as a Management Ideology. http://www.almc.army.mil/alog/issues/JanFeb08/critique_6sig_ideology.html (accessed January 21, 2012).
2. U.S. Department of State. ND. China: Country Specific Information: Crime. http://travel.state.gov/travel/cis_pa_tw/cis/cis_1089.html#crime (accessed January 21, 2012).
3. BBC. 2011. US Geologist Loses China Appeal Over "Spy" Conviction. http://www.bbc.co.uk/news/world-asia-pacific-12502111?SThisEM (accessed January 21, 2012).
4. Ibid.
5. Ibid.
6. Murakami, Haruki. 2001. *Underground: The Tokyo Gas Attack and the Japanese Psyche*, trans. Alfred Birnbaum and Philip Gabriel. 1st Vintage International ed. New York: Random House.

7. Wikipedia. 2011. Nahariya Hospital for the Western Galilee. http://en.wikipedia.org/wiki/Nahariya_Hospital_for_the_Western_Galilee (accessed January 29, 2012).
8. Jewish Federation of Greater Indianapolis. ND. Emergency Response Group ERG Course XI at the Western Galilee Hospital in Nahariya, Israel. http://www.jfgi.org/page.aspx?id=203624 (accessed January 29, 2012).
9. Boumbulian, Paul J. ND. Learning from the Israeli Disaster Preparedness System. https://www.vhafoundation.org/PriorInitiatives/DisasterPreparedness/Documents/israeli_mce_response___web_version.pdf (accessed January 29, 2012).
10. Ibid.
11. Wikipedia. 2012. ZAKA. http://en.wikipedia.org/wiki/ZAKA (accessed January 29, 2012).
12. Israel Ministry of Foreign Affairs. 2002. The Israel Foreign Ministry's Development Cooperation Program. http://www.mfa.gov.il/MFA/Mashav+%E2%80%93+International+Development/Activities/MASHAV-+Center+for+International+Cooperation.htm (accessed January 29, 2012).

9

Into the Uncanny Valley

9.1 KEY TERMS

9.2 OBJECTIVES

After reading this chapter you will be able to:

1. Describe why the next decade will produce the need for decisiveness and dedication in the field of emergency management.
2. Discuss how the current period in which we practice has given rise to a larger undermining force to potential impact assessments than in any other period of history.
3. Illustrate an understanding of ethics and decision making when it comes to serving the organizations and customers.
4. Provide an example of the key dual challenges confronted in the postmodern business impact assessment.
5. Discuss how we might work toward a better means of working both within the context of postmodern businesses and around the issues embedded in them by demonstrating an understanding of the concept of the uncanny valley.

9.3 OVERVIEW: POTENTIAL IMPACT ASSESSMENTS AND REALISM

Well-performed potential impact assessments inform us about *what is in harm's way and what is at risk of being damaged or lost.* The work of conducting a potential impact assessment for the organizations that employ our services is a means to establish remediation and mitigation actions that must be taken to minimize potential impacts. This book has proposed the five guiding principles as a method that produces a higher-quality potential impact assessment (Figure 9.1).

Figure 9.1   Key concepts in this chapter are the uncanny valley, insurrection, and the necessity of an obsessive curation. (Bottom image used with permission, copyright Rob Kints/Shutterstock.com.)

The five guiding principles have been presented as a specific method for addressing the evolution of impacts as described in Chapter 1. Specifically, the postmodern world generates a new set of opportunities and constraints for emergency managers conducting potential impact assessments. Recall in Chapter 1 we introduced that we must consider the context in which many enterprises, both public and private, now operate. This context was referred to as the digital, or information, age. You may also recall that the digital age is the idea that we now operate in a period in which the primary output of the enterprise or organization is information and services. This was discussed as being *fundamentally different* than the industrial age, in which the primary item of output of the factory was a physical product.

Our initial discussion in Chapter 1 highlighted that the digital age includes the globalization of supply and distribution chains, a growth in emerging markets, outsourcing, and a variety of other permutations of new private and public entities purpose-built for these new realities. In addition, business, and perhaps life itself, seems to have accelerated with the arrival of the digital age. We have seen the arrival of real-time reporting, global communications networks, a deeper interdependency between trading and cash systems, and the overarching monetary policies and governance that guides them.

We also discussed the concepts of Fordism and Taylorism—referring to managerial and operational systems that had a high degree of local focus and brought raw materials through the front of a factory, with workers delivering a finished product at the end of a manufacturing factory line. This was framed as the hallmark that informed much of our thinking about the impacts of the industrial age. In both models of factory management, worker output was designed and integrated in highly localized forms, managed by "the numbers" and optimized for rapid manufacture and delivery via a factory. In that context, the potential impacts were much more local, and therefore much easier to measure.

Today, parts, materials, talent, information, and craftsmanship come to most organizations from all over the world, with the digital superhighway of the Internet and private networks enabling the management of vast, globalized supply chains and the delivery of high-skilled knowledge (such as product design, innovation, and management) to low-skilled workers. These products are often manufactured in countries other than the ultimate country of consumption. Even in Chapter 7, new terms such as *labor arbitrage* and the *repatriation of currency* enter our lexicon to be dealt with in the measurement of potential impacts in a postmodern world.

It is the globalized supply chain and the labor arbitrage of the postmodern world that has changed the life cycle of a product, which today can start as design and prototyping in the United States, be outsourced to any number of companies for refinement and sample creation, delivered in pieces to China or India for manufacture, and finally packaged and delivered to the end consumers back in the United States.

These elements of postmodernism were raised early in this book to highlight the primary condition of the economy of the digital age—every piece of the factory is now a globalized point of service, not a localized process. As you will recall, to be postmodern is to be less attached to a static location, and more attached to a time, context, and conditions that are fluid. Throughout this book we've considered and approached the work of conducting a potential impact assessment with a postmodern, global view that is appropriate to the digital age. However, we have not addressed the larger problem of change and innovation that was only briefly introduced in Chapter 1.

9.3.1 A Larger Problem

Change and innovation are synonymous and share a symbiotic relationship—each affecting the other. Radical changes in the markets, capital, and cost models associated with production lead to innovation. Innovation in turn causes radical changes in markets, capital, and cost models. The symptoms of innovation and change may sometimes lead to **insurrection**. Insurrection is a violent uprising against an authority or government, such as an opposition to a new regime. In the current postmodern era, insurrections have taken various forms. The Occupy Wall Street movement, computer hacking groups such as Anonymous and LulzSec, as well as national uprisings and general civil unrest around the globe are examples of modern insurrections (Figure 9.2). Questions about government policy, corporate stewardship, community, and global citizenry arise during times of shifts from one form of workforce to another. These groups, and the insurrectionist doctrines and tactics that they employ, create general mayhem and civil unrest. While often viewed as lofty academic issues, the question of insurrections and the symptoms of change resistance have very real influence on the process of conducting a potential impact analysis.

Building on the presence of insurrections during times of great change and innovation, it is notable that most of the transitional periods between ages, such as that from the agrarian age to the industrial age, are accompanied with the term *revolution*. We had the industrial revolution and we are in the midst of the digital revolution. Revolution embodies not only the concept of a great change, but also the associated insurrections and revolts that occur during the adjustment to radical change and innovation.

* * *

A larger challenge we face, as practitioners conducting potential impact analyses, is that revolutions add turmoil to the already ground-shifting changes to the organizations and enterprises we serve. As the means of

Figure 9.2 Anonymous is a very present threat in the digital age. It takes an active and vocal role in disrupting government operations throughout the world. (Used with permission, copyright Rob Kints/Shutterstock.com.)

production and the distribution of labor and wealth shift from one age to another, insurrections are a natural result of the public, private, and political changes. The digital age is not unique in this manner.

* * *

To better understand this larger challenge, let's return to our musing about Susie's Lemonade Stand in Chapter 1. You'll probably be able to readily recall the rapidly growing digital business she created in under 60 seconds. It is not difficult to remember how one cell phone seemed to transform her friendly, local business into a much larger enterprise. Could it be considered that hidden behind the patina of a lucky kid with a booming business, the larger, modern cultural challenge of the 99% is being represented in this commercial as well?

Recall the loyal, young employee who ruined his bike by riding through wet cement and cutting through a park in order to tell Susie about a machine being out of stock. Do you think it was possible that he became disgruntled by the fact that Susie's technologies and adaption of telemetry made him, for lack of a better term, obsolete?

And what of the truck driver who was rerouted to replace the dwindling stock of that same machine? Was it possible that he viewed his interaction with the phone as nothing more than an automated micromanagement tool? Was his skill as a supply chain logistician suddenly being replaced, and perhaps subsumed, by a computer?

Could it be that we are watching these two employees become the 99% as Susie ascends to her position in the 1%?

We live in an age of economic, military, and political change. Much of this change is driven by information and a shrinking world. This change is also driven by a perceived ever-increasing equality gap. How do Susie's employees view these changes? What is their role, either knowingly or unknowingly, in the broader rumblings of the digital revolution and its associated insurrections and revolutions at hand?

The fundamental flaw of thinking too small in our potential impact assessments is currently being played out against a backdrop of radical social uprising and conflict worldwide, with new hot spots emerging almost weekly. The outcomes of these protests and revolutions create a dual challenge for the practitioner working on a potential impact assessment today. One is the massive set of changes brought on by the digital age within the enterprise, and the other, larger challenge is the social and political unrest roiling in the background outside of it. In 2010 and 2011 alone, the number and scope of revolutions occurring worldwide was dramatic. The Arab Spring, Eurozone conflicts, Occupy Wall Street movement, and recent uprising in Russia are based on social confidence in monetary policy and governance, which has been eroded by the extremely fluid global economies, and how quickly the degradation of one (the U.S. recession of 2008) has a ripple effect on the others.

Figure 9.3 While uncomfortable, riots and insurrection are the state of our modern world as we undergo an economic and governmental shift, as this image from the London riots in March 2011 illustrates. (Used with permission, copyright 1000 Words/Shutterstock.com.)

These facts may be unsettling, but it is important to recall that these revolutionary tones and resulting unrest are *the natural by-product of change*; therefore to take up a political view or stance either for or against these by-products is not the job of the professional business continuity, disaster recovery, or emergency management professional (Figure 9.3). Our job is to protect the assets of the organizations we serve, and not let our personal opinions about the world around us get in the way of our mission. It then goes without saying that this includes protecting our organizations from insurrections, uprisings, civil unrest, activism, hacking, and even revolutions. An interesting result of approaching the work through the application of the five guiding principles is the envisioning of a clear, *high-definition* picture of what is *at* risk.

During the course of an in-depth potential impact analysis, it is completely possible to come across questions such as "What happens if we have to move our business out of the country?" or "How do we insure continuity of government during a complete and modern civil war?" Understanding that a well-crafted potential impact analysis will naturally lead to this type of discussion is to truly understand the insightful power of the five guiding principles.

* * *

Simply put, the five guiding principles force a high-definition view of what is at risk that ultimately leads to what must be done to remediate and mitigate against potential losses. While remediation and mitigation strategies are beyond the scope of the potential impact analysis phase, understanding *how to deal with the realism* that a potential impact analysis puts on the table is not.

* * *

This type of high-definition view of potential impacts will create a reaction within the organizations we serve. Those reactions will be based on the degree of realism and accuracy that is delivered by following the five guiding principles. While many professional disaster recovery, business continuity, and emergency managers are prepared to cope with this level of realism, most enterprises and organizational sponsors we support *are not*.

9.3.2 Realism

We are now going to talk about the resulting realism and accuracy that occurs in reporting potential impacts when working from the five guiding principles. The degree to which the potential impact analysis is defensible is heavily based on how we approach and use data, as discussed in Chapter 6. Recall from that chapter that there are two types of data sources: (1) opinion or interview-based data and (2) big or system-based data. Interview-based data are easier for an organization to dismiss and "not take too seriously." System-based data, on the other hand, are nearly impossible to ignore and will complement the validity of interview-based data.

Generally speaking, the organization that opts for a big, systems-based data approach to data collection in the potential impact analysis is already demonstrating a higher level of maturity. The organization that prefers interview-based data alone is generally less prepared to confront the potential losses captured in the potential impact assessment. Nonetheless, even with the overrides and deviations in place from the discussion and actions we took by applying the fifth principle (as covered in Chapter 8), we are often, at the completion of a sound potential

283

impact assessment, left with stakeholders who are shocked by the realities of what is in harm's way when discovered by this process.

If we are following the broader prescription of understanding risk as described in the author's prior book, *Managing Emerging Risk*, and delivering a risk assessment based on the probable *and* the possible, as well as a high-resolution potential impact assessment as called for in this book, our customers and the organizations we work for are going to be faced with a very real view of risk and potential harm. *These realities may include things that nearly any person who is not a professional emergency manager will shy away from.*

The potential for impacts arising from a civil unrest event will be right there for us to consider, right along with the other impacts. The reality that doing business in the postmodern age has created a natural cycle of rebellion and unrest in society will come into focus.

* * *

Even as we deliver a clear picture there is an undertone of potential revolution and insurrection that is global in nature, which generates a set of impacts that are, in some cases, more profound and more damaging than our stakeholders can comprehend.

* * *

As professional emergency managers we serve organizations that may place profits high in their impact-based response decision making. We also serve organizations that are trusted with public safety and the well-being of society at large. Whatever the case, it is important to always remember that we serve the organization and its constituents, *not the social upheavals* that are embedded in the current shape of postmodern business, capitalism, and governance. In order to completely do our job of understanding impacts, we must come to terms with the background conversation incumbent to the times. Understand the logical and well-ordered arguments they use in protest, rather than heeding the whispers and complaints of a society undergoing a massive shift in its orientation to work and citizenry. By doing this, you understand the thinking behind the revolution, and also (more importantly) the clear and present danger the groups and their reasoning represent to our clients. This is one of the challenges of the realism created by the five guiding principles.

9.4 THE CLEAR CHOICE DURING TURBULENT TIMES

Much of the popular rhetoric found in modern protest movements (such as Occupy Wall Street and the EU protests) is based on the concepts of economic inequality and social injustice. The trade winds of postmodern capitalism and globalization inflict suffering on a population that then feels victimized.

The Tea Party's more radical elements pine for a 1950s' America, where all manufacturing is done at "home." They thereby wish to deconstruct America's system of global trade and production, and decry America's place in the global economy through international trade and manufacturing agreements. These complaints often don't stop at simply "restoring America," but also have a global undercurrent that implies the only way to restore social justice and economic equality is by a global uprising of "the people" against all orders of governance and business.

That said, it is important to note that writing off the protests of a few, or even the populous view of many, as ill informed or "radical" is to miss an important point. The complaints they have resonate with a large group because they are very much true, and based on intelligent reasoning. As long as protest groups are not calling for, or developing, actions that could result in chaos and massive disruptions to society, they should not be disregarded for their complaints about the results of the changes in global and local economies (Figure 9.4).

* * *

To ignore the tactics, motives, and impacts of insurrectionists, radicals, and hackers is naïve. They are spurred on by the actions of the enterprises for which we are measuring impacts. To disregard their intelligent arguments is to move forward blindly because we are protecting the very value that may be generating *further* threats and impacts.

* * *

As we advance our understanding of the nature, composition, people, processes, and technologies that the organizations we serve wish to protect, we may also confront the reality that these same values create a vicious cycle of future impacts and threats in the form of civil unrest and insurrection. While it is often convenient to leave these issues "out of scope," to be dealt with by cyber security professionals, it should be made clear that the author views this approach as akin to leaving virology out of a general physician's hands. At a minimum, it must be recognized by the informed practitioner that interacting with both physical and cyber

Figure 9.4 Whether or not you agree with Occupy Wall Street, it is a fact that this event, and other protests that we see today, are spurred on by the organizations we protect. (Used with permission, copyright Daryl Lang/Shutterstock.com.)

security specialists is required due to the findings of the potential impact assessment. These often tie the unrest and revolutionary undertones of counterculture to the productive globalized organizations for whom we measure potential impacts.

To further this discussion, consider how closely linked the facts presented in this book regarding postmodernism and globalization are to the complaints of radical elements within the global insurrection movement. One text that is simply impossible to ignore in this conversation is *The Coming Insurrection* by the so-called Invisible Committee. *The Coming Insurrection* is a French work that has extreme influence on North American anarchist movements and was written either by the **Tarnac Nine** or those who supported them in France in or around 2007. The Tarnac Nine is a group of anarchists who were arrested for causing delays of over 160 trains through sabotage. With roots deep in the French leftist movement, either the group or a group representing them published *The Coming Insurrection,* a work that has become a popular anticapitalist text.

This book has been handed out in the form of leaflets, spread across the Internet, and is currently published by Semiotext(e).

While the notion that the Occupy Wall Street movement, the Arab Spring, or the EU riots and their associated unrest may be tied to this text would be wildly argued among the protesters themselves, *The Coming Insurrection* is a tremendous, contemporary manifesto regarding the current social contempt for globalization and is a *must-read* for anyone who desires to understand the linkage between the evolution of impacts described in this book and the evolution of unrest widely visible across several revolutionary movements around the globe.

The protesters of Occupy Wall Street, Greece, Spain, and even the fringe group Anonymous have often referenced the text. Understanding its lucid argument, which veers suddenly into radical action, is a key to better understanding the direct link between *what is in harm's way* for our clients and *what these groups perceive as a target*.

The Coming Insurrection gives much attention to globalization and international governance in the form of a "police state," saying early in the text: "What this war is being fought over is not various ways of managing society, but irreducible and irreconcilable ideas of happiness and their worlds. We know it, and so do the powers that be."[1] Here, the war being fought is between the enterprise and the worker, or in Marxist terms, the Bourgeoisie (the upper-class capital owners) and the Proletariats (the lower-class wage worker). The various ways of managing society (ranging from immigration controls to wages and incarceration) are magnified into the "irreducible ideas of happiness," as expressed by the text.

A central problem, as presented in this book, is "two centuries of capitalism and market nihilism have brought us to the most extreme alienations."[2] The alienations referred to are between worker and product, worker and wage, and in the terms of the text, producer and raw materials as spread out across the global supply chain. This is where *Understanding Impacts* and *The Coming Insurrection* intersect: This textbook is based on understanding impacts for emergency managers in a postmodern world and agrees with the premise of a revolutionary handbook arguing that the current state of capital market affairs has created cultural stress. However, *while the basis of the arguments for both books is rooted in fact, it is what to do about these facts that completely separates the two writings*.

For *The Coming Insurrection*, the response is exploitation, sabotage, and terrorism. "They say we are disappointed by business, that it failed to honor our parents' loyalty, that it let them go too quickly. They are lying. To be disappointed, one must have hoped for something,"[3] or so the argument goes for the insurrectionists. Eventually, the call for action is raised: "On the margins of this workforce that is effective and necessary for the functioning of the machine, is a growing majority that has become superfluous, that is certainly useful to the flow of production but not much else, which introduces the risk that, in its idleness, it will set about sabotaging the machine."[4]

This is the counter, repulsive voice of the digital revolution, the argument about what to do about open trade, globalization, and capitalism that have caused change, and thus the shared woes of the revolutionaries. This is also the rogue outcome of the globally distributed supply chain and labor arbitrage that is unearthed during a well-executed potential impact assessment. Within the very people, processes, and systems that the practitioner identifies need to be protected are elements that potentially harbor great dissatisfaction and ill will to the system itself. Our job as emergency managers is to recognize this outcome, and to come to terms with it through advising our enterprises regarding the threats embedded in the very values we are protecting, i.e., that perhaps the largest single point of failure within the enterprise could be a disenfranchised worker who would throw himself into the machine if only to stop it.

The Coming Insurrection highlights the ease with which the enterprise can be ground to a halt by attacking single points of failure, such as laying siege to whole cities by the simple closure of a rail line or a convenient, easily orchestrated strike of public servants. This represents not only a risk (as discussed in *Managing Emerging Risk*) but also a threat buried in the very values we are discovering through the completion of a potential impact assessment. This threat plays itself out not only in the private sector, but also in the public sector, with the likelihood of inside jobs and internal attacks permeating the highest levels of law enforcement.

Consider the recent and apparently ongoing hacking and surveillance of the FBI and Scotland Yard by hackers from Anonymous. Kim Zetter of *Wired Magazine*'s threat level not only described, but also posted a 17-minute conference call between the FBI in the United States and Scotland Yard on February 3, 2012. The call involved several FBI agents from the Los Angeles office, the Washington, D.C., office, and Scotland Yard agents. The recorded conference call, posted by Anonymous, detailed the names of the agents involved as well as a strategy session regarding active cases against other hackers and future investigations. A Twitter post announcing the hack said, "The FBI might be curious how we're able to continuously read their internal comms for some time now."[5]

While the prospect of *outside* hackers being able to conduct counter-surveillance on the FBI and Scotland Yard may be hard to fathom, it might even be more disturbing to think that this type of activity is the result of an inside job. Consider what the Department of Homeland Security had to say about the possibility of such inside jobs in July 2011. According to a CNN report, a bulletin distributed to utility facilities in the United States warned against possible threats to water, gas, and waste facilities. In the bulletin, no specific threat was mentioned; however, it was noted that if "violent extremists" were able to "gain access to an insider or acquire an insider position, this increases the likelihood of success and impact of an attack."[6] Here we see the link between core values found in a potential impact analysis and those values that might actually create a disgruntled employee.

The document did detail a case in 2010 when a U.S. citizen was arrested in Yemen during a roundup of suspected al Qaeda members. The person had worked "for several contractors performing non-sensitive maintenance at five different U.S. nuclear power plants from 2002 to 2008."[7] In fact, by December 2011, the FBI announced a radical increase in electrical grid, gas, water, and waste facilities that had been hacked into through their **supervisory control and data acquisition** (SCADA) control systems. These are low-level control systems for mechanized controls within power grids, water, and waste systems. In a speech given by Michael Welch, the deputy assistant director of the FBI's Cyber Division, Welch announced: "We just had a circumstance where we had three cities, one of them a major city within the US, where you had several hackers that had made their way into SCADA systems within the city."[8]

The threat, which revolves around either the ease of accessibility by instable individuals to passwords, or the lack of controls around password protections, is global. Welch continued: "Because threat actors operate globally, a significant volume of cyber threat activity occurs outside of normal business hours."[9] These types of threats, while normally captured in a risk assessment, may only become clear during a potential impact assessment because they are loosely coupled to the core values and operational structure of the enterprises being analyzed.

* * *

In fact, operational failures in security, infrastructure, and personnel protection are often revealed during the potential impact assessment, along with counterintuitive threats such as those posed by community ill will or perceptions regarding the organization. While not impacts per se, they do further inform the risk assessment and deepen the need to place a higher value on single points of failure, as found in the potential impact assessment.

* * *

This leads us to an important issue: choice. As students, practitioners, and professionals in the fields of disaster recovery, business continuity, and emergency management, do we press the advantage using the insights we've gathered through our potential impact using the five principles? Or do we water down the message, rifling through slides at the end of a project, like so many images collected on a boring vacation, just to leave our customers more confused about the values that are at risk and the *new* risks we've discovered? Or do we spend the time to walk our shareholders through our findings with care and deliberation?

* * *

Rifling through slides at the conclusion of an in-depth impact assessment is akin to rambling through the findings of an intense clinical diagnostic workup of a patient. Not only will the patient not know what to do next, but worse, the doctor will look like an incompetent fool.

* * *

9.4.1 The Choice

Our clear choice as professionals is to protect our clients. If we have taken a role with an organization that we cannot fundamentally agree with in terms of ethics, we must move on. If we do not have an issue with the ethics of the organization we are supporting, then we cannot, for one instance, be on the fence in this regard. We must understand that there *is* an "us" and a "them." The "us" are those who mindfully choose to protect the interest of our clients, and the "them" are those who would mindfully have their radical ideologies destroy it.

* * *

Professional emergency managers do not have the luxury of being on the fence regarding the current political and social discourse when such discourse calls for massive interruptions to trade and threatens the well-being of our clients and society at large.

* * *

What the reader should understand in this regard is that there is a clear choice, no matter how cunning the revolutionary or insurrectionist arguments seem. In fact, in many cases, these arguments seem to mirror the emergency manger's concerns with the current evolution of impact, with one important difference—*what we do about it*. It's important to recognize that much of what constitutes the current sociopolitical uncertainty in our world is based in the very same uncertainties we've been discussing in this book.

Looking back across the application of the five guiding principles, the reader should recognize that when well applied, and *especially* when big data are used, potential impacts leap out at the organization in stunning detail, with all of their inherited complexities and dependencies, with their positive cash flows, negative public perceptions, and happy customers, with an uncanny realism the potential impact analysis is a rendering of the actual values, valuables, and measured outputs of the organization. Some of these are valued by the organization and some are, frankly, not valued by the popular voice of an uncertain public at all.

We are not merely mentioning that what we would protect as professionals based on a sound potential impact assessment is subject to radical social views and revolutionary controversy. We are pointing out the fact that our job, and thus the hard choices we must shepherd our stakeholders through, is to directly face these radical elements in our society and, based on our assessment, the impacts they might create.

* * *

Like it or not, our final functional role in delivering a potential impact assessment is to help our organizations face potential impacts, including the unpleasant reality that they, their business, or their role in society is maybe *the target* of a radical segment of our global society.

* * *

This is the point at which we can separate audit fodder from real potential impact assessments. A potential impact assessment based on the five guiding principles does something that "jumping right in" and gathering several opinions about impact and ranking them *does not do*, such as:

- Illustrates the real values and outputs of an organization
- Documents whether or not those values are aligned with public interests when under duress
- Follows regulations, laws, and local customs

Of course, there are many other items that also come to light using the approach outlined in this book. The five guiding principles generate potential impacts that are so much more realistic than previous methods were able to generate, that we have to consider our professional role in stewarding our organization through our findings. Some disaster recovery and business continuity and emergency management professionals have tried to explain away the need for accurate potential impact assessments with an alphabet soup of acronyms and strange, poorly framed logic. There is the old business impact assessment, known as the BIA. There are rapid impact assessments (RIAs). There are critical resources and materials lists. There is the minimum acceptable recovery criteria, known as MARC. There are executive business impact assessments (EBIAs). Many claim that these quick and opinion-based approaches lead to remarkable accuracy when dealing with clients.

The first mistaken output of these approaches is that they are not accurate at all. Findings based on opinions are called polls—not analyses. The second mistaken output, which really is a fundamental flaw, is they do not think big, and therefore rarely match the reality of impacts when disaster *does* strike. However, the real litmus test of these so-called impact assessments is that they do not capture *potential* impacts that reflect any sort of organizational reality in a postmodern context. If they did, they would require that the analyst spend some time walking the organization through the uncanny realization that occurs when potential impacts are accurately captured.

When delivering a potential impact analysis based on the five guiding principles, the analyst must be prepared to give an in-depth explanation of the uncanny potentials and realities captured during the potential impact assessment. In short, he or she must be prepared to walk with the client through what will be referred to as the uncanny valley.

9.5 THE UNCANNY VALLEY

The reader may recall our discussion in Chapter 1 regarding curating historical impacts as evidenced in past disasters or terror attacks. In that discussion, we introduced the idea that taxonomies and thesauri could be created based on these collections by virtual learning models and real-life displays of past events. We spoke about an imagined reference library of past events that truly demonstrated the impacts of September 11. We also talked about the notion of such an exhibit being uncanny, which you may recall was described as being very similar to reality, but not quite real, thereby making it creepy because the minor differences perceived were not obvious.

While it is true that such a collection of past disasters and terror events that really showed impacts would be uncanny, it is also true that a potential impact assessment performed using the five guiding principles will present the organization with future impacts that may also be uncanny. It is human nature not to do well with uncanny presentations of data or objects. It's the job of the disaster recovery, business continuity, or emergency management professional to be certain that the organization does not "shut down" when faced with these potentials.

It has been said in our field that people who have dreams of falling almost always wake up with a hypnic jerk before they hit the ground because *they cannot imagine the risk*. The author has often used this illustration to break the ice with audiences at conferences. The trick works like this: The speaker asks everyone in the room to raise their hand and hold it up if they have ever had a dream of falling. Nearly everyone in the room does so. The audience is asked to keep their hand up if they "splat" on the ground at the end of the dream. Nearly all hands go down. The speaker then tells them, "It's because you can't imagine the risk."

However, on reflection, we realize that the dreamer *can* imagine the risk; after all, the dream is about the manifested risk of falling. What the people in the room *can't* imagine or visualize at the subconscious level is *the impact*—the splat on the ground. Humans are wired to aspire. We have evolved to thrive and survive, and in our deep animal brain, being able to contemplate, even at the subconscious level, an impact that would result in our death causes a hypnic jerk that saves us from our purely fictitious demise.

9.5.1 Studies in the Uncanny Valley

Dr. Masashiro Mori, a scientist specializing in robotics, has framed much of the contemporary discussion regarding the uncanny through his critical thinking and writing on the subject. And it is only natural in his field, as the term applies to anthropomorphic robots. Interestingly, his writings have influenced other researches in the areas of computer-generated graphics and computer-generated human characters. The subject of the uncanny is deeply explored by 3D animation experts, robotics scientists, and filmmakers who have at their disposal vast arrays of data and rendering tools, but still face the challenge of creating things that are almost real, but somehow off. This is a problem that Mori applied to the subject of human-like robots back in the 1970s and presciently referred to as the **uncanny valley**.

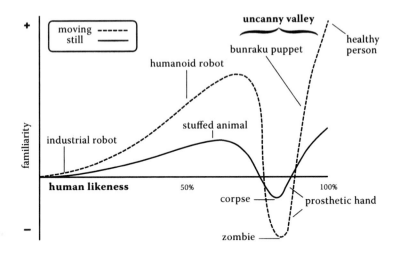

Figure 9.5   Uncanny valley illustration.

Mori created "a hypothetical graph that predicts that as something looks more human it also looks more agreeable, until it comes to look so human we start to find its nonhuman imperfections unsettling,"[10] according to Karl F. MacDorman from the Indiana University School of Informatics. The graph, originally created by Mori in his work "Bukimi no Tani" (The Uncanny Valley) in *Energy* in 1970, has now been applied by MacDorman and others to describe why humans do not do well with the uncanny—from robots to human photorealism, as found in computer-generated imagery (CGI) in movies and computer games (Figure 9.5).

Take a moment to study the illustration of the uncanny valley. Notice how the familiarity factor goes into the negative space of the valley with a prosthetic hand and into the positive space with a puppet or a healthy person. This is the gap between the well rendered and the real. It is also interesting to note that along the bottom axis, which is labeled "human likeness," things that are fake, like a stuffed animal, become "frighteningly real" and fall into the uncanny valley. Finally, notice the trajectory of the "unmoving" solid line. This is the trajectory that would most closely align itself with a well-rendered report from a well-executed potential impact assessment.

It is not that a potential impact assessment *is* an industrial robot, a stuffed animal, a corpse, or a prosthetic hand. It is that the potential impact assessment and the presentation of the data generated from it *become more human*

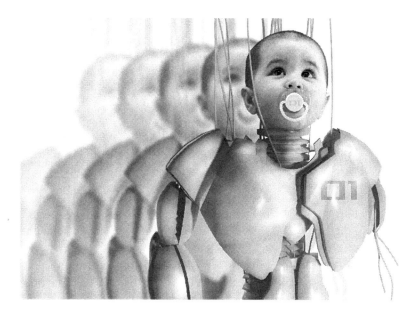

Figure 9.6   Does this image disturb you? It's because you are riding in the depths of the uncanny valley. Viewing this as a possible reality is as difficult as it is for organizations to view the reality of impacts that have not occurred.

and more real in terms of "likeness" when using the five guiding principles. A likeness that, as previously mentioned, can cause the resulting final deliverable to fall into the uncanny valley and cause stakeholders to shut down and neither hear nor see the potential impacts just uncovered (Figure 9.6).

The implications of the uncanny valley on stakeholders who are exposed to very realistic, yet potential impacts to their organizations are part of a theory captured by MacDorman et al., in their article "Too Real for Comfort?" The reaction of "shutting down" we are describing is strongly linked to **terror management theory**. Terror management theory has demonstrated "how subliminal reminders of death can cause a pervasive shift in our attitudes and preferences. In particular, these reminders cause us to favor those who have opinions that support our cultural worldview."[11]

In generating a potential impact assessment, we are presenting cognitive "reminders of death" in a very accurate way. Though the data and findings of the final deliverable of a potential impact assessment are in no way a simulation or rendering, robotic, CGI, or otherwise, they are a written report or set of charts and graphs that illustrate a potential for harm that is much more accurate than the methods used in other approaches. It is this very narrative and set of graphs that "look too real," but are uncertain, that create an uncanny response. Most robotics scientists and animators would argue that written reports have little to do with the uncanny valley problem presented by Mori, but of course they would be missing a history of discussion about the uncanny that precedes Mori by 60 years or more.

In 1919, 60 years before Dr. Mori applied the notion of the uncanny to robots, Sigmund Freud considered feelings of unease associated with the uncanny in a paper of the same name.[12] Freud, writing in a time before CGI, robots, or any real humanoid likenesses, studied literature, from fairy tales to the works of the Greeks, to dig up what "undoubtedly belongs to all that is terrible—to all that arouses dread and creeping horror; it is equally certain, too, that the word is not always used in a clearly definable sense, so that it tends to coincide with whatever excites dread."[13] Freud is looking at written fantasies and stories, much more of the type of material created in a potential impact assessment than the robots and stuffed animals studied in Dr. Mori's work!

In Freud's work about the uncanny, which links the feeling, inspiringly, to all manner of infantile anxieties, such as castration and returning to the womb, we find some glimmers of psychological insight into the very human reaction to what is uncanny and why. Freud writes: "This is that an uncanny effect is often and easily produced by effacing the distinction between imagination and reality, such as when something that we have hitherto regarded as imaginary appears before us in reality, or when a symbol takes over the full functions and significance of the thing it symbolizes, and so on."[14] Here we find an important clue as to why we must shepherd our clients and organizations through the findings of a potential impact assessment.

You'll recall that in Chapter 1 we said, "In short, to conduct an impact assessment is to consider the profanity of havoc. The job at hand requires professionals who are able to measure what happens when things degrade from order and fall into chaos." In Freud's terms, the result is to make the "distinction between imagination and reality." Through the application of the five guiding principles this is achieved.

In these terms, the symbol may be a chart or graph of body counts, financial losses, or the admixture of core values, legal, regulatory, and cultural issues that resulted in our weighted scores and tiers. When based on the five guiding principles, "the symbol takes over the full functions and significance of the thing it symbolizes." Thus, a graph in the final report becomes uncanny for the stakeholders and they are bound to recoil. Reporting the final results of a potential impact assessment based on the five guiding principles leads us to the uncanny because, as Freud writes, "The whole matter is one of 'testing reality,' pure and simple, a question of the material reality of the phenomena."[15]

"The material reality of the phenomena" generated in a potential impact assessment is more than just the impacts measured accurately and aligned so well to the stakeholders we have engaged with, it is (as this chapter points out) the larger problem that some values we seek to protect are not *valued at all by a subgroup of society,* and that *some impacts are so large and far away from the original disaster that they do not appear to be impacts at all, but some other disastrous event.* These are the issues that disaster recovery, business continuity, or emergency management professionals must master.

When we apply the five guiding principles to a potential impact assessment, we are creating a narrative and picture of that which will be harmed. When done well, that story and picture will be finalized into a report that may be difficult for even the most involved stakeholders to consume and entertain because it may be too close to reality, too accurate. We may want to run back to the stuffed animal of the uncanny valley, where there is no expectation for things to be lifelike. We (and they) may be tempted to undo the material reality of the narrative by falling back to the contested and questionable methodologies of interviews and stick with opinion, simply because it is so much easier to digest.

However, applying the five guiding principles and conducting and delivering a well-crafted potential impact assessment is a question of professional ethics and studied critical thinking. If we agree that a fundamental flaw exists and that impact assessments rarely reflect the realities faced by organizations dealing with real disasters or terror attacks, we must consider that the five guiding principles of potential impact assessments lead us to a much more material, albeit uncanny, reality.

Suddenly, the question of the five guiding principles of potential impacts shifts and the work product and its implications become slightly more problematic. If we are to truly analyze potential impacts and understand them in terms of their alignment to the organizations we serve, as well as their capability to generate values to be protected that may insult the sensibilities of radicals and revolutionaries—if we are to expand the impact horizon out to consider the damages of an earthquake 2 years after the fact to distant coastlines, then we are left with a final deliverable that is not only accurate, but uncanny.

9.5.2 The Otaku's Curation of the Uncanny

In Western civilization, many would argue that this need to aspire to greater things, the "wired to aspire" nature of our thinking, has been hijacked by advertising and media geared to constantly offer us what is new, next, and nice. We are, in fact, bombarded with advertisements that claim they will make us better people and that we deserve a better life if we would only purchase this or that product. The need for human beings to be aspirational is part nature and part nurture. The tragic sense of entitlement that explains most of Western culture's ideas about going splat cannot simply be written off as a natural tendency to disregard entropy. It is also the unnatural result of a culture that is highly driven by advertising to have the "next great thing."

In Chapter 1, you might recall that we discussed how Eastern cultures, such as Japan, have a much deeper regard for entropy and the things that are weathered and well worn. We referred to this aesthetic in Japanese culture as Wabi-Sabi. Discussing the keepers of such ephemera in Japanese culture, a contemplation of collectors would not be complete without a discussion regarding the **Otaku**.

Otaku are obsessed by information about a singular subject. There is a strong negative connotation of being associated with this cult. Often a singular topic or genre appeals to them, and their study of that topic nears a feverish "cult of the thing." They have been variously described as "fetishists," "extreme fan boys," and "geeks without rival." Otaku were once a young minority in Japan, but have since blossomed into a middle-aged majority so thoroughly integrated into the mainstream culture that they are no longer viewed as a passing youth trend (Figure 9.7).

The reasons the Otaku are an important component of Japanese resiliency is that they harbor vast collections of knowledge and objects of highly focused categories. There are Otaku worlds for every domain from pop idols, to gaming, to the Internet, to movies, clothes, robots, and even toy trains. The first generation of object-obsessed Otaku have made their way into industrial Japan as young workers, and have brought with them their collecting and organizing sensibilities. There is strong reason to believe that Japan will not so easily give up on its culture or its prequake traditions. Many of these traditions, after all, are based in their acceptance of life and death as a part of the natural order of all things.

Japan reacted to the H-bomb attacks of WWII with Atom Boy, a heroic robot character, and Godzilla, the H-bomb monster. No less than 29 films

Figure 9.7 Anime is one of many obsessions that the Otaku might follow. It is their deep fetish, like curiosity about a given topic, that is important to consider.

have been made about the Godzilla monster, and they continued through 2004. During World War II, Tokyo was burned to ashes by mass carpet bombings. Hiroshima and Nagasaki were flattened by atomic bombs. Fifty years later, Tokyo is a thriving metropolis, perhaps in part because the Japanese people met the horrific visions of destruction with creative explorations of renewal and triumph through their extreme fetish for what is old and, to a certain degree, what can be re-created from destruction. Films, cartoons, and comic books dedicated to the topic of the H-bomb dominate the culture.

Otaku today represents a cultural (not a subcultural) aspect of Japan that is, by all sociological descriptions, a group of obsessive collectors, builders of theory, and protectors of objects. They share a sociological kinship with the Medici, Sebu, and Steve Jobs—the curators we discussed in Chapter 1. The 2011 earthquake will not, in this author's opinion, so easily destroy Japan's national values. However, it will be a vast embarrassment for them.

9.5.3 The 2011 Tōhoku Earthquake

Keeping in mind that the Japanese thinking in these matters is different than that of the United States, we must try to fully understand their view of impacts from the 2011 earthquake, because their view of impacts is so steeped in their traditions that they may not hold the same limits as our American fascination with the opposite matter: the fascination with all that is simply new. *2:46, Aftershocks: Stories from the Japan Earthquake* is a book that was written for the digital age. It began with a simple request by its author, Patrick Sherriff, on the first day of the earthquake. He posted on the Internet a quick request: "If everyone wrote 250 words—one page—or submitted their favorite (original) tweets, pics or artwork, I could edit, publish it in days."[16] This is a request for a fetish-like, Otaku approach to cataloging a shared experience. The book was published in 1 week.

"While the foreign media is obsessed with apocalypse, the Japanese people are already talking of rebuilding."[17] The Otaku are obsessive about their collections, and they see the world around them in a multidimensional way. The quote above is making three statements:

1. Electronic media is faster and more relevant.
2. While official sources of news were talking about destruction and the end, the people of Japan were already talking about rebuilding in the idea of rebirth.
3. "Official sources" were irrelevant based on the speed and availability of Internet-based communications and the will of the people.

In addition to enriching the discussion about the foreign worldview of Japanese culture, the statement also signals the shift in the way people consume media in the digital age. Electronic media is faster and more relevant, and therefore more trusted, than traditional media. In the case of *2:46*, the material is curated from completely new sources thanks to the digital age. Facebook, Twitter, and other forms of social media are

Figure 9.8 The digital age is giving us new forms of media transmission in Facebook, Twitter, and Google. Combined with powerful personal computers we carry in our pockets, the digital age is quickly making traditional print media obsolete and irrelevant.

displacing the traditional sources of media. There are distinct advantages to this shift in the curating of information: The information is more relevant, timely, and distributed more quickly for mass consumption. Ultimately, the point here is that the Otaku embody the essence of an unflinching curator by embracing and distributing news more quickly, and from multiple sources with firsthand knowledge and experience of what is being reported (Figure 9.8).

For the Japanese, the 2011 earthquake was an expression of suffering *and* joy as a fact of life—the manifestation of the natural course of all things. A book that was on the way to its publisher when the earthquake hit, *Reimagining Japan*, is a study of renewal and the need for Japan to reinvent itself. Japan's aging population and the now globalized competition for technological innovation had threatened its once competitive edge. *Reimagining Japan* added a hasty foreword and some quick editing to frame its story of a new vision of the country with the earthquake as a freshly minted introduction.

In the foreword of the book, Yoichi Funabashi writes, "The Earthquake of March 11, 2011, changed the geography of Japan—literally. Digital maps and GPS devices are likely to deviate by more than 5 meters as a result. The country has undergone a cataclysmic realignment."[18] Funabashi offers up many more details of the earthquake, the Fukashima nuclear reactor events, and the tsunami in his introduction of the book. Peter Tasker, another contributor to the work, observes that the earthquake, tsunami, and nuclear contamination crisis were a "triple disaster." In *Managing Emerging Risk*, the events of that day are all discussed as part of a disaster halo effect.

The impact of the March 11, 2011, earthquake and the numerous disaster halo effects that followed are just starting to sink in. The series of events following the quake certainly underscore the disaster halo effect at work, given the number and frequency of aftershocks, two major tsunamis, and the nuclear incident at Fukushima. To call the series of quakes that happened after the initial quake of 9.0 aftershocks (according to most scientists, although Japanese seismologists initially placed the quake as a 7.9) is a fantastic understatement. There was no less than a swarm of quakes that lasted for a week after the first event scenario that ranged in intensities as high as 6.0.

The resulting tsunamis were devastating. There were reported wave heights from 5 meters (16 feet) at Ishinomaki, to an unofficial report of a 30-meter (98-foot) wave at Ryōri Bay. Entire cities and farms were devastated, and what only made the tragedy worse is that several thousand people were struck by the tsunamis in areas designated as tsunami evacuation sites.[19] Here are some impact numbers describing the damages:

- Tens of billions of yen were estimated to be lost within the first few days.
- Twenty-eight hundred people were declared dead within 2 days, and the numbers quickly rose to more than 10,000 fatalities in one province alone. Ultimately, the total loss of life could be well over 100,000.

- Three nuclear power generators lost the ability to cool their cores, threatening nuclear meltdown and exposing thousands to radiation.
- Two million households were left without power on day 2 of the event, and 1.4 million homes were without water.
- By the second day, gasoline was being rationed nationwide.

All of this happened in a country that was more prepared for an earthquake and tsunami trigger event than any other in the world. The scale of the global response could only emphasize the massive scale of the disaster. Over 500,000 people were placed in shelters. Japan's Self Defense Force deployed 100,000 troops. Teams from 13 countries poured into the Island. The USS *Ronald Reagan* (CVN-76) offered medical assistance and was the first American warship that had been allowed into Japanese territory since World War II (Figure 9.9).

The massive earthquake affected the entire northeast coast of Japan, caused rolling power outages in Tokyo, and even affected world markets, with $1.6 trillion being pulled out of Japanese companies that were viewed as unstable because of the disaster. Going forward, it has been suggested that as much as $200 billion will be spent by Japan's government just on basic infrastructure. The damages have also caused a slowing of electronic chip manufacturing, including the Far East movement of watches (popular with fashion brand, lower-cost watch manufacturers like Seiko), vehicles destined for U.S. shores, and other goods. Further, supplies of these and many other items were constrained for weeks, if not months, as the quake tested the globalized supply chain. Computer memory factories were slow to rebuild their base of stable pricing internationally for as long as three quarters, slowing the speed with which new devices—everything from smart phones to digital cameras—entered the world market.

However, there is a more interesting perspective that we want to point out in this chapter. This is the deeper view of the Japanese mind relative to disasters. Tadashi Yani, a particularly rebellious contributor to *Reimagining Japan*, offers this: "My advice to young people is simple: Get out of Japan." This author is not certain that Yani is capturing the mood or resiliency of Japan's youth culture. In 2011 and 2012, the youths of countries from America to Syria fell into protest and rebellion over the inequalities discussed in the prior section. However, Japanese youths have offered no such protest as of the writing of this book, simply ignoring Yani's suggestion.

303

Figure 9.9 Japan suffered multiple impacts in the manifestation of a risk they were well prepared for. What would Japan look like if it never bothered to look realistically at impacts?

Perhaps what Yani and other contemporary thinkers are missing is the aspect of *shame* that still exists in Japan today. Sociologists and anthropologists have referred to Japan as a *shame society*—a society that is deeply dependent on the acceptance of one's place and duty within society and the maintenance of self-respect that results from not choosing what is good over what is evil, but by choosing what is expected of one by society at large. You may recall that none of the victims of the sarin gas attack were keen on blaming the cult Aum Shinrikyo. One of Murakami's interviewees from the attack sums it up for us in *Underground*: "Apocalypse is not some set idea, but more of a process…. I think the gas attack was a kind of catharsis, a psychological release of everything that had built up in Japan."[20]

It is strongly suggested that the reader explore the works of Haruki Murakami, an author mentioned in Chapter 1, to better understand this cultural perspective. His work, *Underground*, about the sarin gas attacks has been discussed in Chapter 8 of this book as a reflection of the *shame culture* we are referring to now. What comes across in *Underground* so clearly is that the Japanese culture of crying for the company, or out of shame for their actions or something embarrassing to them as a people, is akin to a national pastime. There is no American equivalent to the cultural phenomenon we are discussing here other than American patriotism, and that is debatable. Yet, out of the 2011 Tōhoku earthquake and tsunami, a final impact lurches toward America—an impact that is yet to be truly understood either here or in Japan.

9.5.4 The Unexpected Impact—A Sea of Debris

Well beyond the disaster halo effect in the days and months after the 2011 earthquake in Japan looms what may well be its final impact. Body counts, property damage, financial impacts, and other impacts have already been enumerated and reported, but there is one impact that was not expected, and we are only beginning to understand it now—that there is a vast sea of debris floating in the Pacific Ocean as a result of the tsunami, and it is headed directly for the western coast of America.

As of this writing, there is a lot of confusion about this sea of debris. According to some accounts, the floating island of debris is about the size of Texas and is floating in the direction of the West Coast of the United States along the great Pacific current. The debris field is made up of things like "full houses, partial houses, boats, and quite a lot of stuff," according to Penelope Linterman, an emergency management program coordinator in Clallam County, Washington.[21] Most of the debris is currently in the middle of the Pacific Ocean, but it is headed for Washington, Oregon, and California. Some projections bring the debris onshore in the spring of 2013, but others say it could be sooner.

"The bulk of the debris ... is expected to arrive on beaches in 2013, though fishing boat floats from Japan were found on Neah Bay, La Push and Kalaoch (WA) beaches in early December"[22] of 2011. All reports agree that there is about 25 million tons of debris that did not sink into the Pacific (yet), and although the originally large floating mass is breaking up into smaller patches, the debris field still represents a real impact potential for the West Coast of the United States. One oceanographer from Peninsula

College in Washington says that the debris is "possibly in volumes large enough to clog ports."[23]

NOAA is leading the monitoring and will eventually engage with the Federal Family, including FEMA, the USCS, and others, to deal with the cleanup and impact of the debris, making landfall along the West Coast. In a frequently asked questions (FAQ) document published on NOAA's website, the following is offered regarding the potential impact of the debris fields coming ashore in the United States. "It is safe to assume that debris will move across the Pacific, but exactly where, when and how much it will potentially impact the continental U.S. and Hawaii are unknown."[24]

The FAQ goes on to say: "The initial debris field will continue to disperse as they move with ocean currents and winds, essentially becoming scattered and unlike the large 'mats' seen in the days after the tsunami."[25] The International Pacific Research Center (IPRC) offers a slightly different view. "One thing is certain," it offers in a report, "the debris is hazardous to navigation, marine life, and when washed ashore, to coastlines."[26]

A failure to understand the potential impacts of 25 million tons of debris coming onto shore, and perhaps interfering with harbor operations or navigation in the Pacific Ocean off the shores of Oregon, Washington, California, and eventually Hawaii, from a tsunami in Japan represents all of the hallmarks of a failed potential impact assessment as discussed in this book. Further, the notion that we are still uncertain regarding the real financial and quality of life impacts that this debris could have *as the event is unfolding* is uncanny.

We can see the debris fields, we are monitoring them using GPS locators within the debris fields and satellites in space, and yet we remain uncertain. At some point, the debris will arrive, all 25 million tons of it. With the best efforts of NOAA and the IPRC, we may know a week or a few days before each beach or port is impacted. From there, we can only really start counting the number of days until a beach is unusable, the expense of the cleanup, or the financial impact of a port closure.

Taking a step back and considering what we do know about this potential impact, it is both easy to see how we missed it, and hard to see how we did not. On the one hand, it is nearly impossible to imagine a mass of floating debris the size of Texas crossing the Pacific and landing on the U.S. West Coast as the result of a tsunami. Who could imagine that all of that debris would float? On the other hand, who wouldn't? This is not an indictment of the current practices used by NOAA, FEMA, or any other agency. It's just to say that we are still shortsighted in our ability to fully understand and predict impacts.

* * *

At some point, in 2012 or 2013, we will be confronted with real images of surfers, beachcombers, and people who live along the coastline of the Pacific dealing with the impact from the Tōhoku earthquake of 2011. Those days will be sad, to say the least. The cleanup effort will be costly. The shame the Japanese people will feel on this day will be nearly impossible for us to fathom.

* * *

9.5.5 Insurrections and Earthquakes

What both the potential impacts of insurrections and the earthquake in Japan help us understand is that we are not well equipped to see long-term effects, the natural downward causation, or the loosely coupled impacts we are supposed to be measuring in a potential impact assessment. Even though applying the five guiding principles brings us much closer to accurate, data-driven results, we are still faced with something that is "too real, but slightly off" and hard to communicate or present. Something in the data and the resulting potential impact assessment that is hard to put a finger on or understand.

This difficult thing to understand about potential impact assessments is that we are in some cases responsible, yet we do not accept responsibility—that we *can* see the impacts, but often *don't want to*. That our world is headed toward multiple revolutions and insurrections based in the very progress we have created. That we are not a world at peace, and that mother nature is not benign and not yet fully understood by science. However, with the best potential impact assessment in hand, based on the best data we can gather, we are left with a highly realistic picture of potential impacts that our stakeholders may barely understand or accept.

They may accept that the organization might go splat. In fact, the more accurate our potential impact assessments are, the more likely they will be to wake up—just to avoid the realities presented within them. We do not do well with things that are eerily real or slightly off. We do not do well with the uncanny.

9.6 THE ETHICAL CHOICES WE MUST MAKE

This book has forwarded the concept that we can create much more meaningful, insightful, and realistic projections of what is at risk through the application of the five guiding principles of a potential impact assessment. To accept this approach and expand the impact horizon is to accept that we must therefore steward our enterprises through the rough ground of what we have found, and lead them on to a new, firm footing based on these realities and findings. The application of the five guiding principles of potential impact assessments, when considered from a critical vantage point, undisputedly generates a more accurate and realistic potential impact assessment, but to see the job through, new questions arise: What are the ethical choices we must make when delivering the final documentation to our clients or enterprises, and how do we comport these findings without unhinging the broader disaster recovery, business continuity, or emergency management program?

We have established some ethical guidelines along the way that, upon reflection, may assist us in understanding how to deal with the challenges presented by the uncanny valley. Among these assertions are:

- If we find ourselves working with an organization that does not want to establish an impact horizon and scope of impact that includes upstream or downstream business partners and other stakeholders, document this decision.
- If we find ourselves working with an organization that does not want to consider people, processes, and technologies as they relate to their core values, document those choices and consider our own professional position in this regard prior to continuing work with the organization.
- If we find ourselves working with an organization that does not want to consider federal and state laws or industry-specific regulations, we must document them and either continue our work, or choose to move on.
- If we find ourselves working for an organization that prefers interviews and speculation without augmenting them with verifiable facts based on big data, document the process and move on.
- If we find ourselves faced with executive overrides, do not own them! Document them as customer-based choices and stick with the facts as located in our professional examination. Educate those who would advocate process-oriented overrides and deviations with regards to the process of conducting a potential impact assessment. Finally, only apply overrides to outliers and deviations that are based on fact, documenting all others as customer or organizational exceptions.

The approach recommended in this book is to apply the concepts of the five guiding principles of potential impacts with a solid commitment to professional, ethical behavior and a deep personal commitment to unbiased data and fact.

* * *

It is this basic notion (presenting the full breadth and width of potential impacts is the only way to overcome the fundamental flaw of past impact assessments) that drives the five guiding principles. However, without a professional commitment to all of the ethical decisions and actions that are incumbent on the practitioner, the assessment will slide back into the murky waters of uncertainty.

* * *

Our profession is at a crossroads, where we find one path that leads to cheaper business case-based thinking in impact assessments, and another path that leads to healthier organizations with a full picture of potential impacts. The future, specifically the next decade, will continue to press our profession with ongoing globalization and the larger problems of civil unrest and insurrection roiling in the background.

Simply stated, our jobs will not become any easier. Some professionals will become highly skilled at generating a status quo business impact analysis that simply meets the demands of auditors, allowing the business to continue the programs in which they are engaged. Other professionals will begin to apply the five guiding principles of potential impacts with sharp, critical thinking and the appropriate ethical facilities to elevate not only their personal positions within our field, but our profession itself. We should keep in mind that there is no guarantee, no real promise, that our profession will always be regarded as necessary or even valid. The past 30 years of practice in disaster recovery, business continuity, and emergency management has benefitted from the war on terror as much as it has from a political climate of regulation. To take either of these conditions as ongoing certainties would be naïve.

Essentially, the ethical question we must confront is one of professional credibility and value. While it will be easy to keep cost down and customer satisfaction high with the opinion-based polls and fantasy-based business impact assessments that are so prevalent in our profession today, the real credibility and value will come from those who are able to rapidly, and cost-effectively, apply the five guiding principles of potential impacts to better prepare our enterprises and protect our nation.

9.7 SHEPHERDING THE ORGANIZATION THROUGH THE UNCANNY VALLEY

Two questions come to light when the potential impact assessment is completed. One is strategic: How do we know these criticalities are true? The other is tactical: What do we do next? To be clear, this volume is not a book about designing appropriate tactical responses to disasters and terror events, or writing appropriate mitigation plans. That material will be covered in a separate book. What the potential impact assessment delivers is *the right questions* based on criticalities as determined by the five guiding principles. The key issue here is strategic in nature—when presented with the criticalities as scored using the five guiding principles, the organization may respond with repulsion or uncertainty that we have referred to in this text as uncanny.

The first goal for the practitioner is to address the strategic challenge of presenting uncanny data to organizations. It should be clear that postmodern, contemporary life necessitates an understanding of the increasingly complex interactions and the entities that enable them. If we are to recover from disasters and terror attacks at all, we must curate a deep understanding of the wondrous mechanisms of commerce and governance that are unearthed through applying the five guiding principles. A deep trust in the rationale and logic set forth in this book puts up a guard against personal biases. We must inform, but not induce, a view of what is critical to the organization and what is not. Having succeeded in adhering to the five guiding principles, we can help to shepherd the organization through our criticality findings based on the strength of analysis the principles provide.

The practitioner should be clear that he or she has not sought to impart a monolithic organizational reality onto the values of the organization, but rather has defined objects based on both their physical and connected realities to other people, places, and things within the context of the organization's stated values and legal constraints. To be clear, this is the art of looking at objects based on the process of collecting things—curating. As the practitioner curates over the years and applies the five guiding principles, he or she will gain insights into the relationships between people, processes, and technologies that will eventually lead to an inexplicable but palatable insight—the postmodern organization is complex. It is this palatable knowledge that must be used to strategically position the data found as criticalities in the final potential impact assessment, a strong base of qualification and experience that allows the practitioner to say: "You may have never seen things this way before, but I have." Few people ever glimpse the process and glow of capital in the way a practitioner using the five guiding principles will.

A practitioner who is curating a body of uncanny impacts is inspecting issues that many have never even considered. They are gathering information from simply meeting with, listening to, and understanding the postmodern organization—not influencing it.

Strategically, the practitioner who uses the five guiding principles is well positioned to compare his or her findings for the organization against other experiences he or she has had over the years. He or she can then ensure his or her current clients that the criticalities, relationships, and values in harm's way, unearthed through the process of the potential impact assessment, are very similar to those found in other organizations—much like a doctor who sees compound fractures can reassure a patient that as grisly as it seems, the wound can be repaired. This brings us to the tactical issues that the potential impact assessment unearths.

If the potential impact assessment informs us about what value is in harm's way, and in what order, or criticality level, the obvious next question is what to do about it. In short, the topics of remediation and mitigation are our next area of study and practice. What should be clear, however, is that no matter what budget is available to the organization, or what level of will or commitment it exhibits toward the potential impact assessment findings, there is a clear next step—remediate single points of failure and start with the most critical objects first. The tactical execution of protecting against impact may take years. Remediation, mitigation, and testing are only informed by the criticalities found and prioritized in, and by, a potential impact analysis. They are not solved.

The job of the professional practitioner in our field, as mentioned above, is to hold to his or her ethics, deliver a potential impact assessment based on the practiced curating of the uncanny with determination and experience, and inform the next step in the process—prioritized remediation and mitigation.

311

9.8 CONCLUSION

The five guiding principles force a "high definition" view of what is at risk that ultimately leads to what must be done in order to remediate and mitigate against potential losses. While remediation and mitigation strategies are out of this volume, understanding *how to deal with the realism* that a potential impact analysis puts on the table is not. Even as we deliver a clear picture based on the five guiding principles of potential impacts, there is an undertone of potential revolution and insurrection that is global in nature and generates a set of impacts that are, in some cases, more profound and more damaging than our stakeholders can comprehend.

We serve the organization and its constituents, not the social upheavals that are embedded in the current shape of postmodern business, capitalism, and governance. In order to completely do our job of understanding impacts, we must come to terms with the background conversation incumbent to the times, not the whispers and complaints of a society undergoing a massive shift in its orientation to work and citizenry. We come to terms with the logical and well-ordered arguments they use in protest, and also with the clear and present danger they represent to our clients. This is one of the challenges of the realism created by the five guiding principles.

To ignore the tactics, motives, and impacts of insurrectionists, radicals, and hackers is naïve. They are spurred on by the actions of the enterprises for which we are measuring impacts. To disregard their intelligent arguments is to move forward blindly because we are protecting the very value that is itself generating further threats and impacts. As students, practitioners, and professionals in the fields of disaster recovery, business continuity, and emergency management, do we press the advantage using the insights we've gathered through our potential impact analysis using the five principles, or do we water down the message, rifling through slides at the end of a project, just like with the endless photos collected on a boring vacation, just to leave our customers more confused about the values that are at risk and the *new* risks we've discovered? Or do we spend the time to walk our shareholders through our findings with care and deliberation?

Our choice, as emergency managers, business continuity professionals, and disaster recovery experts is *to protect our clients*. If we have taken a role with an organization that we cannot fundamentally agree with in terms of ethics, then we must move on. If we do not have an issue with the ethics of the organization we are supporting, then we cannot, for one instant, be on the fence in this regard. We must understand that there *is* an "us" and a "them." The "us" are those who mindfully choose to protect the interests of our clients. The "them" are those who would mindfully have their radical ideologies destroy our clients' interests. Like it or not, our final functional role in delivering a potential impact assessment is to help our organizations face the potential impacts, including the unpleasant reality that they, their business, or even their role in society may often *be the target* of a radical segment of our global society.

When delivering a potential impact analysis based on the five guiding principles, the analyst must be prepared to explain, in depth, the uncanny potentials and realities captured during the potential impact assessment. In short, he or she must be prepared to walk with the client through the uncanny valley.

What both the potential impacts of insurrections and the earthquake in Japan help us understand is that we are not well equipped to see the long-term effects, the natural downward causation, or the loosely coupled impacts we are supposed to be measuring in a potential impact assessment. Even though applying the five guiding principles brings us much closer to accurate, data-driven results, we are still faced with something that is "too real, but slightly off," and it is therefore hard to communicate or present. There is something in the data and the resulting potential impact assessment that is hard to put a finger on or understand.

This difficult thing to understand about potential impact assessments is that we are *in some cases responsible* for seeing the impacts, yet we do not accept the responsibility to see, and often *don't want to*. We can sometimes see that our world is headed toward multiple revolutions and insurrections based on the very progress we have created. We understand that we are not a world at peace, and that mother nature is not yet fully understood by science. So, even with the best potential impact assessment in hand, based on the best data we can gather, we are left with a highly realistic picture of potential impacts that we can have difficulty accepting, and our stakeholders can barely understand.

In generating a potential impact assessment, we are presenting cognitive "reminders of death" in a very accurate way. Though the data and findings of the final deliverable of a potential impact assessment are in no way a simulation, but rather a written report with sets of charts and graphs that illustrate a potential for harm that is much more accurate than the methods used in other approaches, they appear as a robot or CGI that looks real and convincing, but leaves uncertainties that create an uncanny response.

In these terms, the symbol may be a chart or graph of body counts, financial losses, or simply the admixture of core values, legal, regulatory, and cultural issues that resulted in our weighted scores and tiers. When based on the five guiding principles, "the symbol takes over the full functions and significance of the object it symbolizes." Thus, a graph in the final report becomes uncanny for the stakeholders and they are bound to recoil. Reporting the final results of a potential impact assessment based on the five guiding principles leads us to the uncanny because, as Freud writes, "the whole matter is one of 'testing reality,' pure and simple, a question of the material reality of the phenomena."[27]

Suddenly, the question of the five guiding principles of potential impacts shifts and becomes slightly more problematic. If we are to truly analyze potential impacts and understand them in terms of their alignment to the organizations we serve, as well as their capability to generate values to be protected that may insult the sensibilities of radicals and revolutionaries—if we are to expand the impact horizon to consider the damages of an earthquake 2 years after the fact to distant coastlines—then we are left with a final deliverable that is not only accurate, but disturbingly realistic and uncanny.

It is the basic notion that presenting the full breadth and width of potential impacts is the only way to overcome the fundamental flaw of past impact assessments that drives the five guiding principles. However, without a professional commitment to all of the ethical decisions and actions that are incumbent on the practitioner as stated in this work, the accuracy and value of the potential impact assessment driven by the five guiding principles will slide back into the murky waters of uncertainty.

The approach recommended in this book for dealing with the revolutionary component of our society and the uncanny nature of our findings is to apply the concepts of the five guiding principles of potential impacts with a solid commitment to professional ethical behavior and a deep personal commitment to unbiased data and fact. That commitment is developed through curating. Curate your profession, your client(s), and your society. Collect without discrimination as much as you are able to that pertains to your work. Take on the obsession of the Otaku and know your environment inside and out. Become familiar with all of the positives and negatives surrounding a potential impact assessment, and assemble the information in familiar and newly discovered permutations. Your familiarity and comfort will allow you to discuss the uncanny elements of the potential impact assessment knowledgably and confidently. You will be enabled to take on the role of a doctor to your client, effectively diagnosing your patient, and informing him or her on risks and prevention—thereby shepherding him or her through the uncanny valley into familiarity with his or her business and knowledge about how to protect it.

9.9 QUESTIONS

1. Why will the next decade produce the need for decisiveness and dedication in the field of emergency management?
2. How has the current period in which we practice given rise to a larger undermining force to potential impact assessments than in any other period of history?
3. Illustrate an understanding of ethics and decision making when it comes to serving the organizations and customers we work for.
4. What are the key dual challenges confronted in the postmodern business impact assessment, and what is an example of them?
5. What is the uncanny valley? How can we achieve a better means of working both within the context of postmodern businesses and around the issues embedded in them by applying this concept?

ENDNOTES

1. The Invisible Committee. 2007. *The Coming Insurrection.* Los Angeles: Semiotext(e) Intervention Series, p. 14.
2. Ibid.
3. Ibid.
4. Ibid., p. 48.
5. Zettler, Kim. 2012, February 3. Anonymous Eavesdrops on FBI Anti-Anonymous Strategy Meeting. Threat Level. http://www.wired.com/threat-level/2012/02/anonymous-scotland-yard/ (accessed February 4, 2012).
6. Candiotti, Susan. 2011, July 21. Homeland Security Warns of Potential Threats Against Utilities. CNN U.S. http://www.cnn.com/2011/US/07/21/terror.warning.utilities/index.html?iref=allsearch (accessed February 4, 2012).
7. Ibid.
8. BBC. 2011, December 13. FBI Says Hackers Hit Key Services in Three U.S. Cities. http://www.bbc.co.uk/news/technology-16157883 (accessed February 4, 2012).

9. Wisniewski, Chester. 2011, December 13. FBI Acknowledges More SCADA Attacks, Increases Cyber Budget. Naked Security. http://nakedsecurity. sophos.com/2011/12/13/fbi-acknowledges-more-scada-attacks-increases-cyber-budget/ (accessed February 4, 2012).
10. MacDorman, Karl F., et al. 2009, January 29. Too Real for Comfort? Uncanny Responses to Computer Generated Faces. *Computers in Human Behavior*, 25, 695.
11. Ibid., p. 697.
12. Freud, Sigmund. 1919. The Uncanny First Published in Imago. Bd. V. Reprinted in Sammlung, Fünfte Folge. http://web.mit.edu/allanmc/www/freud1.pdf (accessed February 5, 2012).
13. Ibid., p. 1.
14. Ibid., p. 15.
15. Ibid., p. 17.
16. Sherriff, Patrick. 2011. Introduction. In *2:46, Aftershocks: Stories from the Japan Earthquake*. London: Quakebook.
17. Ibid., p. 22.
18. McKinsey & Company, eds. 2011. *Reimagining Japan*. San Francisco: VIZ Media, p. 8.
19. Wikipedia. 2011, March. 2011 Tōhoku Earthquake and Tsunami. http://en.wikipedia.org/wiki/Japan_tsunami (accessed April 14, 2011).
20. Murakami, Haruki. 2001. *Underground: The Tokyo Gas Attack and the Japanese Psyche*, trans. Alfred Birnbaum and Philip Gabriel. 1st Vintage International ed. New York: Random House.
21. Peninsula Daily News. 2012. NOAA Expert to Talk about Marine Tsunami Debris in Port Angeles, Forks Panel. http://www.peninsuladailynews.com/article/20120122/news/301229995 (accessed February 5, 2012).
22. Ibid.
23. Ibid.
24. NOAA. 2011, December. Frequently Asked Questions: Japan Tsunami Marine Debris. http:marinedebris.noaa.gov/info/japanfaqs.html (accessed February 5, 2012).
25. Ibid.
26. IPRC. 2012, January 25. Tsunami Debris Survey Launched Northwest of Midway. Honolulu, HI.
27. Ibid., p. 17.

INDEX